Studying in English

For a complete listing of all our titles in this area please visit
www.palgravehighered.com/study-skills

Palgrave Study Skills

Business Degree Success
Career Skills
Cite Them Right (10th edn)
Critical Thinking Skills (2nd edn)
Dissertations and Project Reports
e-Learning Skills (2nd edn)
The Exam Skills Handbook (2nd edn)
Get Sorted
The Graduate Career Guidebook
Great Ways to Learn Anatomy and Physiology (2nd edn)
How to Begin Studying English Literature (4th edn)
How to Study Foreign Languages
How to Study Linguistics (2nd edn)
How to Use Your Reading in Your Essays (2nd edn)
How to Write Better Essays (3rd edn)
How to Write Your Undergraduate Dissertation
  (2nd edn)
Improve Your Grammar (2nd edn)
Information Skills
The International Student Handbook
The Mature Student's Guide to Writing (3rd edn)
The Mature Student's Handbook
The Palgrave Student Planner
The Personal Tutor's Handbook
Practical Criticism
Presentation Skills for Students (3rd edn)
The Principles of Writing in Psychology
Professional Writing (3rd edn)
Researching Online
Skills for Success (3rd edn)
Smart Thinking
The Student's Guide to Writing (3rd edn)
The Student Phrase Book
Study Skills Connected
Study Skills for International Postgraduates
Study Skills for Speakers of English as a Second
  Language
The Study Skills Handbook (4th edn)
Studying History (3rd edn)
Studying Law (4th edn)
Studying Modern Drama (2nd edn)
Studying Psychology (2nd edn)

Success in Academic Writing
Teaching Study Skills and Supporting Learning
The Undergraduate Research Handbook
The Work-Based Learning Student Handbook (2nd edn)
Work Placements – A Survival Guide for Students
Write it Right (2nd edn)
Writing for Engineers (3rd edn)
Writing for Law
Writing for Nursing and Midwifery Students (2nd edn)
Writing History Essays (2nd edn)
You2Uni: Decide. Prepare. Apply

Pocket Study Skills

14 Days to Exam Success
Analyzing a Case Study
Brilliant Writing Tips for Students
Completing Your PhD
Doing Research
Getting Critical (2nd edn)
Planning Your Dissertation
Planning Your Essay (2nd edn)
Planning Your PhD
Posters and Presentations
Reading and Making Notes (2nd edn)
Referencing and Understanding Plagiarism
Reflective Writing
Report Writing
Science Study Skills
Studying with Dyslexia
Success in Groupwork
Time Management
Where's Your Argument?
Writing for University (2nd edn)

Palgrave Career Skills

Excel at Graduate Interviews
Graduate Entrepreneurship
How to Succeed at Assessment Centres
Social Media for your Student and Graduate
  Job Search
Work Experience, Placements and Internships

Studying in English

Strategies for Success in Higher Education

Second edition

Hayo Reinders, Marilyn Lewis and Linh Phung

 palgrave

First published 2017 by
PALGRAVE

Palgrave in the UK is an imprint of Macmillan Publishers Limited, registered in England, company number 785998, of 4 Crinan Street, London, N1 9XW.

Palgrave® and Macmillan® are registered trademarks in the United States, the United Kingdom, Europe and other countries.

ISBN 978–1–137–59405–1 paperback

This book is printed on paper suitable for recycling and made from fully managed and sustained forest sources. Logging, pulping and manufacturing processes are expected to conform to the environmental regulations of the country of origin.

A catalogue record for this book is available from the British Library.

A catalog record for this book is available from the Library of Congress.

Printed in China

For Sachiko—
Hayo Reinders.

For all the students and teachers I have worked with—
Linh Phung.

To all the children who inspire me—
Marilyn Lewis.

Contents

List of Figures and Tables

Introduction

The second edition of this book is for students who speak English as a second language and who are studying or planning to study a degree taught in English, either in their home country or overseas. The book focuses on strategies and skills that you can use and develop in order to succeed in your university studies.

The book is based on our own experiences as teachers and as students in various countries. All three of us have gone overseas for university study and know what it is like to study in a second language. We have also listened to the stories of university students who speak English as a second language and to their teachers. Their experiences and ours helped us to write this book.

Because this is a reference book, and because different chapters will be of interest at different times, you can turn to whatever section suits you. First have a look at the table of contents and see if a chapter fits your interest. If you don't find exactly what you want there, turn to the index. Here you can look up any topic you want to know more about such as *note-taking* or *tutorials* or *homestay*. Use the index for new words you hear everyone using at university such as *faculty* or *discussion boards*. The other place to look for word meanings is the glossary at the end of the book. This section is arranged like a small dictionary, giving you simple meanings of terms used throughout the book. If you want to know more about the meaning of any of these words, you can go back to the index to find the page where they are explained in more detail.

We hope that you find what you want somewhere in these pages. Although we have tried to give you the big picture, we know that there are differences from one university to another and from one country to another. For a more detailed picture you can read the books and websites suggested throughout the chapters. We hope that wherever you are reading this book and whatever stage of your university life you have reached, you will find the ideas helpful. Happy reading!

Hayo Reinders
Linh Phung
Marilyn Lewis

What's New about Studying in English?

Everyone's experience of learning English is different. Below you will read about the language learning experiences of three students and compare their stories with your own. This will help you to find out what you like about studying English and other subjects in English, and how best to use this book.

Three language learners' stories

We are starting this book with three language learning stories that will help you to write your own. The three learners had very different experiences, at different times and in different places. But there are many similarities, too. As you read the stories, compare your experiences with theirs – there are some questions to help you do this at the end of each story. When you have read the three examples, we encourage you to write your own story.

Story 1: The challenges and joys of learning English in the US

My name is Mohammed. I came to the US to learn English in 2012. I used to learn English in Saudi Arabia, but it was not effective because I did not use English often. I faced many challenges in learning English, yet I found different ways to overcome them. When I first came to the US, I would talk for an hour with a native speaker, and at the end of the conversation they would ask me, 'What are you talking about?' As you can imagine, it was difficult to find a native speaker who was willing to spend time talking with me. It was natural that they were more interested in talking with people they could have a smooth conversation with. Thus, to attract them to have a conversation with me, I invited them to parties and restaurants so they would come and enjoy the parties and meals and I would enjoy speaking with them.

The second challenge I faced was learning the meaning and the use of words. When I learned new vocabularies by translating them from English to Arabic and vice versa, I often thought I had got the meaning, but in fact the uses of the words were different. For example, in Arabic the word 'calendar' has two different meanings: dates and dental braces. So when I went to the dentist in the US, instead of asking for braces, I asked him for a calendar and he gave me a folder. I realized that he had misunderstood me because of my English.

The third and biggest challenge was learning English pronunciation. For instance, in English they have the two different sounds *p* and *b* while in Arabic we have only the sound *b*. One time I had an appointment with a native speaker, and he called me and asked, 'Where are you?' I said, 'I am outside.' When I arrived, he asked me again, 'Where have you been?' I said, 'I was *barking* on Fifth Avenue.' He said, 'Why didn't you come and *bark* here!' I did not understand what he meant. After three months he said, 'Your English is getting better. Do you still *bark*?' I could then answer, 'No, now I am *parking*.' After several semesters of studying English, my English greatly improved. I got admitted to study a Master's degree in biology. As a biology student, I now know words that many native speakers do not know, such as anastomose, decussate, osteoclasts, and lipolysis. After looking back at my experience, I can confidently conclude that you never fail until you stop trying.

Now start thinking

1   What difficulties did Mohammed have in his language learning? Do you have the same difficulties?
2   What did he do to create more opportunities to use English? Why do you think opportunities to use English are important for success in language learning? List three things you can do to find more opportunities for using the language.

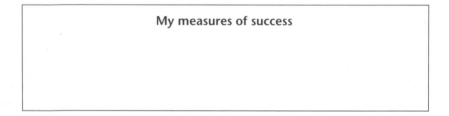

Three things I can do
1.
2.
3.

3   Did Mohammed succeed in the end? What was his measure of success? What are your measures of success in your studies?

My measures of success

4   What are you doing now to succeed? What else can do you?

Story 2: Competitiveness, motivation and opportunities in English language learning in Vietnam and the US

My name is Linh. I started to learn English in middle school in Vietnam when I was 11 years old. My class specialized in English, so I had more English lessons than any other subjects. I remember we studied grammar and did a lot of exercises. I also remember having fun; the teacher taught us songs and told us Sherlock Holmes stories. We also performed plays and sang songs in English. We all felt she cared about us. I adored her and loved English. As I became more successful in my learning, I was determined to become the top student in class, and so I studied with great intensity. During those years, I wanted to be extraordinary, was extremely competitive, and was keen to do well in school. I maintained my number one ranking throughout my high school year and won third prize in the national English contest. However, because of my competitiveness, I was frustrated that I couldn't remember long lists of words I created from the reading I did. I didn't know why my writing didn't earn as high a score as I thought it should. I was not as successful as I wanted to be.

After graduating from high school, I chose the College of Foreign Languages to continue my specialization in English. During the first two years of college, my coursework focused on developing English skills, including listening, speaking, reading and writing. I had more opportunities to communicate orally in English through class discussions, debates and presentations. However, I still spent a significant amount of time studying test preparation books including TOEFL and IELTS because course exams were often similar to the tasks in those books. Also, there were not many other English materials. I didn't really connect to the content presented in those materials, but I was convinced that more practice would lead to better language skills and exam scores. In addition, for classwork I had to listen to the radio more often. One of the activities I remember was listening to the BBC or the VOA, recording a piece of news, then transcribing it. I found the activity to be time-consuming, but useful. I also liked watching American movies; I watched them in the library and rented them to watch at home whenever I had the chance.

With high scores in the TOEFL and GRE tests, I moved on to do a Master's degree in the US. My language development continued through interaction with others in English. During my MA, reading articles in the field was difficult because of the new content, as was following group discussions. I was mostly quiet in the first year of my MA, and I knew I needed to continue to improve my English. I found chatting useful, so I made friends online and chatted often. I also watched popular TV shows like *Friends* and *Everybody Loves Raymond*. When I had to write papers for class, I spent time reading and taking detailed notes. I earned As in most of my classes because of my papers.

Now, as a professional living in the US, I use English comfortably for a variety of purposes. I know that my English is still changing as I continue to learn new words, new ways to talk about certain topics in my field and new ways to relate to other people. I have more confidence in many professional circles, and I'm more outspoken. I've never made it my purpose to sound like a native speaker, but I do wonder how my English will evolve after years of living in the US.

Compare and contrast

Do you think Linh was successful in her language learning? What helped her to succeed? Complete the following table to compare your experiences with hers. Fill in Column 2 from Linh's account, then fill in your own ideas in Column 3. Note that the points are not in any special order.

	Linh as a language learner	You as a language learner
Learning goals	To be number 1 in her class. To compete in the national contest. Not to sound like a native speaker.	
Feelings towards English and English-speaking communities		
Actions to help learning (learning strategies)		
Challenges		
Ways of measuring success		
The learner's personality		
Factors contributing to success		

Story 3: Far, far from home

My name is Marilyn. My experience of changing countries, languages and ways of learning happened when I had the chance to go and study in France. Although you might think that the main challenges would be the language and, perhaps, new ways of learning, my first obstacles were more about everyday life.

First I had to find a place to live. The university supplied a list of homestay families who were happy to have fee-paying international students, but the students had to find the houses themselves from the addresses they were given and then negotiate the arrangements. Remember that this was all in a language I had studied formally but had not used before in everyday life. While waiting to find the right place, I was staying in a cheap and rowdy hotel where soldiers used to come in drinking downstairs each night. My goal was to leave there as soon as possible. I was very fortunate to find a place to stay within walking distance of the university. 'Madame' turned out to be quite strict with her boarders. In fact, I was lucky because she had recently boarded a couple from my country and they had made a good impression on her, so she welcomed me in.

The second challenge was the language. The way we had learned French was to focus on the grammar, so my sentences were very correct but not very idiomatic, which was a bit of a problem when I had to listen to other students. They used to ask me to say certain sentences so they could listen and laugh, because I was using verb tenses from long, long ago that were no longer in use in France. When it came to lectures, though, the language was more formal than students used in conversation, and this made it easier to listen and take notes.

A number of things made my stay a very happy one. On the language side, I found that listening for the general meaning of something, whether it was a lecture or a conversation, helped me more than concentrating on the details. Once I understood the big picture, then I could guess at most of the details.

On the social side, I decided to try to meet some local people apart from university students. I found a church within walking distance, and this led to some invitations home to meals. Since the university was in one of the provinces, not Paris, travelling round to see rural France was part of the fun. Some of the other international students had the same idea, so we used our limited funds to travel by bus out to the countryside on Saturdays, although I had decided beforehand not to spend too much time with other foreigners because of the temptation of using English. In fact, a mixed group of us, including people from Germany and French-speaking Canada, used French anyway as our means of communication.

I haven't mentioned much about the study side. It was really a case of getting used to the system, especially their means of assessing us. For example, the written examinations were VERY long: four hours. Maybe that's changed now, but it was a long time to sit writing on one topic.

All in all, I would recommend international study to anyone who has clear focus about what they want to study and is willing to participate in the social side, too.

What's different?

1   How does this story differ from the previous two?
2   Do you think the social side of learning English is important? How is it important in your context?

Now you write

Start writing your own language learning story. Think about the challenges, joys, strategies and incidents that have changed the way you think about the nature of learning English. Imagine who you want to be in the future and how you're going to use English later in life.

Conclusion

As we said before, language learners are different from each other. We hope that, by reading the stories in this chapter and writing your own language learning story, you understand yourself better as both a language learner and a university student. The following chapters in this book will provide you with further advice, resources and tasks that you can explore to determine what will best help you to achieve success in your university studies.

How to Become a Better Language Learner

One of the most important steps in becoming successful in your studies is to make sure your English is good. Having a low level of English often means getting lower scores and failing courses. So it is a good idea to invest your time in improving your English as much as you can. In this chapter we will look at some ways to do that.

This chapter will help you to:

- find out which language skills are the most important for you
- find out your current English level
- set your English language learning goals
- find out what kind of learner you are
- find the best language school
- get to know about your university's language support
- build a language portfolio
- keep a language journal
- find excellent ways to learn English while having fun!

What language skills do you need to improve?

Improving your English starts with knowing what your strengths and weaknesses are. The better you know what to focus on, the less time you will waste and the better you will know where to look for help.

How will you know what areas to work on first? Here are some ways to find out.

Ask your teacher or a previous teacher for their feedback on your language skills. Write down his/her comments here.
Look at your (university) grades and especially any grades from English classes you may have taken. Write down your grades here.
If you are already taking courses at university, look at the feedback from your lecturers on your writing. Are there any comments specifically about the language? Also look out for

(Continued)

words like 'unclear', 'messy', 'difficult to follow', 'unstructured', 'chaotic', 'imprecise'. Copy the comments here.
Take a test such as IELTS or TOEFL. Many libraries have books with practice exams and answers so you don't have to pay to do the test. Often these give you an overall score as well as a component score for different English skills. Write down the overall and the individual scores here.
Overall score:
Listening:
Speaking:
Reading:
Writing:
Vocabulary:
Others:
Rate yourself (see below) or ask others to rate you.
Do a needs analysis (see below).

Rate your own English

You can use the self-assessment grid below to rate yourself in different areas of English. You can then use this to decide what to work on first.

Level	Listening	Speaking	Reading	Writing
Basic	I can follow simple instructions that are spoken very slowly, but I cannot understand long speeches.	I can interact with other people by using simple phrases, but I can't produce long sentences.	I can understand very simple signs, emails and instructions.	I can produce very simple sentences, but I can't produce long sentences.
Intermediate	I can follow simple instructions and longer speeches when the speaker talks very slowly.	I can introduce myself in a paragraph. I can tell a simple story. I can write paragraphs.	I understand simple newspaper articles and short passages about familiar topics.	I can write about familiar topics in paragraphs. I can connect ideas. I can write a variety of sentences.

(Continued)

Level	Listening	Speaking	Reading	Writing
Advanced	I can understand news on the radio, speeches and lectures.	I can interact with people comfortably. I can tell a story in the past easily. I can express my opinion and support my opinion with examples and explanations.	I can understand news articles, stories and college-level texts.	I can write essays with clear organization, unity of ideas and complex language on a variety of topics.

Planning your learning: setting goals

Now that you have an idea of level, it is time to set some specific goals. This will help you to keep track of your progress so that you know exactly how much more work you have to do. Use these steps to find this out.

1 Write down all the skills you want to improve (both general English skills such as 'pronunciation' and 'listening', as well as academic English skills such as 'speaking in tutorials' and 'writing an argument essay').

2 Write down both the level you have now and your goal level. Your goal level is how good you think you will have to be at that skill. You could give yourself a score from 1 to 10: 1 means 'very bad'; 10 means 'excellent'. You do not need to have an excellent level for all skills, certainly not in your first year! After you enter your current level and goal level, subtract your current level from the goal level (goal level – current level) to come up with the difference. This tells you how much effort you need to make in order to achieve your goal level.

3 The next step is to find out which skills to work on first. For this you choose how urgent each skill is (1 – not urgent; 2 – somewhat urgent; 3 – very urgent). For example, even though your speaking skills may be poor, if you expect to study mainly online this would not be a very urgent skill for you to improve. However, if you know you will need to do a lot of reading from the first week, then reading might be a more urgent skill for you.

	General English skills	Current level	Goal level	Difference	Urgency
G1					
G2					
G3					
G4					
	Academic English skills	Current level	Goal level	Difference	Urgency
A1					
A2					
A3					
A4					

Now that you know your difference (goal level – current level) and the urgency of each skill, you can decide what skills to focus on first and how much effort you should put into improving them.

4   The final step is to set some specific goals and list the ways you intend to improve your top priority skills. Let's focus on the top four skills. Write them down in order of priority. Next, write down what it is you find difficult about each skill and what you can do to improve.

Skill	What I find difficult about this skill	What I can do to improve

With this information you can start studying in an effective way. Read the rest of the chapter for tips on how to start.

What kind of learner are you?

Everyone learns in a different way. Some of us study lying on a couch with the TV on in the background while others can only study sitting down at a desk in absolute silence. The same is true for language learning. There is no one right or wrong way but it is good to know what your own preferences are. Answer the questions below and then add up your score. You can look up your results in the answers section at the end of the book.

	0. I don't know	1. I disagree	2. I partly agree	3. I strongly agree
A. The most important part of learning English is to study grammar rules.				
B. Learning new words by using vocabulary lists is helpful.				
C. I need to learn new words and grammar rules by heart.				
D. Having a good teacher is very important.				

(Continued)

	0. I don't know	1. I disagree	2. I partly agree	3. I strongly agree
E. When I read, I look up all the words I don't know in a dictionary.				
F. When I make a mistake, I want to have it corrected immediately.				
G. I often feel I don't have enough time to think before I speak.				
H. It is important to keep a well-structured notebook when learning English.				
I. It is important to take every opportunity to speak English.				
J. Languages follow grammar rules, but, because native speakers often don't know these rules, I don't need to learn all of them.				
K. Listening to the radio and watching TV are good ways to learn English.				
L. The best way to learn English is to pretend to be an English speaker and then act out a dialogue with a partner.				
M. When I read, I usually just guess the words I don't know.				
N. It doesn't matter if you make mistakes; the important thing is to speak as much as possible.				
O. Whenever I meet a native speaker, I try to practise my speaking.				
P. The teacher can help, but I am the one responsible for my learning.				

Are you a strategic learner?

If you can understand the English in this book you have already come a long way as a language learner. Do you know how you did it? Probably you attended courses, read a lot, memorized words, maybe listened to music and watched English movies. But you did much more than that. You also used *language learning strategies*. Strategies are techniques or ways that help you to learn faster or learn more. An example is when you learn new vocabulary by writing it down or by forming new sentences with it. Often we are not even aware of the strategies that we use. We know, however, that strategic learners are far more successful than non-strategic learners. Let's look at some types of learning strategies. You will find more examples of strategies throughout this book.

Memory strategies

When you meet someone new, how do you try to remember their name?

- I write it down.
- I repeat it in my mind.
- I find a word it rhymes with.

These are examples of memory strategies, and we use them every day. We also use them for language learning. In order to understand how best to memorize new language, let's look at the figure below to understand how our brains work.

As you can see, your brain has three memory stores. The first one is called your 'sensory memory'. Sensory means anything to do with your senses, i.e. anything you touch, smell, hear, or see. This memory store can hold information for only a very short time, often even less than one second. If you do not pay attention to the information you hear or read, say, for example, a new word, your sensory memory loses it very quickly. However, if you do pay attention to it, the new word has a chance to move on to your 'working memory'. It is called this because your working memory works for you. Maybe you repeat the word silently for yourself, maybe you

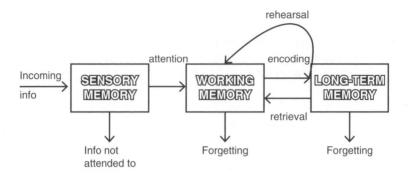

Figure 2.1 Types of memory

quickly write it down, maybe you spell it out – whatever you do, by working with it you are transferring it to your third memory store, your 'long-term memory'. Items in your long-term memory can be remembered for a very long time.

Many learners make two mistakes.

1 They do not pay enough attention to the language. They think that watching a movie while drinking a beer or half-falling asleep will help them learn English. Maybe you will learn a little bit but unless you try actively to pay attention to the language you hear (or read in the subtitles) during the movie, your sensory memory will not keep that information. In other words, it has no chance to move on to your working memory.

2 Many learners also do not use their working memory. They listen to a teacher explaining a new grammar point and maybe even pay close attention. But then, as the teacher moves on to a new point or as the class finishes, they forget about that point. The brain then does not have time to work with the new information and cannot transfer it to the long-term memory. They will probably forget a lot of what they heard.

So, if you want to learn something you have to be active, concentrate and pay attention to the language.

Another point is that without reviewing, whatever you learn will be lost quickly. Have a look at the graph in the next page. It shows you how quickly you forget things. The other thing it shows you is that one review is not enough. You need several reviews and they need to be spaced so that they are further and further apart. Do you do this in your language learning?

Communication strategies

Ken has recently arrived in Pittsburgh, Pennsylvania, USA and will start studying soon. He has studied English for many years but this is his first time in an English-speaking country on his own and he finds it hard to communicate with people. Read this brief conversation between him and Susan, who will soon be his classmate. What strategies do you think Ken is using? Think about them as you read the conversation. The answers are in the text below so you may want to cover that while you read the conversation.

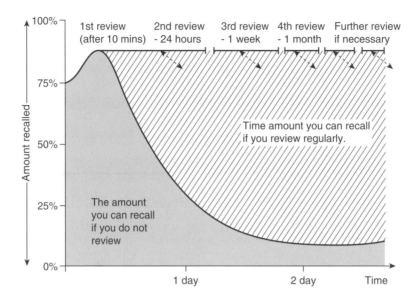

Figure 2.2 The importance of reviewing

Ken:	Hey, Susan.	
Susan:	Hi, Ken. What's up?	
Ken:	I am just going to complete my registration.	
Susan:	What subjects are you taking?	
Ken:	Subjects?	Ken repeated the word that he did not understand with a question tone so that Susan could rephrase the word.
Susan:	Yeah, what courses?	
Ken:	Ah, I am taking chemistry 101 and physics. How about you?	
Susan:	Same here. I am also taking a minor in engineering.	
Ken:	What's a minor?	He specifically asked what a minor was. Don't be shy to ask questions.
Susan:	It's like your second subject. What's yours?	
Ken:	My minor is biology.	Ken used the word 'minor' in the conversation after he understood what it meant.
Susan:	Cool. Did you know they offer an exchange programme with a university in the UK?	
Ken:	No, I didn't. Sounds interesting.	
Susan:	Yeah. Hey, by the way, have you got a computer account yet?	
Ken:	Yes, I got it. I can use computer network in library, but I can't, eh … you know … use it with my laptop, outside.	
Susan:	I see, you can't use the wireless network. You need to get a separate account for that.	Ken did not know the word wireless, but he successfully expressed what he wanted to say by giving an explanation.

These are all excellent communication strategies. One of the most successful ones is to simply get out there and speak without worrying about mistakes! We have often found that our students who make very little progress are those who do not leave the house or only mix with students from their own countries and do not speak very much English outside their classes. This will not help you in the long run. It is good to realize that by using some simple strategies, you can improve your understanding.

Strategies for managing your learning

One important type of strategy is how you *manage* and organize your learning. Good language learners are people who are good at managing themselves and their learning. This becomes even more important once you move overseas. When you start studying your main subjects, you may not have time to take language classes and you will do most of your learning by yourself. Take the brief questionnaire below to see how strategic you are about managing your learning.

Which of the strategies below do you use? Write 1, 2, or 3 next to each statement.

	1 = Never, 2 = Sometimes, 3 = Often
I plan my language learning.	
I know how to check if I have improved and regularly do so.	
I work on language learning tasks with other people (e.g. friends, people on my course) as well as on my own.	
I try to find opportunities to practise speaking (even to myself) to improve my fluency.	
I set specific weekly or monthly language learning goals.	
I try to adopt an active approach towards my language learning; I don't just study when I have to.	
I think about what I need to learn to meet my goals.	
I think about how I learn so I can improve my learning methods.	
I am willing to take risks and be adventurous with language to try out my skills.	
I try to learn from the mistakes I make.	
I motivate myself to learn and to keep learning even when it is not going well.	

Adapted from http://www.lang.soton.ac.uk/resources/key.html.

When you are finished, add up the total number. If your score is under 24, see if any of these strategies sound as if you might want to try them out. Although being a strategic learner is not just about the number of strategies you use, it certainly doesn't hurt to know a few more. You can use the tips in this and other chapters to help you use some of the other strategies.

Choosing the right language school and course

Choosing the right place to study is a very important decision. You are likely to spend considerable time and money so take the time to get the choice right. But choosing a school is not enough. You also need to know what the right type of course is for you. For example, do you need to work on general English skills first or go straight into academic English? Do you need an intermediate or an advanced course? Use the earlier sections in this chapter that help you find out your English level. Schools will also test your English to find out which class you should go into. Then use the following checklist to help you decide the best school. Only fill in the first part once and then the rest for each school you are considering.

Content
My current overall level is:
The most important skills for me are: 1. 2. 3. 4.
I will use English in the following situations, for the following purposes:
I need practice for the following language test:
I need to reach the following level:
I have (…) weeks/months to reach this level:
Quality
Average teaching experience of the teachers:
Maximum and average class sizes:
Nationality mix of students:
Teacher qualifications:
Reviews (from other students or the internet):

(Continued)

Facilities and services		
Does the school have:		
a resource room?	Yes □	No □
resources you can borrow?	Yes □	No □
good computer facilities?	Yes □	No □
a self-access centre?	Yes □	No □
a common room/lounge?	Yes □	No □
tutoring services?	Yes □	No □
conversation partners?	Yes □	No □
Is there a language/course advisor to help you plan your learning? Yes □ No □		
You may also want to ask about activities and other services. Does the school:		
help with finding homestays and accommodation?	Yes □	No □
offer trips?	Yes □	No □
offer after-class activities?	Yes □	No □
Practical and financial questions		
The maximum amount I can pay per week is: Price for this school: Extras:		
Can I get a refund if I stop early? Yes □ No □ If yes, then what percentage?		
Can I attend some classes to see if I like the school? Yes □ No □		
Do students at this school have conditional admission into a specific university or college? Yes □ No □		
Are the course times suitable for me? Yes □ No □		
Other comments/observations:		

What kind of English course do you need?

Whether you need to do an English course before your university course will depend on the level of your English. However, even if you have a high enough TOEFL or IELTS score to start your university studies, it may still be a really good idea to spend some time taking English classes beforehand to build up your confidence, get used to using English all the time and, particularly, improve your academic English skills. Remember that once you start your university study, you may have little time to fully concentrate on improving your English. Here are some different types of course.

1 A general English course aimed at improving your English communication will help you with skills (reading, writing, listening and speaking) and language (grammar and vocabulary). Many English-speaking countries offer intensive English programmes where you study for 18–24 hours a week in class.

2 An EAP (English for academic purposes) course is similar to a general English course except that the topics studied will be more academic and the skills and language you will learn will be more like the skills you will need at university and those covered in this book. These courses are taught by language teachers (not academics) and the other students may all plan to do different courses at university. Often you will need to be at intermediate level or above to enter one of these courses.

3 An exam preparation course (IELTS or TOEFL) will teach you about the exam you are going to take and give you practice in answering exam-type questions.

4 A foundation studies programme or a pathway programme is a much more general academic programme, so it will include other content as well as English language classes.

Read the following case studies. Decide which type of language course would be most suitable for each student. Then read the advice given by an academic counsellor. Do you agree?

Waleed (Saudi Arabia): My English is low-intermediate level and I need 6.0 at IELTS as soon as possible to go to university. I don't have much confidence in my English – my speaking and listening are okay – but my writing and my spelling are bad. I think I will go to another country to study English so I can go to university. My parents expect me to start my university course next semester. What English course should I take?

Counsellor: *6.0 IELTS is high-intermediate level. It means it will take you several semesters (14–15 weeks each) to achieve the high-intermediate level. It is a good idea to start an intensive English programme as soon as possible. These programmes offer about 20 classroom hours a week, which will help you to improve both your general English and your academic English.*

Li Ping (China): I need 6.5 IELTS to get into university. I've done an IELTS preparation course and studied hard for IELTS, but my scores are not improving and I'm bored with preparing for IELTS. What sort of course should I do?

Counsellor: *Taking lots of IELTS tests may help your test-taking technique a little, but your English probably won't improve that much and you are already getting bored. Also remember that to succeed at university you need much more language than is tested in the IELTS test. You should think about taking an academic English course. This will help you with your IELTS scores and will be more interesting than just doing more practice tests.*

Sun Woo (Korea): My English is roughly upper-intermediate level, but I haven't studied at university before. I graduated from high school last summer. Of course, I need to do IELTS, but I am also worried. My friends say that studying at university in an English-speaking country is very different from studying in high school in Korea. I would like to know what other students know before I start university.

Counsellor: *You could attend a bridge programme, a foundation programme, or a pathway programme for international students at a university. In these programmes, you will have language and content-based classes, such as mathematics or a class related to your future degree. In addition, you may be able to transition to a degree programme at the same university without having to take IELTS. You should check with the department at the university where you want to study and ask them if there are specific programmes that they would recommend.*

Ekaterina (Russia): I think my English is good enough to get the TOEFL score to get into university, but I'm not sure if I have the skills to write long essays, read articles and give presentations. I previously studied at university in Russia so I know what it's like! I have three months before my course starts. Should I take a TOEFL preparation course?

Counsellor: *First, you should try taking a TOEFL test to see what your current score is. It may be better for you to take an academic English course aimed at providing you with the language skills you will need at university. This course will also help you to improve the academic skills measured in the TOEFL test. Attending a language programme based at your desired university before your degree programme starts may be a good idea. Many universities now have summer programmes for international students.*

Getting to know your language centre

When you are enrolled at a university, your university may have one or more places where you can get help with your English. These places can have different names in different universities:

- self-access centre (SAC)
- independent learning centre
- writing centre
- language centre.

These are excellent places to improve your English, ask questions and get feedback on your progress. Take a bit of time to get to know your centre. It will be well worth your time.

Take the sheet below and find out the answers to the questions. This way you will get to know about the resources available in your centre. Perhaps you can give your answers to a staff member there.

Using the SAC	What time is the SAC open?
	When are there staff members to help you?
Finding materials	How can you find the right materials? See if: • there is a computer catalogue to search for materials by topic, level, or skill; • you can browse through the materials on the shelves. Find out how they are organized (e.g. by skill or topic).
Getting help	Is there someone in the centre who can help you with the following? • borrowing a book • looking at the work you complete in the centre • helping you plan your independent learning • providing feedback on your writing or presentation.

(Continued)

Managing your learning	Successful learners plan and reflect on their learning. Many self-access centres offer students help with this. Does the centre have:
	• books on 'learning to learn' or 'study skills'; • worksheets that help you develop your language learning strategies; • staff who you can ask questions; • a language 'consultant' or 'advisor' who will help you to develop a language learning plan; • computer resources such as a 'needs analysis' that will help you identify the areas you need to work on and develop a learning plan?

Building a language portfolio

A portfolio is a tool to help you record your language learning achievements. It is a way for you to record your progress and to show this to others, such as your language teachers (if you have them) and future employers. Here are some reasons to keep a portfolio:

- to get feedback from a teacher
- to show to your new language school or teacher
- to include when sending your CV for a job interview.

A Sample Portfolio

Here is a sample language portfolio that you can photocopy and fill in, or use to make up your own. In this example we use English as the language, but of course you can use it for other languages too.

LANGUAGE PORTFOLIO	
NAME: LANGUAGE: ENGLISH	
Years I have studied English	0–1 years ☐ 1–2 years ☐ 2–5 years ☐ More than 5 years ☐
Total time I have spent in English speaking countries	0–1 month ☐ 1–6 months ☐ 6–12 months ☐ More than 12 months ☐ For each overseas stay describe: Country/place visited: Length of visit: Main purpose of trip (if English course, describe course level and aims):

(Continued)

I use English...	... minutes/hours per week (you can include time spent reading newspapers or watching movies in English) My main purpose for using English is to ...
Experience in using English	Describe any other experiences you have with using English. For example, you could mention writing with an English-speaking pen pal, or doing a project in school where you had to produce materials in English.
Courses I have taken	
Certificates and diplomas (English)	
Self-study courses I have completed	Name of course: Date:
Test scores (e.g. TOEFL, IELTS)	Test: Score: Date: Test: Score: Date:
Other scores	My reading speed for academic texts is ... words per minute (see Chapter 7). My vocabulary is at the 3000 word level (see Chapter 4).
My skills	My strong points in English are: 1. 2. 3. The points I want to improve are: 1. 2. 3.

(Continued)

My goals	My goals in studying English include (include a target date/year): 1. 2. 3. 4.

Keeping a language journal

Keeping a language journal can be a great way to record what you learn and to see your progress. A journal can help you to:

- plan your learning
- record your progress
- think about what went well and what did not
- find out what areas you need help with
- make sure you are working on the right language skills
- make sure you meet your goals
- practise your writing skills.

A Sample Journal

Here is a sample language journal that you can photocopy and fill in, or use to make up your own.

<table>
<tr><td colspan="2" align="center">LANGUAGE JOURNAL
NAME:
DATE:</td></tr>
<tr><td>Today/this week I studied the following skills:</td><td></td></tr>
<tr><td>I used the following materials:</td><td></td></tr>
<tr><td>Time planning:</td><td>Times I planned to study:
Mon \| Tue \| Wed \| Thu \| Fri \| Sat \| Sun
Times I actually studied:
Mon \| Tue \| Wed \| Thu \| Fri \| Sat \| Sun</td></tr>
<tr><td>I did/did not have a chance to practise my spoken English.</td><td>If you did, describe the situation where you used the language.</td></tr>
<tr><td>The things that went well were:</td><td></td></tr>
<tr><td>The things I want to improve are:</td><td></td></tr>
</table>

(Continued)

Some ideas I can try out are:	
I would like someone to help me with:	
Now re-read your previous journal notes. Did you work on the points you wanted to improve last time/last week? Did you try out some of your ideas? Did you get help from a teacher?	
My goals for next time/week are:	
The amount of time I intend to spend is:	Mon | Tue | Wed | Thu | Fri | Sat | Sun

Learning English the relaxed way

Learning English does not have to be all hard work. Many successful learners say they have picked up a lot of new words from reading magazines, improved their speaking skills over a coffee with friends, or become better at understanding different accents by watching movies. Here are some useful tips on improving your English, the relaxed way.

Listening

Listening to podcasts on your phone is a great way to improve your English. There are also many podcasts specifically aimed at language learners. Here is a great collection:

http://iteslj.org/links/ESL/Listening/Podcasts/

In addition to these podcasts, you can also learn a lot through music. When you listen to music, search for the lyrics of a song and read along while listening.

Another excellent site is by the BBC. They have a section on learning English with music, interviews with artists, video clips and more:

http://www.bbc.co.uk/worldservice/learningenglish/help/

If you would like to practise your listening skills, but can't find any good podcasts or instead want to listen to your own texts, then either download an audio-book or use a text-to-speech programme to have any text on your computer read out to you by a computer voice. The better voices sound very natural. So, for example, you could copy the text from any website (say a newspaper or an online magazine) and then have the computer read it, save that as an audio file and play it while you are waiting for the bus!

A good programme is: www.nextup.com

Using English online

If you use social networks such as Facebook and Twitter, participate in conversations in English.

Watching movies and TV

Movies are a great way to improve your listening skills. By using the tips below you can get even more out of your movie-watching experience.

Movies	Strategies for watching movies
	Watching a movie in English can be quite difficult, especially when people speak with an unfamiliar accent or speak fast. Just watching movies and trying to understand them will definitely help you, but by using some strategies you can make it easier for yourself to understand what is being said. It may take a bit more time this way, but you'll learn a lot more!
	Before you start watching
	Because English is not your first language, you need to prepare for watching a movie. Try to find as much information as possible about the movie that can help you to understand what it is about. For example, you can use:
	• the title of the film – what do you think the movie will be about?
	• the blurb information about the movie that appears on the cover of the video/DVD
	• any other information you can find such as the scripts and the characters of the movie – one good place to start is: http://www.simplyscripts.com, where you'll find movie and TV scripts and information about the characters, etc.
	• your background knowledge of the topic the movie addresses – what do you know about the country where the movie takes place, the people and their culture?
	While you watch
	Of course, you can just sit back, relax and enjoy the movie. But you'll learn more if you're a bit more active. Research has shown that the best language learners are actively involved in the learning process. They are constantly looking for new information and comparing it with what they already know. Here are some hints.
	• Ask yourself what will happen next – challenge yourself.
	• If you don't understand, then stop the movie and rewind. Don't do this too often, though.
	• Watching movies helps to improve your *extensive* listening skills. Therefore, you should try to keep listening and not focus on vocabulary too much. If an unfamiliar word keeps coming back or seems to be very important, then you can look it up.
	• Use the subtitles if you have difficulty understanding the movie. If, after having used it for a while, you feel more comfortable, turn the subtitles off again.
	• Try to focus on specific language aspects when watching a film. This could be a particular accent, or particular forms of language use (e.g. types of greeting, compliments, thanking, etc.).

(Continued)

After you finish watching

Your learning is not over when the movie finishes. By reflecting on the story and actually *doing* something with what you have seen and learned, you will remember much more.

- Talk to your friends about the movie.
- Email a friend and describe what happened in the movie and your opinion about it.
- If you had to use the subtitles (and liked the movie!) then try watching it again sometime but this time without the subtitles. How much can you understand now?
- Stop to think for a moment what you found most difficult about the English in the movie. Was it the accent? Words you didn't know? The speed with which the characters spoke? Thinking about this helps you know what to work on next.

In addition to the general guidelines above, here are some further exercises you can do to work on specific skills.

Summarizing

How can you improve your English by watching a movie? Summarizing is a skill that is important at university. You will often have to read a book or article and then summarize and analyse it for an assignment.

1 Select a movie.
2 Write down some key words or phrases while you watch the movie.
3 After you have watched the movie, write a summary of it. The key words that you have written down will help you remember.

Possible ideas to include are:

I liked/didn't like the movie because ....
It made me feel ....
I'd recommend this movie to .... because ....
The main character is ....

Describing and comparing

Use the prompts below to think about what you saw.

1. What is the name of the movie?
2. Describe the main character.

(Continued)

3. Would you like to meet this character? Why, or why not?

4. Write a paragraph to compare this person to someone that you know. Think about physical appearance, mannerisms and personality.

Building vocabulary

1 As you watch the movie, write down some words or expressions that you find interesting that you do not know. Next, rewind the video or DVD a little and listen again. How is the word or expression used? Does it sound polite, impolite, or neutral? Is it used between friends or in a more formal situation?
2 After you finish watching the movie, spend a few minutes looking the new words up in the dictionary. Did you get the meaning right? Then start using them in your speaking or writing.

Working with a friend

This is a really good exercise to practise your listening and also your speaking skills. You each watch half of the movie and then meet to find out what happened in the other half.

Student A:

1 Choose a movie that neither you nor your partner has seen.
2 Sometime during the week watch the **first** half of the movie only.
3 Make some notes to help you remember what happened.
4 Write down a list of questions to ask your partner to find out what happened in the second half.
5 Meet with your partner and ask each other your questions. You can both only answer questions with 'yes', or 'no'. You can take notes.

Student B:
    The same as student A but watch only the **second** half of the movie.

Language exchanges

Another great way to learn a language in a fun way is to do a language exchange. You find a partner who speaks English and who wants to learn your native language, and then you speak in each language half of the time. This has advantages for both of you as you can practise conversation (and other) skills without having to pay. Some students meet face to face while others prefer to meet online. This works well if you want to start practising before you go overseas.

    This site is a great starting point to find a partner:

    www.mylanguageexchange.com

Some people prefer to just talk, but exchanges work best if there is a little bit of structure. Before you start, answer these short questions.

My first language is: _____

My English level is: _____

The areas I want to improve are: _____

The topics I want to talk about are: _____

Make sure to keep track of the time so that each of you gets to practise for half of your meeting. It is best to decide beforehand what you will talk about so that you can both prepare. It may be useful to talk a bit about your preferences:

Do you prefer to be corrected every time, or would you rather your partner take some notes and you go over them later?

Do you want your partner to speak naturally, or a bit more slowly?

Would you like your partner to explain English points, or would you rather have a natural conversation?

By talking about these points beforehand you will not be disappointed.

Playing Computer Games

Can you learn English through computer games? You certainly can! You can buy special English 'educational games', but many students do not find these very exciting. A better alternative may be to use the games you normally use as a way to practise your English.

If you normally play games in your first language, see (on the setup screen) if it lets you change the interface language, such as the language of the instructions, to English.

With games that you play online against others, change the language in your profile to English. This way you will meet others who speak English and you can interact with them, for example via chat or Skype. Some games are based on communicating with others, such as the Sims, and these may be your best bet.

Some computer games require you to use language, for example, to persuade others to do something. 'Ace Attorney' is a good example. In this game you are an attorney who has to come up with good arguments in order to win cases. Great fun and great learning!

Materials for further study

The websites below are all good sources for further practice. The last time we checked they were all free (and had been for several years).

General English. Learn English with the BBC through this week's news – including sport, music and work-related topics. You can do quizzes, watch video clips, listen to singer-songwriters and LOTS more. Enjoy exploring!

http://www.bbc.co.uk/learningenglish/

General English. If your English is quite good and you're ready for a laugh, read the 'news' on this site. Be warned: some of the language on this site may be offensive.

www.theonion.com

General English. There are 17,000 free e-books on the Project Gutenberg Online Book Catalogue and you may download them. In fact, they are books of various types, not only for learning English. You can find novels and books involving language learning there. If you don't live in the United States, please check the copyright laws of your country before downloading an e-book.

http://www.gutenberg.org/

IELTS. Thinking about taking IELTS? Or do you just need to check a few details before your test? Before you do your IELTS, you should familiarize yourself with the official homepage. Basically all the information in the handbook is on screen for you.

http://www.ielts.org/

This website provides you with practice materials and hints for IELTS preparation:

http://www.askynz.com/ielts/preparation.htm

TOEFL. This gives you the inside information about the TOEFL exam.

http://www.toefl.org/

Grammar. These websites provide you with some useful grammatical explanations and exercises:

http://www.grammar.com/

http://owl.english.purdue.edu

http://www.englishpage.com

Grammar. These self-study grammar quizzes provide lots of grammar and vocabulary exercises for elementary, intermediate and advanced learners. Why not test yourself? Some of the areas tested are prepositions, articles, idioms and sentence structure, among others.

http://a4esl.org/q/h/grammar.html

Pronunciation. Search for Rachel English on YouTube or on the internet. You will find useful videos to practise certain sounds and other pronunciation features in English.

Spelling. This site deals with the most frequently misspelled words. If you want to work on your spelling, spend a few minutes a day on this site. You can check the meaning and pronunciation of frequently misspelled words, then try to remember the spelling and do the quiz.

http://www.esldesk.com/vocabulary/misspelled-words

Mixed skills. This provides lots of grammar and vocabulary exercises for elementary, intermediate and advanced learners. Why not test yourself?

http://iteslj.org/quizzes/

Study skills. Read how four successful language learners learnt to speak English to a very high standard using a computer program called Supermemo. It is interesting to read about their experiences.

http://www.antimoon.com/

Study skills. This site gives suggestions about writing, reading, note-making, managing time, assignments and exams. Under 'Time management' there is advice on how to get motivated and organize your studies and language learning in the context of life.

http://learnline.cdu.edu.au/studyskills/

Conclusion

This chapter introduces various strategies, tasks and resources that we hope have helped you to learn more about yourself as a learner, set your goals, plan your studies and monitor your progress. As you will see, success in your study depends on what you want to achieve and how you work towards it. You will have to work hard to make progress, but we hope you will find ways to have fun as well.

Studying Abroad

You have decided you want to study abroad. Good for you! This will be one of the most exciting and rewarding times of your life. To make the most of that time, it is important that you carefully consider what to study and where.

This chapter will help you to:

- explore different study abroad options
- find out where to go and how to choose the right university
- write a good application letter for a scholarship
- choose the right language test
- learn how different language tests (and your scores) compare
- learn about foundation programmes and conditional admission
- learn from other students' experiences in choosing their studies
- make sure you submit all the necessary information when applying
- prepare for your departure.

Study abroad options

Many universities around the world welcome international students to their various programmes and majors. You can apply to a degree programme such as a bachelor's degree, a master's degree, or a doctoral degree. A bachelor's degree is usually called an undergraduate degree. A master's or a doctoral degree is called a graduate or a postgraduate degree.

Apart from these degree programmes, you can apply to an English language programme to study English for one or more terms. One term can be as short as a few weeks or as long as 15 weeks. Many programmes offer multiple start dates throughout the year. If you're interested in studying in the US, websites such as studyusa.com list hundreds of English language programmes for you to choose from. Even when your main goal is to complete a degree programme, enrolling in an English language programme before you start can be a good opportunity for you to adjust to the new environment.

If you are an undergraduate or a graduate student in your home country, you can also go to another country to study for a term or longer. Your university may have agreements with many foreign universities. Ask the International Student Office at your university for information about these opportunities. Governments from many countries offer scholarships to excellent students to go to their countries to study for one term or more. Ask the embassy of the country where you want to study about these scholarships.

Where to go?

Before you go, it is good to explore the reasons why you want to study abroad. Here are some common reasons for deciding to study abroad. How important are these reasons for you?

	Importance		
Reason	**Not at all**	**A little bit**	**Very**
To improve my English			
To study at a famous university			
Because the study I want to do is not available in my country, or the quality is not good enough			
To experience another culture			
To take a break and study at the same time			
Because the study I want to do is easier to enter/complete in another country			
I will be able to get a better job in my home country if I have studied overseas			

Knowing your reasons for going overseas will help you decide where to go. Look at the most important reasons for you from above. And then ask yourself further questions to narrow down the choices. There are some examples for you in the chart below.

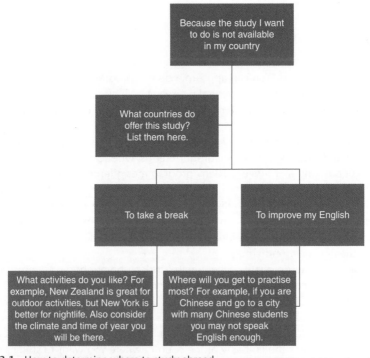

Figure 3.1   How to determine where to study abroad

The above chart will help you come up with an ideal list of places. If you need to find out more information about particular countries, universities and degrees, try one of these ideas:

- Go to a website such as: https://educationusa.state.gov. This is one of many sites with information about universities in the United States.
- Go to the university's website.
- Contact the Admission Office or the International Student Office of the university you're interested in. Most of the time, the employees from these offices will try to answer all the questions that you have.
- Ask people who have been there.
- Although it is expensive, some families visit the universities they are interested in with their sons and daughters. There may be some study tours organized by some travel agencies.

You have your own reasons, but there may be a lot of practical reasons that affect your choice. When you have a few universities in mind, use the table below to find out how some practical points affect your choice. First list your top three ideal choices:

University 1 =
University 2 =
University 3 =

Next, consider each of the following practical points. For example, if tuition fees are an important issue for you, and one of your preferred universities has very high tuition fees, that university gets 0 points. If its tuition fees are reasonable, it gets 1 point. If its fees are low, then it gets 2 points. If a question is not important for you (for example, whether you can meet people of your own culture), then simply don't answer that question.

	Uni 1	Uni 2	Uni 3
What are the tuition fees like?			
How much does it cost to live in that city?*			
Is it possible to get a scholarship to go there?			
How easy is it to get a visa?			
Are there people who speak your language?			
Do you know anyone there (friends or family) who can support you?			
Is it dangerous to live there?			
Is the climate right for you?			

(Continued)

	Uni 1	Uni 2	Uni 3
How difficult is it to be accepted at the university?			
Are the start and finish dates suitable for you – for example, if you want to continue to study in your own country when you finish?			
Is it a city with activities and opportunities you like to have or is it a small town with few activities?			
Total score			

* See the answers section for ways of finding out the cost of living in a country.

When you are finished, add up the score for each university. Do you have a clear winner? Then you know which option is the best one for you.

Applying for a scholarship

For many students, a scholarship is a necessity if they want to be able to study overseas. Luckily there are many opportunities available to eager students (see below). Your chances of getting a scholarship depend on many things, including the quality of the documentation you submit. If the information you prepare is well written, looks as if it has been prepared carefully and gives a good impression of you, your chances are that much better. Your cover letter (or 'personal statement') is particularly important to show why you are the right candidate for the scholarship. Have a look at this sample letter from one student. What do you think of it?

Hello!

My name is … and I am a student at … in ….

I am very interested in the … scholarship. I love to study and to travel abroad. My dream is to be a … one day. I have studied … for three years and next year I hope to graduate.

The … scholarship is right for me as my family is poor and I don't have a chance to study overseas. I hope you will give me the money. I will be a good student and work very hard.

Thank you very much

Stu Dent

What do you feel is missing from this letter?
   Here are some key things to include:

- the reason why you want the scholarship (your motivation)
- why you are the best candidate to get it

- why this scholarship is the best one for you (compared with others)
- what you will do after you complete the scholarship
- how you meet all the requirements.

Consider including an audio or video recording as a supplement to the documentation.

In addition to this, your letter needs to be clear and well written. You want to check very carefully for language mistakes. Always ask someone (preferably a native speaker) to proofread your letter. Also, make sure you include all the relevant documents such as recommendation letters, copies of your qualifications, etc.

A model letter

In the model letter below you will find all the elements listed above. But there are some gaps. Fill them in with information about yourself and your studies. Also make any other changes to the text you find necessary. There is no answer key for this task as your 'answers' will depend on the specific scholarship you are applying for.

What do you think? Is this an improvement over the other example?

Dear Madam/Sir

In a recent newsletter from the University of … I read about the … scholarship. Having nearly completed my undergraduate degree in the area of … I am now very keen to get the practical experience the scholarship will give me. It is my goal to one day work as … and be able to make a difference in …. I think this scholarship will give me a wonderful chance to develop myself further and to learn ….

I am a hard-working student. I have received … grades and taken several extra courses, including …. In addition, I have been a class representative three times, been a member of the student board and have assisted with producing our department's magazine. During the last summer I worked as an intern at …. Although I did not get paid for this job, I was eager to learn the practical skills in this field. During my internship I have learned … and further developed my … skills.

The information about the … scholarship says it aims to '…' and I feel that I fit this description. It also specifically mentions candidates who have experience in …, and from my attached CV you will see that I have taken courses in all these subjects. I strongly agree with the scholarship's goals to …, as these are also some of my personal goals.

After I finish the scholarship I plan to … and to put into practice the skills I will have learned from this scholarship by ….

Please find attached a copy of all the required documentation. I have checked and am eligible to apply as I am under … years of age and have already completed my … degree. I hope, through this letter, I have shown you some of my enthusiasm and motivation in applying for this scholarship.

Yours sincerely

Scholarships   TIP

Your own government may sponsor people to study overseas by paying travel expenses as well as tuition fees. A good place to look is at the website of the Ministry of Foreign Affairs or the Ministry of Education in your own country.

There are also scholarships given by international organizations such as the United Nations, the British Council, the World Bank, the Ford Foundation and so on. These are usually awarded to students from certain countries or students who cannot afford the tuition fees. A good place to start looking is one of these sites:

http://www.iefa.com

Here, international students can search for scholarships by area of study, by their country of origin, by the region where they want to study, or by the name of the university that they want to attend.

http://www.globalgrant.com

Although this site charges a fee to help you find a scholarship, this kind of service may be useful when you don't have access to a university or if your university does not have someone to help you with your scholarship.

Ask the embassy of the country where you want to study. You can also ask the university you apply to for scholarships, teaching assistantships and research assistantships.

Which language test is right for me?

There are many language tests in use around the world. Below are the most common ones that are used internationally. Here is some information about them.

	Where is it used?	Which version?	Other information
TOEFL	Around the world, especially in the United States	There are three versions. More and more testing locations use the internet-based test (iBT), while others still use the computer-based test (CBT) or the paper-based test (PBT).	This is a test of your academic English proficiency. The internet-based test includes four parts: listening, speaking, reading and writing. toefl.org
TOEIC	Worldwide	Most countries use only one version of the TOEIC. Japan and Korea are now using an online version, which will gradually become available in other countries too.	This is the Test of English for International Communication. It is also a test of your global English proficiency, but it covers more business, rather than academic, topics. It includes both spoken and written components. ets.org

	Where is it used?	Which version?	Other information
IELTS	Great Britain, Canada, Australia, New Zealand and many other countries that also accept IELTS	There are two versions: one general and one academic. You will need the academic one for entry into most universities.	IELTS tests either your general or your academic English proficiency. There are four parts: reading, writing, listening and speaking. ielts.org
Cambridge	Worldwide, especially in Europe	KET: elementary level PET: intermediate FCE: upper-intermediate CAE: advanced CPE: very advanced Others include tests for legal or business English.	These are general English (not academic English) exams. There are five parts: reading, writing, listening, speaking and use of English (which includes grammar and vocabulary). cambridgeesol.org/exams/index.htm

Which one is right for you depends on what you need to take the test for. Simply to get an idea of your level you may just want to borrow a practice book from your school or library to avoid having to pay for an expensive test. If you need a test score for university entrance or for immigration purposes, they will be able to tell you which tests they accept.

How do scores on TOEFL and IELTS compare?

Table 3.1 compares the possible scores for the two most commonly accepted tests by universities, the TOEFL and the IELTS tests. It also shows you common minimum scores for university entry. Ask the university that you plan to apply to about the tests they accept.

Table 3.1   Comparison of IELTS and TOEFL tests

	Possible scores	Common scores required for university entry
TOEFL (paper-based version)	310 to 677	550
TWE	1–6	4.5
TOEFL (computer-based version)	0–300	215
TOEFL (computer-based version) writing section	1–6	4.0
TOEFL (internet-based version)	0–120	79 The requirement may vary from 61 to 100. Check with your university.
IELTS	1–9	6.0 (No band below 5.5.)

Table 3.2 shows you what the various scores mean and how they compare between IELTS and TOEFL.

Table 3.2   How do IELTS and TOEFL tests compare?

IELTS scores and description	TOEFL (paper)	TOEFL (computer)	TOEFL (Internet)
9.0 expert user	(700)	300	120
8.0 very good user	630–650	267–280	94–106
7.0 good user	607–627	253–263	86–93
	553–603	217–250	81–87
6.0 competent user	503–550	177–213	65–85
	500	173	
5.0 modest user	450	133	66

Adapted from 'What is IELTS?' – htttp://www.ielts.org/format.htm and LSE Language.

Conditional admission

Even when you do not yet meet all the requirements from the university you want to attend, you can ask for conditional admission. Conditional admission may be given to applicants who meet most of the requirements. If your grade average from your previous degree(s) or your English score is not high enough, you may be asked to enrol in programmes that allow you to increase your grade or your English level. These programmes may be foundation programmes, bridging programmes, pathway programmes, or English language programmes. Below are some common questions about these programmes.

What is a foundation programme or a bridging programme?

These are programmes run by either a university or a college linked to a university that some students need to take before they start their degree programme at the university. They may be called bridging or pathway programmes in countries such as the United States.

Why do students have to study in a foundation programme, a bridging programme, or an English language programme?

It may be because you don't have the academic qualifications to study at university and/or your English is not good enough. For example, you may come from a country where most students study for 12 years at school and you want to study in a country where it is normal to study for 13 years before starting university. You may not have completed high school or your high school grades may not be good enough for university entry. For international students, you often learn English at the same time.

What do you learn in such programmes?

Depending on your needs, you can learn a combination of:

- **Content courses:** These courses are relevant to the university programme you want to attend – e.g. calculus or trigonometry, chemistry, basic statistics. This is usually at the same level as in year 13 at school in the country where you wish to study.
- **English courses:** You may enrol in an English language programme at the university where you plan to attend. You will study academic English in order to be ready for your college study in English. For example, you will learn how to write an essay or a research paper, listen to a lecture, give an academic presentation, or read college-level texts. Alternatively, you can study any English language programme, take a language test and apply to a degree programme after you finish your language study.
- **Study skills:** e.g. critical thinking, how to use a library, how to manage deadlines.
- **Information technology:** e.g. using word-processing software or spreadsheets.

How long does this programme last?

Usually a year, but sometimes longer or shorter. It depends on your academic skills and language skills when you start. For example, you may need to study for 12 months if your IELTS level is 4.5 but only six months if your IELTS score is 5.5.

What happens at the end of the programme?

You are assessed based on your performance in the programme and your English level. Sometimes you may need to take an IELTS or a TOEFL test. Ask the university to see if these tests can be waived for you because you have enrolled in their foundation, bridging, or English programme. If you are successful, you may go directly to university. If you are not successful, you may need to keep studying and retake some courses.

How do I find out more?

Contact the International Student Office or the Admission Office at the university where you want to study. Tell them about your academic record and your language level. They will tell you if you need to enrol in certain programmes and possibly recommend one or more places.

Case studies

One way of thinking about your university studies is to learn from the experiences of others. Here are some examples of students at different stages of their studies. After each one we have put some questions to help you consider your situation. There is no answer for this section because choices about study do not have just one right answer.

Before your study

Vijay is at the stage of enrolling for university. His family really wants him to be a doctor, but he knows that medicine is not an easy degree to be accepted on to. Also, his uncle is a doctor who works very hard for long hours and he's not sure if that's the

> life for him. The university offers a number of other courses, such as a year's study in bio-medical subjects, which could lead to medicine or to other fields of study.

Questions for you

- Is there anything about Vijay's story that sounds like your situation?
- How many options does Vijay have?
- If you were Vijay, what option would you take and why?

> Malwina has always been good at languages and had imagined she would study them at university, but now her friends have raised some doubts. 'What could you do with languages for a job later?' they say.

Question for you

Which of these steps would you recommend for Malwina?

- Go to discuss the future with a careers counsellor.
- Look on the website of the languages departments to see what careers they mention.
- Study just one language, but choose other subjects that seem to have a more professional focus.
- Talk to someone who has studied languages and ask them about their career.
- Ignore the friends and study the subjects you are good at.

> Miyako has already completed her undergraduate degree in commercial law. She is now considering doing a master's, but her friends don't agree. They think she should get some work experience first.

Questions for you

If you were this student's friend, or if you are in a similar position, here are some questions you could ask:

- Are you eligible for a master's programme? Were your grades good enough?
- What do you hope to get out of it? Do you enjoy studying or is your goal to get a higher salary or a better job?
- Have you spoken with someone who works in your field? What do they think doing a master's will do for your career opportunities?

During your study

> Robert has just completed the first year of his degree. He passed all but one subject. He is being given different advice by different people.
>
> His lecturer says, 'Plenty of people miss one subject in their first year. It doesn't mean anything. Just keep on with your second year subjects and repeat the one you missed.'
>
> His friend says, 'This course obviously doesn't suit you. How about changing to something easier?'
>
> His older sister says, 'You only took that failed subject because someone else thought it would be good for you. Drop that and continue with the others.'

Questions for you

Talk about this advice with a friend.

- What do you think of each comment?
- If you were Robert, which would you follow? Why?

> Ly had planned to major in certain subjects. She had had this idea ever since her schooldays. When her first year results came out, the head of department called her in and said that she had done extremely well in one particular subject and that she would be eligible for a scholarship for her fees if she advanced it. Actually this was the subject she had been least interested in all year, mainly because she found the lecturer boring.

Questions for you

Which of these options would you recommend? Why?

- Take the scholarship and hope to get a different lecturer.
- Check out who would be teaching the course before agreeing to the scholarship.
- Ignore the offer and drop the subject.

> Ahmed has started a postgraduate diploma and now has a choice between doing coursework only or doing some coursework and writing a thesis. He is not sure what to do.

Question for you

What would you want to know about this student before recommending either of the options?

- Whether he is disciplined enough to work on his own.
- Whether he likes doing research.
- What his writing skills are like.
- What he will do after completing his studies.

After your study

> Ricardo has completed his degree. Now his parents have said they would like him to continue and do a PhD. In his opinion he is only an average student, and, anyway, he wants to start earning money.

Question for you

With a friend, work out all the options for Ricardo. If that were you, which would you do?

Applying to a university

It is not always easy to enter the university of your choice. There may be only limited places available and you will almost certainly have to meet a large number of requirements. Here is a checklist that will help you to make sure that you include all the relevant information when you submit your application. Check for specific information with the department.

Information to submit	Type of proof/documentation	OK?
English language level	An official copy of your IELTS, TOEFL, or other **accepted** test result.	
Previous qualifications	Diplomas and certificates. These often need to be (1) translated and (2) verified (in the case of copies) by a Justice of the Peace or similar.	
Transcripts	In addition to (a copy of) your qualifications you will generally need to provide official transcripts that show the courses you took and your results.	
Previous work experience	Some studies, especially at postgraduate level, require evidence of work experience in a relevant field. You will need to provide some sort of evidence, for example in the form of a statement from the employer.	
References	Some universities require one or more references. These can be academic, personal, or professional. An academic reference gives comments on your abilities as a student – whether you are conscientious, prepare your work on time, work well with other students, etc. A personal reference gives information about you as a person – your social and communication skills, etc. A professional reference gives information about your work experience.	
Personal statement	Many programmes require you to give information about yourself, your reasons for choosing this study and university and your personal and professional goals. You can use the tips earlier in this chapter on how to write an application for a scholarship for this part.	
Copy of passport	Almost always needs to be a verified copy. This means that a Justice of the Peace or a solicitor needs to view the original and the copy and needs to sign it.	
Evidence of your ability to obtain a visa	It often happens that students cannot travel to their chosen country because they cannot get a visa. Some universities require you to show that you are eligible to enter the country.	
Financial situation	You may be asked to give evidence of your ability to support yourself financially during your studies. You may have to submit a bank statement or a scholarship letter as proof of funding.	

How to work out your cost of living

Many universities will tell you on their website how much you can expect to pay for living expenses, such as rent, transport, food, entertainment, etc. as well as student fees. Many of them have useful cost of living calculators. When using these cost of living calculators, check what is included and what is not. Also, remember that while all international students at a university taking one course will pay the same basic course fees, there may be a big difference between two students' weekly expenses!

A currency converter is a useful online tool:

http://www.xe.com/ucc/

Type in the amount in one currency, choose a second currency and it works out the value using today's exchange rate.

Pre-arrival preparation and orientation

After you get admitted to a university abroad, preparing to go to another country can be exciting and overwhelming at the same time. Often, the International Student Office from the university will send you necessary information to help you get ready for your departure. Usually, you will receive information about:

- how to apply for a visa (if necessary)
- when to arrive on campus
- what to pack
- orientation
- airport pick-up
- housing arrangements
- vaccination requirements
- campus life
- city life.

Make sure to check and answer your email about all the important steps you may need to take before leaving your country. Ask questions if you are not sure about something. When you are in a new country, be open to new experiences.

Conclusion

Studying abroad is many students' dream. However, the process of applying to a university can be overwhelming. If it is your dream, you should take steps to find out as much as possible about the university that is the best fit for you. The key is to do thorough research and ask questions when you need help. The following chapters in this book will also provide you with information on cultural adjustments and life in a foreign country.

Academic and Technical Vocabulary

Words, words, words – why are there so many in English? No one knows for sure exactly how many words there are and how many of those the average person knows, but we do know that the average person has a *working knowledge* of about 20,000 word families (for example, words like 'study' and 'student' are in the same family).

Luckily we don't need that many words to be able to understand and use the English language. The 1000 most common words in English cover over 70% of all words in academic texts, and the estimate for the total number of words we need to understand entry-level academic texts is about 7000. This will give you enough knowledge to be able to understand most of the other words from their context. A good point to realize is that the more words you know, the more you will learn from the context, with little or no effort. So, it pays to increase your vocabulary!

This chapter will help you to:

- find out what 'knowing a word' means
- learn about different types of vocabulary
- find out what your vocabulary level is
- find out how to learn new words
- work out the meaning of new words
- use flashcards to remember words
- make the most of a dictionary and a thesaurus
- learn how to use a corpus.

What does this word mean?

Do you know the word 'commendation'? Your answer depends on what the question means, as you can see below.

1. Do you know the meaning of the word and are you able to translate it into your language?
2. If so, do you know it for sure, or approximately?
3. Do you know the word well enough to *use* it in your own writing or speaking?
4. Do you know if the word is normally used in writing or speaking?
5. Can you pronounce it? Spell it? (Don't look back at the word!)
6. Do you know what words normally go together with this word (which words 'collocate' with it)? For example, do we *give* a commendation or *offer* a commendation or can we use either?
7. Do you know whether it can take a preposition? (e.g. is it 'a commendation for', or 'a commendation with'?)
8. Does it have a positive or a negative meaning? Would you use it in formal or informal situations?

As you can see, there is a lot to knowing a word completely. The question is: how much of each word do you *have to* know? Do you really need to be able to *use* each word or is it okay to only be able to *recognize* some of them?

Even if you don't know this word, you probably know the word 'recommendation'. Knowing that word, you can probably partly figure out the meaning of the word 'commendation'. At least you will know that it is probably something positive. So, even if you don't 'know' the word, you know more than you think you do!

TIP

By not having to learn everything about every word, you can save yourself a lot of time! Some dictionaries give you information about which words are more or less common. For example, the Collins Cobuild uses little symbols in the shape of diamonds to show how common words are. Other dictionaries use other systems. This is very helpful information when you have to learn a lot of words.

Different types of vocabulary

You have probably found that some words are more common in some situations. Words like 'okay' and 'great' are common to conversations, for example. Other words are only used in written English, and some are mainly used in formal situations such as lectures, or in informal situations, for example when talking with friends.

Researchers have found that some words (like 'the' and 'is') are very common in all situations. In fact, even in academic texts, the same 1000 words make up over 70% of the text. So make sure you know these words before all others (see below to find out what they are). You probably already do, if you can understand this book! The second 1000 words occur about 5% of the time, so together you have more than three-quarters of the text covered.

Academic words are, as you would expect, very common in university texts. They make up about 10% of the total, but these words carry a lot of the meaning so you will certainly need to know them. Below you can complete some exercises to make sure you do.

University texts also include technical terms that are specific to your subject. Examples include words like 'merger' in the area of finance and 'osmosis' in the area of biology. These words are usually explained in your textbooks and many of them will be new to native speakers too, so they are often a bit easier to learn as the lecturer is likely to cover them in class or they are explained in your coursebook.

Four categories of vocabulary

So, to summarize, vocabulary can be categorized into the following types:

Type	Description	Examples
Everyday vocabulary	These are the most common words in general use. They are not specific to academic vocabulary.	and, so, but, because, the, big, must
Academic vocabulary	These are words that are used frequently in academic writing but are not specific to any subject.	research, define, analyse
Technical subject-specific vocabulary	These are words that will be extremely important for your university subject, but may not be very frequent. The words may be used in a technical sense.	(for anatomy students) metatarsal, mesothorax, cadaver, glottis
General low frequency vocabulary	These words are not specific to academic texts, and not very common.	cronyism, mewling, crowbar

Now you try

Read the following text from a paper on motivation in language learning. What are the types of motivation mentioned in the text?

Dornyei (2010) reviews three phases of L2 motivation research: the social psychological period (1959–1990), the cognitive-situated period (during the 1990s), and the process-oriented period (recent years). According to Dornyei, the social psychological period was marked by the work of Gardner and associates and their socioeducational model of second language acquisition. This model outlines how integrative motivation is related to other ID variables and language achievement. Integrative motivation has three main components: integrativeness, attitudes toward the learning situation, and motivation. Integrativeness comprises integrative orientation, interest in foreign languages, and attitudes toward the L2 community. Attitudes toward the learning situation consist of attitudes toward the language teacher and the L2 course. Motivation refers to effort, desire, and attitude toward learning. Instrumental orientation, which concerns the benefits that L2 proficiency might bring about, has been interpreted as part of Gardner's model.

Now look at the words in the text. Try to find three examples of each of the types of vocabulary listed above.

Type	Examples
Everyday vocabulary	1. 2. 3.
Non-technical academic vocabulary	1. 2. 3.
Technical subject-specific vocabulary	1. 2. 3.

Check your answers at the end of the book.

Formal and informal language

In addition to the different word types and frequencies, words also differ in how formal or informal they are. For example, you could say:

I need to exit the premises in order to purchase supplies.

Or you could say:

I'm going out shopping.

Academic language is often rather formal because the meaning needs to be as precise as possible and we would not use academic words in everyday conversations very often. When you write academic texts, consider using academic words.

Can you tell which word in the following pairs is more likely to be used in academic texts?

think about	consider
summarize	put together
investigate	find out
determine	figure out
describe	talk about
very small	minute

Check your answers at the end of the book.

Formal text is often less 'emotive'. In other words, it is based more on facts and less on our feelings. A good exercise is to look at the difference between a political speech and a research paper. Which sounds more emotional? Which sounds more objective? What are the differences in the use of language?

You will need to get a feel for which words have greater emotive value than others. For example, the words can mean the same thing, but they do not have the same 'feeling'. Which one is stronger, do you think?

kill / assassinated / butchered

Here are some other words. Can you put them in order from less to more emotive? Check your answers at the end of the book.

explosion / growth / big increase
huge success / successful outcome / victory
great / fantastic / good
insulted / trashed / embarrassed

However, it is not just about the individual words, but also about the tone of the whole sentence or text. Have a look at these examples. How would you rewrite them to make them sound less emotive? Check your answers at the end of the book.

The argument is over the top.

_____

That is nonsense.

_____

I don't like this.

_____

This is a bad research project.

_____

One thing we do is 'hedge' our language by using words like 'could' and 'might', 'maybe' and 'it appears that' to show that there may be other explanations and possibilities. By using these words and phrases, you express your opinion on the topic without using language that occurs more often in conversations such as 'I think' or 'In my opinion'.

What is your vocabulary level?

Without a good level of vocabulary your life at university will be much harder. But what exactly is your level? Here is an easy way to find out:

1 Go to: http://www.lextutor.ca/tests/.
2 Choose Vocabulary Level Test (VLT) 2k–10k.
3 Choose the word level you want to test. For example, 2000 words means that the test only looks at the 2000 most frequent words in English.
4 Make sure to include the University Word List.
5 Write down your answers below.

Level	Score
2000	
3000	
5000	
University Word List	

The website recommends that you get at least 83% on each test. As a university student you will want to pass the 5000 and University Word lists. You may want to work on the 10,000 word list too.

What vocabulary do you use?

What is your vocabulary use like? Your word processor will tell you how many words are in your essay, but it will not tell you how many different words you use, or how often you use the same word. For that we can use the free VocabProfile website:

1 Go to http://www.lextutor.ca/vp/eng/.
2 Copy and paste your text in the textbox.
3 Click 'SUBMIT_Window' to get your results.

The results can be a little confusing, but if you scroll down, you'll see what vocabulary level (1000, 2000, 3000, 5000, Academic Word List and other lists) your own words belong to. Here's an example:

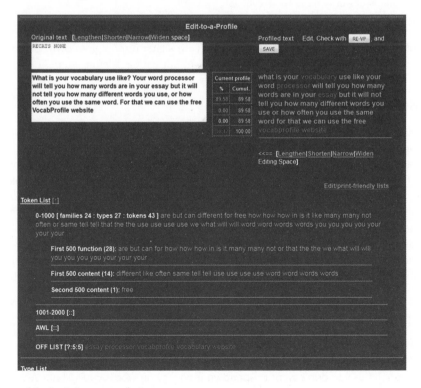

Figure 4.1   Lextutor screen shot

As you can see, the text mostly has words belonging to the first 1000 words. Moving to the left-hand side of the screen, we get some very valuable information. Some words are function words, which do not carry as much information as content words. There are no words belonging to the next 1000 common words and no words belonging to the Academic Word List (AWL). There are words that belong to other lists that the program does not store. This analysis tells you the kinds of vocabulary used in our very short example. However, if this is your own academic writing, you may see more content words and words in the AWL because usually academic texts have denser information.

Practising with the VocabProfile website

Now that you know what vocabulary you use, how is this different from a native speaker? Ask a friend if you can analyse his/her essay and write down the results here. What differences can you find? (If you can't find anyone to give you a copy of their essay, perhaps your teacher has a model essay you could use). Complete the following table to show the differences.

Criteria	Your essay	A native speaker's essay
The number of words in the first 1000 word list		
The number of function words		
The number of content words		
The number of words in the 1000–2000 list		
The number of words in the AWL		

Another approach is to compare a first draft with a later draft of your own. Do you use more words or more types of word? How about your academic words?

How to learn new words

Having learned another language you will know how important it is to learn vocabulary. It is just as important as learning the grammar of the new language. Some people would even say learning words is more important. But with so many words in the English language, you have to learn smart, not just learn a lot. Focus on the most frequent words first, then the academic words and the words specific to your subject (see above). It is also important to think about *how* you will learn (and remember!) new words, as there are more and less efficient ways.

Students have told us they use many different ways to learn new words. Here are some of them. Do you use these? Put a tick in front of every technique you use and at the end add them up. Think about what new tips you would like to try to further improve your vocabulary.

To find new words...

1 *I highlight or copy words I don't know from my textbook and other readings.*
This is a good idea, but be careful (at first) to choose only words that are quite frequent, as you don't want to spend your energy on words you will not see or use again.

2 *I try to write new words down during the lecture or tutorial.*
This can work, but be careful; it is difficult enough to follow the lecturer without also having to worry about new vocabulary, so unless a word is repeated again and again, it may be more important to get the overall message, rather than focus on individual words. It may be better to set aside specific time to learn vocabulary.

3 *I read newspaper articles, stories and academic texts every day.*
Excellent! Reading different kinds of text regularly is one of the best ways to learn vocabulary and also the grammar of a new language. The more often you see some words, the more likely you will remember them.

4 *I study lists of words and phrases we are provided with.*
Words given out by your lecturers (usually in the form of glossaries, or lists of (usually) subject-specific words with a brief definition) are important to learn as they are very relevant to the subject.

5 *I use the 1000, 2000 and Academic Word lists on the internet and check I know those words well.*
This is an excellent strategy. You can find the links to the 1000 and Academic Word lists below.

URL

The 1000 most common words can be found here:
http://esl.about.com/library/vocabulary/bl1000_list1.htm
The Academic Word List can be found here:
http://www.englishvocabularyexercises.com/AWL/

To remember new words ...

6 *I group words by their meaning.*
This works well as it is the same way our brain stores information. Words that go together often are easier to remember together. Below is an example. You could add many more words.

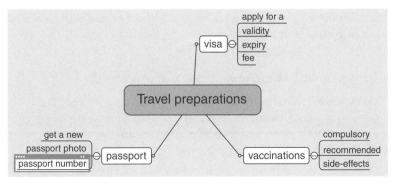

Figure 4.2 Grouping words by their meaning

7 *I try to create a story with the words I want to remember.*
Some students use memory techniques like story-telling, such as this one: 'I am going on holiday and will bring … <add the new words here>. Others use the new words to describe a person (especially good with adverbs and adjectives) or a process (good for verbs).

8 *I classify words.*
For example, cats and dogs are both 'animals' so they can be grouped together. Animals and humans are both 'living creatures', and so on. Remembering words in relation to other words like this can help.

9 *I link new words with pictures.*
Some learners are more visual than others, and, for them, associating words with pictures is a good way to remember them. For example: 'The bumblebee [an insect] sat on the newsreader's nose and read the newspaper.' Or you can simply think of the image of a bumblebee when learning the word.

10 *I review regularly.*
This is probably the most important one. Research has shown that without review we forget up to 75% of new information within ONE DAY (see Chapter 2)! So it is extremely important to have a schedule. This is especially difficult if you are studying hard, but the truth is simple: if you don't review them, you may as well not learn new words in the first place.

11 *I use a flashcard system.*
This is one of the best ways to learn new vocabulary! See further down in this chapter.

To use new words …

12 *I choose five new words in the morning and remind myself to find a way to use them that day.*
This works well for many students as there are so many words and you won't be able to start using all of them straight away. Choose words that you think are important to be able to use yourself, rather than to be able to recognize only.

13 *I keep a list of words near my desk or on my computer so that when I am writing an essay, it reminds me to use those.*
Great! And don't forget the glossary your lecturer may have given you.

Did you get 13 out of 13? If so, well done! If your score was lower, see if any of these suggestions sound like they might work for you. Perhaps do this with another student so you can help and remind each other.

How to work out the meanings of new words

When you meet new words in context they will always seem difficult, but by looking at the meaning, it will be easier to remember the word. Look at this sentence and imagine that *******s is a new word. What might it mean? Write down as many words as possible that would make sense.

The albatross deaths have attracted attention at international *******s.

Look at the end of this paragraph to find the word that was in the actual article. Many of the words you wrote down will have similar or related meanings to the original word. They will be like synonyms. Trying to think about the meaning will help you remember the new word. (The word was 'conferences'.)

Now look at your textbook and find a word you don't know. Try to work it out using these clues:

How do the words in the rest of the sentence help?
Do the parts of the word remind you of other related words?
Take a guess at the possible meaning.
Use a dictionary as a last resort.

One technique is to look at the different word parts. Many words in English are made up of words from other languages. Sometimes knowing this can help you recognize their meaning.

For example, have you heard people talk about 'the post-modern age'? The word 'post' here comes from Latin and means 'after', so 'post-modern age' refers to a period in history after the modern period. We call 'post' a *prefix* because it comes *before* the word.

Can you recognize the others below?

Prefix	Meaning	Example
ante- & pre-		pre-war period
anti-	= against	
auto-		autonomous, autocrat
bi-		bicycle
inter-		interaction
intra-	= inside	
mis-		misinterpreting (interpreting the wrong way)
mono-	= one	
multi-	= many	
neo-		neo-colonialism
pan-	= all	
ele-		telephone, television

Check your answers at the end of the book.

English also uses many *suffixes* which come at the *end* of a word. Here are some examples:

Suffix	Meaning	Example
-ance, ence N	state of being	residence, permanence
-age N	belonging to	percentage, coverage
-ful A	with	doubtful, meaningful
-less A	without	doubtless, purposeless

Learning academic vocabulary

Above we talked about different types of vocabulary and discussed the importance of academic vocabulary for your university studies. Here we look at where to find out which are the most important words and how to learn them.

Researchers from New Zealand have created the Academic Word List (AWL) of the 570 most frequent words found across different academic fields.

URL

The Academic Word List can be found here:
http://www.englishvocabularyexercises.com/AWL/

Download the list and assess your own knowledge of it, by giving a score next to each word.

0 – I do not know this word.
1 – I recognize the meaning, but I'm not sure.
2 – I know the meaning, but I've never used it.
3 – I know the meaning, and I can use it in my speaking and writing.

Practise the words you do not know well and check your progress regularly. In addition, there are a lot of websites on the internet with exercises for the list. This is one of them: http://www.englishvocabularyexercises.com/.

Learning vocabulary with flashcards

Learning words is one thing; remembering them is another. Flashcards (little paper cards) can be of great use as a way of keeping track of words you want to learn. There are many mobile phone apps that can help you, but as they are different, we are describing how paper flash cards can be created and used.

SIDE A	SIDE B
Word or expression	Definition Sentence with that word Collocations Translation Pronunciation Any other information

On one side of the card you write the new word, expression or sentence you want to remember. On the other side you write a definition, an example of its use (perhaps as you encountered it yourself), a translation, collocations (words that go together) and any other information you want to remember about that word (e.g. pronunciation, where you heard it, etc.).

The cards should be written in such a way that if you look at them again after a long time, you know what the word means and how to use it.

Here's an example:

SIDE A	SIDE B
To be fed up with something or someone	Definition: 'If you are fed up, you are unhappy, bored or tired of something, especially of something you've been experiencing for a long time' (Collins Cobuild) 'We're fed up with having to clean up behind the tourists' (police officer in *The Herald*) Collocation: fed up with something or someone Translation: ergens zat van zijn

Here's a good system for using the flashcards to help you learn new words.

1 Put all the new flashcards in one pile.
2 The next day, practise them again. Put the ones you know into a new pile, number two. The ones you don't know stay in pile number one.
3 The next day, do the same thing. The words you know from pile one should go into pile number two, the ones you know from pile two should go into a new pile, number three. Words you don't know stay in their original pile. If you learn any new words in the meantime, put these in pile number one. Do this until you have five piles.
4 Practise all the words every day until they are in pile number five. The good thing about this method is that words that are very difficult take more time to get to pile number five, whereas you don't spend a lot of time on easier words.
5 After a word has arrived at pile number five and you still know it, put it into pile number six. This is a special pile because you only practise it once a month. If you practise these and you still know them, put them into pile number seven. This one you only practise once every six months. If you still know a word then, you will probably remember it forever.

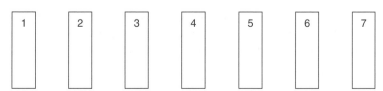

Figure 4.3 Piles of flashcards

Learning vocabulary through games   TIP

Wordcards are excellent to do vocabulary games with. For example, you could take 20 cards and test each other. If your partner gets the answer right, he gets your card. If not, you keep it. The first person to get all 20 cards is the winner.

URL

https://quizlet.com/ is an excellent website for you to create electronic flashcards. Based on the words you submitted, the website will also create games and tests for you. You will also find sets of flashcards that people already created and shared with others.

How to make the most of a dictionary

One tool you will be using a lot is your dictionary. Most people use them to look up the meaning of an individual word, but few realize that dictionaries give far more information than that. Before we look at the uses of a dictionary, let's see what different types exist.

Translation dictionary

This is the most popular type of dictionary with international students. It is quick and you get an immediate idea of the meaning of a word through your own language. There is nothing wrong with occasionally using a translation dictionary, but they are more useful as a practical tool rather than for learning vocabulary.

English–English dictionary

This is where you will find a wealth of information about not only the meaning of a word, but also how it is used in practice. We will look at some examples below. Learners' dictionaries often include study pages and information on how words are related to other words. A learner's dictionary is not the same as a vocabulary book. A dictionary's main function (even a learner's dictionary) is to help you find out the meaning of words. A vocabulary book's main function is to help you learn words.

Special dictionaries

If you study medicine you will probably want a dictionary that explains all the medical terms you are likely to come across. Luckily, such a dictionary exists and there are others for law, science and many other subjects. Having one of these can be very valuable.

Thesaurus or dictionary of synonyms

A thesaurus is a dictionary that gives you a word's synonyms (other words with the same or similar meaning), such as the words 'flat' and 'apartment'. (The opposite of a synonym is an antonym. Examples of antonyms are 'good' and 'bad'). Using a thesaurus is great for when you have to write an essay and can't think of another word to avoid saying the same thing over and over (see below). However, make sure you check the meaning of the synonym before using it.

Collocations

Collocations are words that go together. So we say that we 'have' an argument, not that we 'do' an argument. Getting collocations right is a difficult task for non-native speakers, but not paying attention to them can result in very different meanings and often makes your speech sound unnatural. There are special 'collocation dictionaries' and they are a great help for your writing.

If we look at a collocation dictionary, we may find the following information for the word 'flower':

Adj.	colourful, fragrant…
Quant.	bouquet, bunch
Verb + flower	have, produce…
Flower + verb	seed
Flower + noun	petal, stem…
Prep.	in flower
Phrases	(some example phrases …)

As you can see, you will find examples of adjectives commonly used with 'flower'. It also shows you which quantifiers we use (so we say 'a bunch of flowers', not 'a group of flowers'). Next, you can see examples of how to combine a verb with the word flower, flower with a verb and flower with a noun. Finally, we learn that the preposition used with 'to flower' is 'in' and some common phrases with the word. Very helpful, especially when you are writing an essay.

Phrasal verbs are another difficult area for learners. A phrasal verb is a verb followed by a preposition or adverb:

Bring (something) up
Hurry up

These have a specific meaning; for example, 'to bring something up' can literally mean to bring (say, a book) up (for example, to another room in the house). But often it means 'to start a new topic' or 'to mention something in a conversation'. So even though you may know the meaning of the verb ('bring') and the preposition ('up'), if you didn't know the special meaning of 'to bring something up', you probably couldn't guess it.

Another thing to know about phrasal verbs is that some are *transitive* (they can take an object), like in our example. In the sentence, 'He brought up a new topic,' *a new topic* is the object. Other phrasal verbs are *intransitive* such as 'to show up' (meaning 'to arrive') and do not take an object. There is nothing in the phrasal verbs themselves to tell you if they are transitive or intransitive and you will need a dictionary to tell you.

Similarly, some phrasal verbs are *separable*, which means that the object can come between the verb and the preposition. An example is 'to make up a story'. You can say:

I made the story up.

but also:

I made up the story.

Again, you will need a dictionary as for most verbs it is impossible to tell. Several of the major publishers sell phrasal verb dictionaries and workbooks.

URL

A free website that will help you with phrasal verbs is this one:
http://www.phrasalverbdemon.com/

What information does a dictionary give?

Have a look at the example below, taken from the Collins Cobuild dictionary, and see if you can list the different types of information that are included.

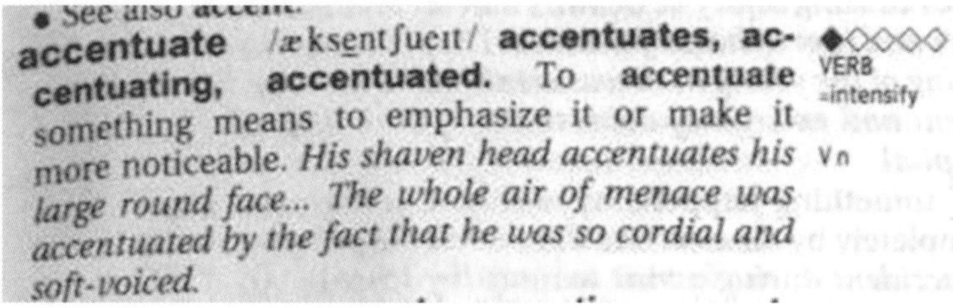

● See also accent.

accentuate /æksˈentʃueɪt/ **accentuates, ac-** ◆◇◇◇◇
centuating, accentuated. To **accentuate** VERB
something means to emphasize it or make it =intensify
more noticeable. *His shaven head accentuates his* Vn
large round face... The whole air of menace was
accentuated by the fact that he was so cordial and
soft-voiced.

Figure 4.4   An example from a dictionary
Reproduced with the permission of Collins Cobuild.

1   pronunciation _____

2   _____

3   _____

4   _____

5   _____

6   _____

Check your answers at the end of the book.

There are others, but you get the picture: a dictionary gives you a lot of useful information. Some words may have more information, such as different entries for different meanings, phrasal verbs, as well as information about whether the word is formal or informal, spoken language only, offensive or technical.

URL

A good learner's dictionary is the Macmillan English dictionary. You can find more information here:
http://www.macmillandictionary.com

Can you find the answers to these questions?

Now that you know how much information a dictionary can give you, see if you can answer these questions. You will need a full-sized (not a pocket) dictionary. Check your answers at the end of the book.

1. Can you say 'the meeting was called by the leader'?
2. Is 'furniture' a countable noun?
3. Is 'darn' an offensive word?
4. What is the difference between the phrasal verbs 'break out' and 'break away'?
5. What sound in the word 'legislature' is stressed?
6. What is a synonym for 'appalling'?

Using a thesaurus successfully

As mentioned above, a thesaurus is a reference book or website that gives lists of words of similar meaning. It can be really useful if you are trying to use a wider and more interesting range of vocabulary; however, a thesaurus needs to be treated with care. Almost no two words can ever be used with exactly the same meaning in exactly the same way all the time. And so it is important to use a dictionary in order to check the words that your thesaurus gives and find out if they are suitable in the contexts in which you want to use them. This task takes you through the necessary steps.

Task

Imagine this situation. You have been asked to write an essay about the ways that you have learned vocabulary in another language. You write the following sentence:

One of the best **ways** to learn new words is by using vocabulary cards.

However, you realize that you have used the word 'way' many times already and want to use a different word.

You go to an online thesaurus to look for other words. Follow these steps:

1 Go to the online Merriam Webster dictionary at http://www.m-w.com/. Enter the word *way* and choose 'thesaurus'. From the results, there are ten different meanings of *way*. Which one is relevant here? See the answers section at the end of the book.

2 Click on the relevant entry word at the end of this definition. It is a link. It gives the following text:

Synonyms: approach, fashion, form, manner, strategy, style, system, tack, tactics, technique, way
Related words: mode; blueprint, design, game, ground plan, intrigue, layout, line, plan, plot, programme, route, scheme; expedient, move, shift, step; practice (*also* practise), process, routine; project, proposal, proposition; policy

Start with the synonyms. Which of these look possible in the original sentence in terms of word meaning? You may need to use your dictionary to do this.

Related words   TIP

Often it may be best to stick with the suggested synonyms. The key to using the related words is to take a step back and rethink what you are trying to say. They can give you different ideas, but they may take you in a different direction and may not fit in with the point that you are making.

---

3 Now use these words to write alternative sentences. Think about how you might need to change the grammar of the sentence.

4 How is the meaning different in each of these sentences?

Using a corpus to learn new words and improve your writing

A corpus is simply a large collection of texts. An English corpus can be a great help to learners to see how the language is used by native speakers in authentic situations, such as in newspapers, books and articles, but also in spoken contexts such as in lectures, or on TV. A corpus is different from a dictionary in that it does not give translations or explanations. Instead, it gives you a wealth of information about what words are most common in English and how they are used. The types of question a corpus can help you answer include:

What prepositions does 'scared' take in spoken British English?
Can you say 'x scared y'?
When do I use 'scared' and when do I use 'afraid'?

Let's see if we can answer some of these questions.

The easiest way to see how a corpus works is by using an example. One free website that we recommend is this one:

URL

http://lextutor.ca/conc/eng/

Here you get access to a concordancer, or a programme that lets you search through a corpus. Let's try to answer the first question above. Go to the above website and you will see the following screen.

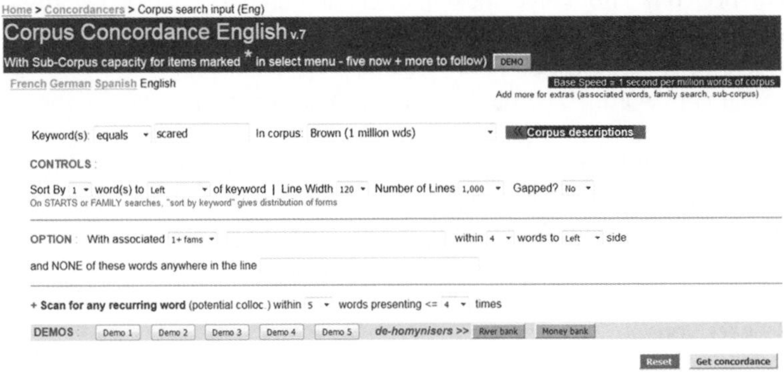

Figure 4.5 How to search for concordances

It may look a bit complicated at first, but let's go through it step by step. We are interested in the word 'scared' so this is what we type in the first text box. In addition to 'equal to', which looks up only the word you type in, you can choose 'begins with' or 'ends with' or 'contains'. This is helpful when you are interested in finding examples of all words that begin with, say, 'inter', such as 'international' or 'interaction'. You could also look for words that contain, for example, 'tion', such as 'education' and 'nation'. In this case we will use 'equal to'.

Next we need to select the corpus we want to use by clicking on the drop-down box. There are several listed. The most useful ones include:

University Word List	Particularly useful when you are writing an academic essay.
BNC written	If you are only interested in written language.
BNC spoken	Likewise, if you are interested in spoken English.

In this case we will use BNC (this stands for British National Corpus) spoken. If we were interested in US English we could use the US TV Talk, but it is much smaller. This is all the information you need to select to get started. You can leave the other options as they are and choose 'get concordance'. Here is an example of the output.

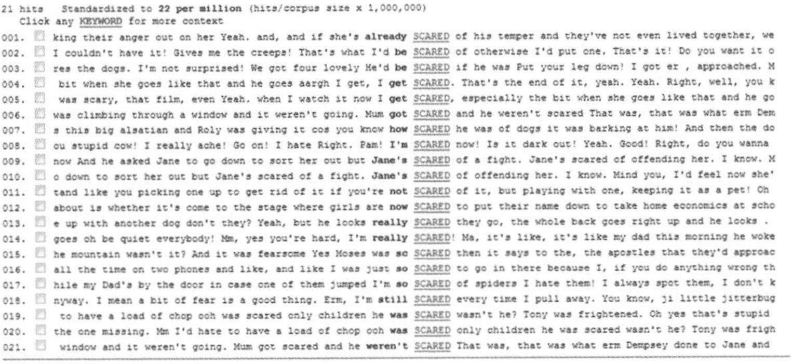
21 hits Standardized to **22 per million** (hits/corpus size x 1,000,000)
Click any KEYWORD for more context
001. king their anger out on her Yeah. and, and if she's **already** SCARED of his temper and they've not even lived together, we
002. I couldn't have it! Gives me the creeps! That's what I'd **be** SCARED of otherwise I'd put one. That's it! Do you want it o
003. res the dogs. I'm not surprised! We got four lovely He'd **be** SCARED if he was Put your leg down! I got er , approached. M
004. bit when she goes like that and he goes aargh I get, I **get** SCARED. That's the end of it, yeah. Yeah. Right, well, you k
005. was scary, that film, even Yeah. when I watch it now I **get** SCARED, especially the bit when she goes like that and he go
006. was climbing through a window and it weren't going. Mum **got** SCARED and he weren't scared That was, that was what erm Dem
007. s this big alsatian and Roly was giving it cos you know **how** SCARED he was of dogs it was barking at him! And then the do
008. ou stupid cow! I really ache! Go on! I hate Right. Pam! **I'm** SCARED now! Is it dark out! Yeah. Good! Right, do you wanna
009. now And he asked Jane to go down to sort her out but **Jane's** SCARED of a fight. Jane's scared of offending her. I know. M
010. o down to sort her out but Jane's scared of a fight. **Jane's** SCARED of offending her. I know. Mind you, I'd feel now she'
011. tand like you picking one up to get rid of it if you're **not** SCARED of it, but playing with one, keeping it as a pet! Oh
012. about is whether it's come to the stage where girls are **now** SCARED to put their name down to take home economics at scho
013. e up with another dog don't they? Yeah, but he looks **really** SCARED they go, the whole back goes right up and he looks .
014. goes oh be quiet everybody! Mm, yes you're hard, I'm **really** SCARED! Ma, it's like, it's like my dad this morning he woke
015. he mountain wasn't it? And it was fearsome Yes Moses was **so** SCARED then it says to the, the apostles that they'd approac
016. all the time on two phones and like, and like I was just **so** SCARED to go in there because I, if you do anything wrong th
017. hile my Dad's by the door in case one of them jumped I'm **so** SCARED of spiders I hate them! I always spot them, I don't k
018. nyway. I mean a bit of fear is a good thing. Erm, I'm **still** SCARED every time I pull away. You know, ji little jitterbug
019. to have a load of chop ooh was scared only children he **was** SCARED wasn't he? Tony was frightened. Oh yes that's stupid
020. the one missing. Mm I'd hate to have a load of chop ooh **was** SCARED only children he was scared wasn't he? Tony was frigh
021. window and it weren't going. Mum got scared and he **weren't** SCARED That was, that was what erm Dempsey done to Jane and

Figure 4.6 Search results for 'scared'

Each sentence comes from BNC spoken. By clicking on the underlined words you can see the whole sentence, but usually it is enough to just look at the part you see on the first screen. The 21 examples only use one preposition: 'of'.

By clicking on 'wordnet' entries you can see a dictionary definition of the word 'scared'.

You can also search for words used with another word by typing it in the 'with associated word' text box. For example, if we search for 'scared' associated with 'of' we find the same ten examples as we found in the 21 results we got above.

Your turn!

Now let's see if you can do this. Can you find the answers to the other questions above? Check your answers at the end of the book.

1 What prepositions does 'scared' take?

_____

2 Can you say 'x scared y'?

_____

3 When do I use 'scared' and when do I use 'afraid'?

_____

_____

URL

Another great corpus to explore is the Corpus of Contemporary American English (COCA). You'll find examples of how words are used in many different types of text: **http://corpus.byu.edu/coca/**

Check collocation with a corpus

You can use a corpus to check the prepositions that follow some verbs and adjectives. For example:

I am really interested … finding out more about music from Cuba.

If you wanted to check this, follow these instructions:

1 Go to **http://lextutor.ca/conc/eng/** or **http://corpus.byu.edu/coca/**.
2 Type 'interested' in the keyword box.
3 Submit the search.

Look through the list and find examples with a similar grammar structure and similar meaning to your sentence. Which preposition follows 'interested' most often?

Use the same procedure to find the missing word in the following sentences. These three words are all words from the Academic Word List. Check your answers at the end of the book.

a. The **implication** … this theory is that companies should do all they can to keep their staff motivated.
b. The boom experienced in the mid 1990s **coincided** … the fall in the value of the dollar.
c. They decided to **concentrate** … their core markets in the following decade.

Sort your concordance search   TIP

Some concordance samplers such as the one at www.lextutor.ca allow you to sort your search left or right. If you are interested in the word that follows your keyword, order by right. If you are interested in the word before your search term, order by left.

Vocabulary resources online

Apart from the resources already mentioned in this chapter, there are many other great resources available on the internet, many of them for free. Here is a hand-picked selection. Internet links do change so we can't promise all of them will still work at the time you read this book. However, most have been available for years and we think they will stay accessible for some time to come.

Vocabulary learning sites

General service list: This list contains the 2000 most useful word families of English. It has been estimated that these words make up 80% of the words used in academic texts so it is important that you check that you know all of them. Click on 'The actual 2284 words, with frequency numbers' to see the list.

http://www.jbauman.com/aboutgsl.html

English Daily: This website has information and exercises on different aspects of English. For vocabulary, read the idiom sections.

http://www.englishdaily626.com/

Self-study quizzes for ESL students: Lots of grammar and vocabulary exercises for elementary, intermediate and advanced learners. Use the quizzes to test yourself.

http://iteslj.org/quizzes/

Merriam-Webster: this online dictionary has a daily podcast and exercises.

http://www.m-w.com

Visual Thesaurus: This helps you find related words.

http://www.visualthesaurus.com/online/index.html

Vocabulary for academic purposes: This website contains lots of useful information on academic vocabulary.

http://www.uefap.net/

Compleat Lexical Tutor: Here you will find many vocabulary exercises and tests to find out your level. Recommended!

www.lextutor.ca

Word and Phrase Info: Click on 'Input/analyze text'. Write or copy and paste a piece of writing in here. This program will analyse it in terms of the frequency of the words used.

http://www.wordandphrase.info/

Dictionaries

Cambridge international dictionaries:

http://dictionary.cambridge.org

Merriam-Webster dictionary:

http://www.merriam-webster.com/

Newbury House dictionary:

http://nhd.heinle.com/home.aspx

Thesaurus:

http://www.thesaurus.com

Free dictionaries, translation dictionary:

http://www.dicts.info/

Urban dictionary:

http://www.urbandictionary.com/

Wordsmyth dictionary:

http://www.wordsmyth.net

Specialist dictionaries

Chinese/Korean/Japanese to English dictionary:

http://www.chinalanguage.com/dictionaries/

Dictionary of acronyms:

http://www.ucc.ie/cgi-bin/acronym

Dictionary of cell biology:

http://www.cellbio.com/dictionaries.html

Dictionary of psychology:

http://allpsych.com/dictionary/

Internet glossary of statistical terms:

http://www.animatedsoftware.com/statglos/statglos.htm

Lexicon of linguistics:

http://www2.let.uu.nl/UiL-OTS/Lexicon/

Nolo's legal dictionary:

http://www.nolo.com/lawcenter/dictionary/wordindex.cfm

Conclusion

Vocabulary is an important aspect of language learning. It is especially important when you need to read academic texts in English, listen to academic lectures, give academic presentations and participate in class discussions. You will pick up new words when you read and listen to English. However, you will also need to assess your vocabulary knowledge and learn vocabulary purposefully. This chapter has provided strategies and resources that we hope you have found useful.

Listening to Lectures

We have called this chapter *listening to lectures,* but if listening was all you had to do then the problem would not be so big. In lectures students have to do many things, which we could summarize as listening, looking, writing and (we hope) understanding. In this chapter we make suggestions for these four skills.

In this chapter you will learn about:

- the purpose, structure and language of a lecture
- lecturing styles that change from country to country
- what you can do before the lecture
- what you can do during the lecture
- what you can do after the lecture
- note-taking tips and what you do with your notes
- becoming a better listener.

What's the problem?

Let's start with some of the problems that students report about listening to lectures. In order to see which parts of this chapter you need to look at, tick the things that are difficult for you. Then turn to that part of the chapter.

If this sounds like your problem ...	... go to this section of the chapter
The lecturing style is very different from what I am accustomed to.	'Lecturing styles from country to country'
I find it hard to make sense of the overall shape of the lecture.	'The parts of a lecture'
How can I know whether a point is important or not?	
I can't tell when the lecturer is moving on to the next point.	
The lecturer talks too fast for me to get everything down.	'Note-taking'
Some lecturers talk as we are trying to copy the PowerPoint slides.	
I can't read my handwriting later when I look back at my notes.	
I don't know how to spell the words.	

The purpose of a lecture

What's the main purpose?

Respond to each of these statements according to your ideas of whether this is *probably* or *probably not* a reason for having lectures. Then check the answers at the end of the book.

The purpose of a lecture is to ...	Probably	Probably not
Make sure that students are serious about their studies.		
Check attendance.		
Give information that can't be found anywhere else.		
Make university learning interesting.		
Let students ask questions.		
Bring together information from many sources.		
Let students get to know one another.		
Present information in a new form from the textbook.		

Why else are lectures useful?

Why do you think lectures are useful? Write down five ideas here and compare your ideas with ours.

1 _____
2 _____
3 _____
4 _____
5 _____

Lectures are useful because listening can make the content memorable. The lectures often extend the content covered in the reading. Lecturers may also give important handouts or carry out interesting demonstrations. Sometimes lecturers show how the topic of the lecture is linked to an upcoming exam. Lectures are also a good place to meet other students.

Lecturing styles from country to country

We asked some international students for their experiences of lectures. Here is what they said. For each comment, note down the main difference in lecture style that the student noticed.

Antonina (from Italy): There were 300 people in a lecture and we couldn't fit in the room so I listened to the lecturer on an intercom in another lecture theatre. We just listened. It was very passive. I was amazed that in lectures in NZ, the lecturer liked to be asked questions at any time and she would give us things to talk about.

Ahmed (from Saudi Arabia): I sometimes feel the lecturer looks down on the students. There is a big distance between 'us' and 'them'. They certainly wouldn't talk to us outside the class. Here in Singapore it is much more open. It is much easier to approach the lecturers.

Jose (from Mexico): My lecturers seemed to make it difficult for us students. They never tried to make things easy or understandable for us and they weren't worried if we didn't get it. In America my lecturers want me to tell them if I don't understand something and they try to make things as clear as possible for us.

As you can see, there are differences in how lecturers and students interact, in their attitude towards students and also in how approachable they are outside the classroom. However, not all of these differences can be explained culturally. Within one country there are many differences between individual lecturers. Later in this chapter you will read about specific listening problems and how to overcome them.

Preparing for a lecture

It's a good idea to spend a few minutes thinking about a lecture before you go in. This is important if the lecture is in your first language, and even more important if you are listening to a lecture in a second language. If you can predict what the lecturer will talk about, you will find it easier to follow the lecture and get more out of it. You will also have a clearer idea of what information you want to get from the lecture and that will make listening easier. You can use reading handed out by the lecturer beforehand and also lecture titles to help you prepare.

Do the assigned reading before the lecture

If the lecturer gives recommended reading (either a handout or chapters from a textbook) for you to read before a lecture, make sure you read it, even if you don't understand everything in it. Lecturers usually talk about the reading in the lecture. Try using this worksheet to prepare for a lecture.

Thinking about the reading	During the lecture
Is there anything you didn't **understand** from the reading and want explained in the lecture?	I am confused about .... /I don't understand ....
What do you want **more information** about in the lecture?	I understand the topic in general but I want more details about ....
Was there anything **controversial** in the reading? Would you like to hear an alternative opinion about this?	I want to hear the lecturer's opinion about ....
Were there any **problems** with the ideas in the reading? Do you want these expanded in the lecture?	I disagreed with the point about ....
Often textbook reading is **theoretical**. Do you want to hear the lecturer discussing the **application** of an idea?	I want to find out the real-life application of ....

(Continued)

Thinking about the reading	During the lecture
Sometimes a textbook gives evidence from one **situation**, but you may want to hear if this is true in another **situation**.	I want to hear if ... also applies to / when ....
Do you need ideas of where to find **further reading** about a topic?	I want more references to read about ....

Predict the content from the lecture title

You may also have questions you want answered simply from the title of the lecture. Coming up with questions will prepare you mentally for the lecture. This section looks at lecture titles and encourages you to come up with questions you want answered in a lecture.

Look at the following lecture title. It is the third lecture in a course on economic development in South East Asia.

Week 3	Wednesday 29 September	Development and Standard of Living in South East Asia: Accounting for the Variation in the Region and the Challenges for the Future

Write down three questions you would like answered if you went to this lecture.

1 _____?
2 _____?
3 _____?

Now compare your questions with these:

1 How does the lecturer define 'standard of living'?
2 How do they measure this? What data do they cite?
3 Which countries have the highest standard of living in the region?
4 Which have the poorest quality of life?
5 Why is there such a variation?
6 Which historical factors affect the standard of living?
7 What specific challenges will the region face in the 21st century?

Summary

It is just as important to become a critical listener as it is to become a critical reader or writer. Being prepared and going into the lecture with clear ideas of what you want to learn is a key part of this.

Assignments   TIP

If you have an assignment due in the next few weeks, you may have questions you want answered by the lecture. For example, you may have an idea of what to write in the assignment and want to check in the lecture that you are on the right track.

Note-taking

At first, note-taking in a second language is very hard. It is tempting to write down everything you hear because you are so pleased with yourself that you heard it (and even know how to spell it!) whether or not it is important. You think 'Okay, at least I will be able to look at my notes later and work out what was said!' This is a bad tactic because note-taking has become a brainless task and you have stopped thinking about the content of the lecture. Note-taking is supposed to help you follow the lecture and then remember and think about the content later. If your notes are not useful, then you are better off concentrating on trying to understand the general meaning of the lecture and forgetting about the details. Let's assume that you really do want to take notes that are useful to you later. If so, read on.

Different ways of organizing your notes

Note-taking does get a lot easier with practice. This section gives some examples of how you can organize your notes more effectively. First, we will present some models that you can use. Then we will list some ways that you can develop your note-taking.

Linear notes

This is when you make notes down the page of the main points in the lecture. It is probably what most students do most of the time. Look at these notes from the beginning of a lecture about the business side of professional sport. What makes these notes easy to follow? Note down your observations and then check the answers at the end of the book.

Professionalism in sport: Are footballers worth $X million per week?

last 20 years' sport: pass-time   big business – **entertainment $**
– ticket sales (less important now?)
e.g. Turkish football grounds – ads … one side of ground only (cameras from other side)
free entry to Wednesday games (Italy)
– TV rights / satellite TV subs
pay-per-view boxing
e.g. highlights on news? <25 seconds – goal / try only (who has TV rights?)
– corporate hospitality (@ sports stadium)
– bar sales (in pubs)
beer / cigarette / junk food advertising $ v. important 4 sport
– advertising – at stadiums / on players / ad breaks on TV / team – stad. naming rights e.g. v. warriors ~ t. clear dome
– shirt / scarf / accessory sales (China – Crystal Palace shirts – 2 Chinese players)

Professionalism in sport: Are footballers worth $X million per week? *(Continued)*

RESULT: Players $$$$$ (celeb. culture) fuel all sales. Commodity?
– transfer fees
– wages
– TV ad contracts – sports shoes / razors / aftershave etc.
– bad (!) autobiographies
– etc.
(sports media – slaves to business?   lack of critical comment on sport?)
The man, the brand. How much does he earn?
per game?
per goal?
per shirt?
per ad?
per razor sale?

Using diagrams to organize your notes

Diagrams are often easier to review than linear notes and visual learners find information in a diagram easier to remember in an exam because they can picture the graphics. Also they are useful for referring to when you are writing assignments. The idea is to use organization that fits the lecture content. Here are three examples.

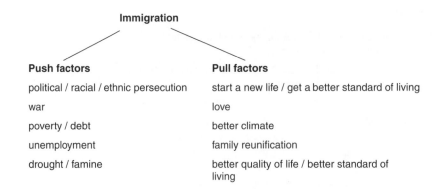

Immigration

Push factors

political / racial / ethnic persecution

war

poverty / debt

unemployment

drought / famine

Pull factors

start a new life / get a better standard of living

love

better climate

family reunification

better quality of life / better standard of living

Figure 5.1   A simple classification diagram

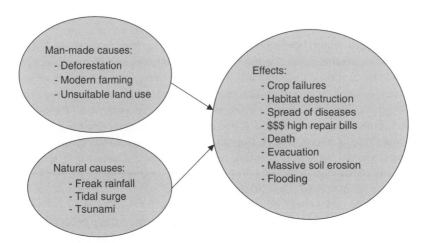

Figure 5.2 A mind map

Example 3: The Cornell note-taking system

Date of lecture	Topic
CUES *Main ideas *Questions that link points *Diagrams *Prompts to help you study WHEN? After class during review 5 cm	NOTES *Record the lecture here, using: – Concise sentences – Shorthand symbols – Abbreviations – Lists *Skip lots of space between points WHEN? During class 5 cm
SUMMARY *Top level main ideas *For quick reference WHEN? After class during review	

Adapted from http://lifehacker.com/software/note-taking/geek-to-live--take-studyworthy-lecture-notes-202418.php

Explanation: how to use it

- Notes column (right): Record the lecture here during class using short sentences and fragments that transcribe the facts you'll need. Miss out all unnecessary words such as *the* and *a*. Use bulleted lists for easy skimming, and as much shorthand as possible (without sacrificing readability.) Develop a vocabulary of abbreviations, like 'e.g./ex' for 'for example', 'v' for 'very', 'cf' for 'compare with'. These abbreviations are special to you. It doesn't matter if nobody else can read them. Another type of abbreviation is to use a capital letter for the key terms in the lecture. Thus in notes from a lecture on immigration you would write simple [I] every time that word appears, or [P] if the word 'problems' was used often. You'll see some more abbreviations in the next section.
- Cues column (left): After class, review your notes and jot down questions and memory joggers in this column that help connect ideas listed in the notes section. When you're studying, you'll look at these cues to help you recall the salient facts in your notes.
- Summary area (bottom): After class while you create cues, sum up in the bottom area the notes on each page in one or two sentences that encapsulate the main ideas. You'll use the summary section to skim through your notes and find information later.

Summary of good note-taking practice

Here is the script from an excerpt from a seminar on note-taking. First of all highlight the beginnings of new sections. The first section has been underlined as an example. You can check your answers at the end of the book. Make notes of the main points. You could try to use one of the organizing systems above and as much of the advice in the seminar as possible.

Seminar on Note-Taking

Okay. Thank you all for coming. Today our seminar is about good note-taking practice.

At the beginning of last year, I did a small study of the note-taking habits of successful students looking at the techniques they use when taking notes in lectures and then I asked them for their advice to students who wanted to improve their note-taking. I will present some of the findings of this study and then at the end of this presentation, there will be an opportunity for you to talk about the note-taking strategies that you found the most effective.

First of all, let's look at what you should make notes on – I mean the paper – not the topics! Now, lots of students use notebooks for their lecture notes. This is fine but some students find it easier to use a loose-leaf notebook – that means one that you can take the pages out of – rather than one with fixed pages. This means that you can take the pages out and put them into a folder with your course notes. Then you can collect notes and course reading for each course in one place, in a separate notebook or section of a notebook – write the name and date of the lecture. Sometimes lecturers give out a handout with the main points from the lecture. You could find it useful to make notes on the handout in the margins – this will help you organize the notes you make. Also, some lecturers put their own notes on the course website after a lecture. You can print these out and put them in your folder next to your notes.

(Continued)

Seminar on Note-Taking

The appearance of your notes is really important too because you will need to refer to them later. If you find yourself making doodles or writing notes to your partner on your lecture notes, remember that not only is this manual activity stopping you from concentrating, but it will also be annoying and confusing when you look back at your notes – i.e. when you are using them to revise for an exam.

It is worth losing a bit of speed in order to write legibly – this saves time in the long run. If you find you don't have time to write neatly, then you are probably writing too much. Note only key words, not every word – and think critically about what you write down. If it is not going to be useful later – don't write it! The other thing you can do if you can't keep up is to leave gaps [ ] when the speaker is moving too fast. You can always check with a friend later if you see a gap in your notes.

In fact, it's a really good idea to review your notes as soon as possible. You could do this with another student. Read through and improve the organization as necessary. Look at the layout – some students make the mistake of writing all their notes in the top quarter of the page. Leave space between points. Indent. Spread it out. Mark ideas that the lecturer emphasizes with an arrow or some special symbol. Put a box around assignments and suggested books so you can identify them quickly.

In terms of developing your listening skills, pay attention to signals for the end of an idea and the beginning of another. If you hear these, they will help you follow the flow of a lecture and lay out your notes logically. Transitions such as 'Therefore', 'finally', and 'furthermore' usually signal an important idea. Also, pay attention to the lecturer's voice. It will often go down in pitch at the end of a section and then up at the start of a new section.

As a final point, often the most interesting and useful things you can gain from lectures are the examples, sketches and illustrations that the lecturer presents. Lecturers often talk about their research in relation to points they make or tell stories from their experience. You can get the theory from a textbook, but often this experience is unpublished and cannot be got from books. These stories are often the most interesting parts of lectures and you can use them in your assignments and exams – so although stories may seem off the point, they may be worth noting down.

Okay. Now, I'd like you to look back over your notes and ....

Symbols and abbreviations for note-taking

Here is a list of common symbols and abbreviations to use when taking notes.

Symbols

@	=	at
↗	=	rise, increase by, grow to / by
↘	=	fall, decrease by, decline
&	=	and
$	=	money
$$$	=	lots of money
~	=	approximately
>	=	is more than

<	=	is less than
∵	=	therefore, so
∴	=	because
♂	=	man; men
♀	=	woman; women
#	=	number (phone # / case #)
/	=	per (kb/s = kilobytes per second)
>1980	=	since 1980
<1980	=	1980 and earlier

Abbreviations

e.g.	=	for example
etc.	=	and so on
i.e.	=	that is
no.	=	number
sth	=	something
s.o.	=	someone
NB	=	note that
ref.	=	reference
doz.	=	dozen
Ks	=	thousands (she earns 89k)
C	=	century (C21st = 21st century)
m.	=	million
esp.	=	especially
c.f.	=	compare with / contrast with
w/	=	with
govt	=	government
w/o	=	without

Ways of developing your note-taking

Here are four ways that you can develop your note-taking.

Method	Details
1. Use published English for academic purposes (EAP) materials	There are a number of good EAP textbooks with recorded lectures and note-taking tasks. One is the 'Contemporary Topics' series published by Longman. There are three books in this series at intermediate, upper intermediate and advanced level and they contain graded lectures with tasks. Because the language is graded, they are useful for developing note-taking skills. Beglar & Murray. 2009. *Contemporary Topics 3*. Longman Salehzadeh. 2005. *Academic Listening Strategies*. Michigan University Press
2. Use lecture scripts from the internet	Google your subject and the words 'lecture scripts' and you will find lecture scripts on the internet. Use these to practise note-taking.

(Continued)

Method	Details
3. Go to some low-stakes lectures	You don't want to develop your note-taking with lectures on your course that really count so why not sit in on some courses that you are not enrolled on? This is great to do if you have not yet started at university. Most lecturers are happy for you to do this so long as you ask first.
4. Record your lectures	Use your phone to record your lecture and then make notes when you listen back to it. This is much easier because you can stop your recording when you need to. This takes time, but it is a great strategy if you cannot follow the live lectures.

Notes   **TIP**

Notes need to be *good enough* so that when you look back you can work out what the lecture was about. They don't need to be perfect. Don't waste time making them look beautiful – they will only be used by you.

The organization and language of lectures

What is the lecturer saying?

When lecturers are speaking, their remarks may be one of the following seven types. The table below shows lecturers' words and their meanings. The left-hand column below tells you the words the lecturer is saying. The right-hand column tells you what to expect next. Thus, with the first words, 'And that leads to …,' you can expect to hear a new topic next.

Listen for these words …		In other words …
And that leads to …. *We now come to look at ….* *Right. Well, if we move on ….* *What I'd like to do now is ….* *Okay now ….*	1	Here's a new topic.
For instance …. *For example ….* *One way this works out is ….* *Let me give you an illustration ….* *This means ….*	2	Here's an example or an explanation.

(Continued)

Listen for these words …		In other words …
According to …. *X would have us believe ….*	3	This is what someone else thinks.
I think this is …. *The most interesting point here is ….* *Let me just say in parentheses ….*	4	This is what I think.
By the way …. *I might say here ….*	5	This is interesting but not important.
So where was I …? *Well, anyway ….* *To get back on the track ….*	6	Now I'm getting back to the topic.
So …. *What I'm saying is ….*	7	Here's a summary.

Adapted from J.R. Nattinger and J.S. DeCarrico (1992) *Lexical Phrases and Language Teaching*, Oxford University Press.

Here is a three-step task for you.

1 Read the columns from left to right.
2 Cover over the right-hand column and see if you can recall what the words mean.
3 Now look at some more examples of what the lecturer means to say.

> *Explaining something he or she has just said in a different way.*
> *Giving an illustration of something that's just been said.*
> *This is not part of the main lecture.*
> *This is the same as something.*
> *These are opinions rather than facts.*
> *A new subtopic is coming.*
> *This is different from something else.*
> *Announcing the topic.*

These words …	mean …
I'd like to talk about …. *What we're doing today is ….* *This morning we'll start looking at ….*	
In other words …. *So the question is ….* *So…. / What I'm saying is ….*	

(Continued)

These words ...	mean ...
That's not the same as .... *The catch here is ....* *That's not what we really mean by ....*	
And that leads to .... *We now come to look at ....* *Right. Well, if we move on ....*	
For instance .... / For example .... *One of the ways this works out is ....* *Let me give you an illustration ....*	
According to .... *I'm a great believer in ....* *X would have us believe ....* *The most interesting point here is ....*	
By the way .... / I might say here .... *As a sidelight ....* *But I'm getting a little ahead of myself ....* *So where was I?* *Well, anyway ....* *To get back on the track ....*	
That would go for X as well as for Y .... *Along the same lines ....*	

Hearing signposting language

Effective lecturers use pauses and intonation (changing the pitch of their speech) to signal the transitions in their lecture. Try the following task.

1 Sit in on a lecture and record it.
2 Try to get the main idea about the lecture, but don't worry too much about the details. In your notes, write down any of the signposting language that you hear from the task above.
3 When you listen back to the lecture, listen to the pitch of the lecturer's voice when he/she uses these signposting expressions. You could indicate pitch change like this:

So ... what I'm saying is ... try to find what patterns you can.

A lecture transcript

The following extracts come from a lecture to students on the topic of English language teaching. In the left-hand column you will find the text of the lecture. Try writing your own commentary in the right-hand column. Your commentary should describe what is happening in the lecture at that time. The first three examples have been done for you. Check your answers at the end of the book.

The lecturer's words	The purpose of the words
Today we are going to have some information about how students can help themselves learn a language. In other words, I'll be talking about what we call language learning strategies. One definition of these strategies is on your handout. Cohen (1998:4) defined them as 'processes which are consciously selected by learners'.	To announce today's topic
In today's lecture I'll be starting by discussing the need for strategies and some definitions of them. I'll be passing on some theories as well as providing you with some examples. Finally there will be some general points about how you might apply the ideas from today's lecture.	To introduce a technical term
Let's start with a question. Why is this topic important to you?	To remind students that they needn't write it down
We have various categories of learning strategies. These are social strategies, cognitive strategies, organizational strategies and metacognitive strategies.	To define a technical term
Now let's turn to some examples of cognitive strategies for learning vocabulary. You have probably used some of these yourselves. Let's see, how many of you try to remember a word by linking it to another word you know in any language?	Start from here
Another aspect that students say they need to learn better is listening. Think of all the contexts where you need to listen: on the telephone, in a social conversation, at a public place and, of course, in a lecture like this one. In some of these places you have to practise selective listening. What we mean by this term is that a person decides to block out much of what is said and listen just for some information that they need. Some of the occasions when you might practise selective listening are	
Etc.	

Visuals

TIP

Visuals are really helpful – they help you follow the main points in the lecture and often have useful quotations or diagrams. Sit by the front so you can see them. Ask the lecturer to post them on the course website or email them to you so you can download them. Don't waste time copying them down if you can get them later.

Some students use their phone to take pictures of the whiteboard and the presentation visuals. Please check with your lecturer first!

Asking questions in lectures

If you have questions to ask of your lecturer, you have different times when this could happen such as:

- one to one later with the lecturer (see Chapter 12 on 'Communicating with lecturers')
- at the end of the lecture
- during tutorials (see Chapter 10 on 'Small group learning')
- in lectures when the lecturer asks, 'Any questions?'

Ranking questions for usefulness

When you think about whether or not a question is worth asking during lectures, you could try running it past a short test:

A. The question is useful to more than one or two students.
B. It is not just about repeating something the lecturer has just said.
C. It is about the lecture content, not something organizational like assignment dates.
D. It refers to what has been said, not what is going to be said later.

There are other things to look for as well:

Has the lecturer just answered a similar question from someone else?
Has the lecturer invited questions?
Is he or she looking at the class and waiting for questions to be asked?

Four of these next questions probably should not be asked in lectures. Read them, and decide which question is a good one to ask. For each of the others, explain why it should not be asked.

1 Is it okay if we email you about changing the time of handing in the next assignment?
2 Excuse me, what was that point again?
3 I have a problem with reading your handwriting on the board. My eyesight isn't great.
4 Will you be telling us more about that shortly?
5 How does this point compare with what you said earlier about ...?

Now check the answers at the end of the book.

Becoming a better listener

So far in this chapter we have concentrated on telling you about lectures. From here on we have ideas to make you a better listener in general. This should help you in lectures and in many other university tasks.

Overcoming listening problems

Here are some of the problems people report when they are listening to a new language. These problems can make listening to lectures especially difficult. For each problem we suggest some ideas for you to try.

1   I can't work out where one word stops and the next one starts. For example: Lennonnmcartney; BondandBond; Centralafrican Republic; HeartofMidlothian.
    What to do
    Write down what you think you hear but write a question mark over the word or words you are unsure about. Later ask yourself which words are most likely in this place. Some students arrange to meet a friend after the lecture to do this task together.
    Learn about features of connected speech – e.g. how words run together in fast speech. A good pronunciation book for this is:
    Hewings, M. (2007) *English Pronunciation in Use: Advanced*, Cambridge University Press.

2   For me it's the intonation that's most difficult to recognize. I never know if the lecturers are asking something or telling me something.
    What to do
    In lectures the difference between a question and a statement is often not very important. Lecturers often ask questions that are more like headings. For example they may say, 'What do we know about the spread of this virus?' as an announcement of the next topic: 'I'm now going to tell you what we know about the spread of this virus.'
    The key thing is to notice the transitions in the lecture. For example, the lecturer's voice may go down at the end of a section and go up again when he/she starts the next section. Lecturers also stress really important points with intonation – so listen for these signals.

3   Most of the time there are many words in the lecture that I don't understand.
    What to do
    Understanding the words that relate to the subject is a very important part of your studies. Your textbook is a good place to find definitions of key topic words.
    Often when lecturers use technical words for the first time, they explain them. So, pay attention to times when lecturers give definitions, e.g. '**Photosynthesis** – by this I mean the process by which plants get their energy from the sun.'

4   I understand individual words and phrases but often I can't follow the overall topic of the lecture.
    What to do
    Prepare yourself for each lecture. How many of these things do you usually do?

    - Look at the lecture schedule for the semester.
    - Glance at last week's lecture for hints about what will come next.
    - Read the relevant chapter in your textbook.

    During the lecture: Record it, and just focus on understanding the main ideas. Write down the topics the lecturer covers. If you need to understand the details about one of the topics the lecturer talked about, listen back to the recording and make notes from that. The advantage of this is that you can listen as many times as you want.
    After the lecture: Talk to another student about the lecture. This will help you put the pieces together.

5 The most annoying thing for me is to hear everyone laughing and know that I
  have missed a joke again.
  What to do
  Understanding jokes in another language is very, very difficult. Sometimes the
  joke depends on knowing what events are in the news or on TV at the moment.
  At other times the joke depends on cultural references. We don't have any quick
  suggestions for understanding jokes in a new language. It is probably better to
  concentrate on what you can understand. However, if everyone else laughs and
  you don't get it, make a note of the joke and ask a native speaker about it
  afterwards. The chances are that the joke was not essential to understanding the
  lecture.

Summary of advice

Three types of 'active listening' are important for lectures:

1 listening for the general meaning that you are expecting in today's lecture
2 listening for details if the lecturer is speaking carefully or with emphasis
3 listening for answers to questions you expect to be answered for this topic.

Keep a journal of your progress with lectures   TIP

After each lecture, reflect on how effectively you listened. You could write about whether you
understood the main points; if you got the details; if you were able to understand any jokes; if you
asked a question; how well you were able to make notes. This will help you see your progress.

Conclusion

To end the chapter we are adding ten tips that students say have helped them. You
may already use some of these suggestions. We have mentioned some of them
during this chapter. Tick the ones you already use. Think about whether you would
like to try some new tips.

1 Find out what the lecture is on before you go. Predict what you think the lecture
  will be about.
2 If there is recommended reading to do before the lecture, make sure you do it.
3 At the beginning of the lecture, lecturers may revise what they said the week
  before and give an overview of what they are going to talk about. Pay attention to
  this overview – it will help you follow the lecture.
4 Don't worry if you don't understand everything. Make a note of topics / subjects
  that you need to read up on. You can always check later.
5 Don't try to write down everything. Often lecturers will post their slides or notes
  on the course website (especially if you ask them to). This is particularly helpful if
  the lecturer has been talking at the same time as showing the slides.

6 Record the lecture. This allows you to listen for the main idea in the lecture and keep up. You can listen again to sections of the lecture that were difficult or very detailed later.

7 Take a team approach to lectures. Work with a partner. Compare your notes afterwards over a coffee. Talk about the most important parts and any bits that you couldn't understand.

8 If you can't understand a part of the lecture, but don't want to ask a question, write to your lecturer afterwards and ask him or her.

9 Often lecturers say what the next lecture is going to be about at the end of a lecture. They may tell you what to read to prepare for next week.

10 You don't have time to use your dictionary. If there are words you do not understand, do your best and check them later.

References

Beglar, D. and Murray, N. (1993) *Contemporary Topics 3*, 2nd edn, White Plains, NY: Longman.

Hewings, M. (2007) *English Pronunciation in Use: Advanced*, Cambridge University Press.

Lewis, M. (1999) *How to Study Foreign Languages*, London: Macmillan.

Lewis, M. (2000) 'ESOL students' notetaking in lectures', *The TESOLANZ Journal*, 8:79–91.

Nattinger, J.R. and DeCarrico, J.S. (1992) *Lexical Phrases and Language Teaching*, Oxford University Press.

Academic Presentations

Giving oral presentations in a second language can be quite scary, yet this might be an important part of your study.

This chapter helps you to:

- prepare for your presentation
- practise your presentation
- improve the delivery of your presentation
- improve your general presentation skills.

Prepare for your presentation

Understanding your assignment

Giving a presentation is a common form of assignment in many courses in higher education. As with a writing assignment, your lecturer wants to see whether you understand the materials in the course and are able to analyse, interpret and evaluate what you have learned. He or she probably also wants to evaluate whether you can communicate ideas clearly to an audience. The first step is for you to understand the instructions for your presentation. What do you have to do exactly? What are the lecturer's expectations? How is your lecturer going to grade your presentation? You can only answer these questions by carefully examining the lecturer's instructions and asking questions if necessary.

You may have listened to many lectures and academic presentations and developed your own understanding of the qualities of an effective presentation. Below, list some of the features that make a presentation great.

1.

2.

3.

4.

Examine the instructions of a presentation in a graduate course below and compare your criteria with this lecturer's criteria. Do the criteria focus on the *content* or the *delivery* of the presentation? What aspects of delivery are mentioned?

Assignment 3: PowerPoint Presentation of Qualitative Research Study (60 Points)

Select from one of the posted qualitative research articles to critique. List the complete APA reference at the top of the paper. Use these points for the headings.

1. **Descriptive vividness (5 points)**

   Was the significance of the study adequately described? Was the purpose of the study clearly described? Were interpretations presented in a descriptive way that illuminated more than the quotes did?

2. **Philosophical or theoretical connectedness (10 points)**

   Did the researcher identify a philosophical or theoretical basis for the study? Was a clear connection made between the data and potential application to nursing practice?

3. **Intuitive recognition (5 points)**

   Can the reader recognize phenomenon described in the study?

4. **Adequate documentation of the participants and context (5 points)**

   Were the study participants described in sufficient detail? Was the selection of participants reasonable? Was the context and location of the study described with sufficient detail to determine if findings are potentially applicable to other settings?

5. **Careful attention to procedural approach (5 points)**

   Did the researcher identify a philosophical or theoretical basis of study? Were research questions clearly articulated? Did the researcher ask questions that explore participants' experiences, beliefs, values and/or perceptions? Was the data collection process adequately described?

6. **Adherence to ethical standards (5 points)**

   Was informed consent obtained? Were participants' rights protected?

7. **Auditability (5 points)**

   Was the decision trail used in arriving at conclusions described in adequate detail? Were participants' quotes included to support findings? Were the findings validated by data to support conclusions?

8. **Analytical and interpretative preciseness (5 points)**

   Do the categories, themes, or findings present a whole and meaningful picture? Did two or more researchers participate in data analysis? How were disagreements about data analysis handled?

9. **Relationship to the existing body of knowledge (5 points)**

   Did the researcher adequately examine an existing body of knowledge? Did the researcher compare and contrast findings with those of other studies?

10. **Applicability to nursing practice, research, or education (5 points)**

    Are the findings relevant to nursing practice, research, or education? Are suggestions for further study identified?

11. **Formatting and delivery (5 points)**

    APA formatting, grammar and spelling, delivery (maintain eye contact most of the time, use notes but not directly read from them).

You probably noticed that this assignment mostly focuses on students' ability to analyse an article. Note that 55 out of 60 points are given for the content of the presentation, while only five points are given for formatting and delivery. However, it is not always that easy to separate content and language, or content and delivery. After all, the lecturer has to understand clearly what you say in your presentation in order to evaluate your content!

How about these criteria? What does the lecturer look for?

Presentation Evaluation Form			
	Good	So-so	Needs improvement
Content Is the information suitable for the audience? Is the content worth presenting?			
Introduction Does the introduction attract the audience's attention? Does it provide an overview of the presentation?			
Organization Is the content divided into different parts in a logical way? Are there transitional signals to guide the audience?			
Conclusion Does the conclusion summarize the main points? Does it give the audience a sense of completeness?			
Body language Does the presenter keep eye contact with everyone in the audience? Does the presenter use his/her hand gestures effectively to draw the audience's attention?			
Voice Does the speaker talk loudly enough? Does the speaker sound relaxed and confident?			
Speed Does the speaker speak with an appropriate speed (not too fast or too slow)?			
Intonation and pronunciation Does the speaker emphasize important information with his/her intonation? Is the pronunciation clear?			

As you can see, this lecturer looks for both appropriate content and effective delivery. However, the emphasis is on the various aspects of delivery, such as body language and voice qualities.

Understanding the audience

After carefully examining the instructions for your presentation, you will have a sense of the purpose of your presentation and what your lecturer expects. The next step is to consider your audience.

Who are you speaking to?

Are they students, teachers, or a general audience? People you know well or strangers? In each case you will probably *pitch* your talk differently. By 'pitch' we mean ways in which you change the tone or content of your talk to suit the audience. As an extreme example, think of how you would explain to a child how a car works. This would be different from how you would talk to an adult. In a presentation you do the same.

What is the audience's interest in the topic?

Why would they want to listen to your presentation? Your lecturer will, of course, be looking at the quality of your work, but how about other students? Are they in the same class and do you know if they are interested in the topic, or are they students from other classes or faculties? In that case you may have to make them enthusiastic about the topic, for example by giving an interesting or funny example.

What do they know about the topic? What don't they know about the topic?

If people have little or no knowledge of the topic you will need to explain the topic first. Explain and give examples of all technical terms and give more background information.

Use this diagram to start planning your presentation.

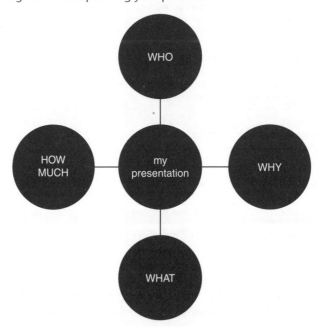

Figure 6.1   Planning your presentation

Preparing the different parts of the presentation

Based on the requirements of the assignment and the knowledge of your audience, you will decide on the content and the organization of the presentation. Just like a writing assignment, you will need to do research on the topic, brainstorm for ideas, organize the ideas and develop the content of the presentation (see Chapters 8 and 9 for more information). It's a good idea to be clear about the main parts of your presentation and allocate the appropriate amount of time to each part. You can adjust the allocation of time as you practise your presentation.

The example below shows how a presentation may be structured.

2 mins   introduction
4 mins   background: what is 'attrition'?*
4 mins   my study: attrition in younger learners
4 mins   results of the study
2 mins   conclusion
4 mins   questions

* One of the meanings of attrition is 'forgetting'.

Introduction

It is important to plan your introduction carefully because it is when you make your first impression on the audience. Consider the following tips for giving an introduction to a presentation.

1 Introduce clearly your name and the topic or title of the presentation. Pause after the title for the audience to absorb the idea. Sometimes when presenters are nervous, they speak too quickly.
2 Explain why you chose the topic and your personal connection with the topic.
3 Indicate clearly what you are going to cover in the presentation and what the audience will learn.
4 Engage the audience with a question. However, remember when you ask a question, give them time to think about the question and respond. Don't just ask the question and move on quickly.
5 Comment on what is happening at the time if that is what everyone is thinking of. For example, if it is the first day after a big holiday, you can mention the holiday. If your presentation is the last one and it is very late in the evening, you can mention that as well.

The language of presentations

As for the language of presentations, it is important to remember that spoken language and written language are very different. Imagine you are studying physiotherapy and you need to give a presentation explaining why runners suffer from frequent injuries.

This is what you wrote in an assignment:

One of the causes of lower-leg injuries amongst road runners who increase their training load rapidly in the build-up to a competition is the hard surfaces on which they do much of their training load. The constant impacts that occur when training on the road result in conditions like shin splints* and ....

* Shin splints is a very painful lower leg injury.

What would you say in a presentation? Turn to the answer key for a solution.

Speaking and writing: what are the differences?

Now answer these questions about speaking and writing.

1 Which one uses more words to say the same thing? *speaking or writing*
2 Which one uses more complex sentences? *speaking or writing*
3 Which one uses shorter and more frequent sentences? *speaking or writing*
4 Which one uses the most complicated vocabulary? *speaking or writing*
5 Which one has more repetition? *speaking or writing*
6 In which one do you need to be the most accurate? *speaking or writing*

Check your answers at the end of the book. Here are the explanations for the answers:

- When you are reading, you can re-read a section if it is difficult to understand. When listening, if you miss something, you've really missed it, so speakers use less complex grammar and vocabulary and simpler sentences when speaking. This helps listeners understand as they listen.
- In writing, the reader cannot say if they don't understand. Writers have to be accurate. Speakers can make their language easier to understand with gestures (using their body language) and pronunciation to stress important words. And if their audience doesn't understand, they can say it again.
- When you are writing, you need to meet a word limit. You cannot write forever and ever. When speaking, there is sometimes a time limit, but no word limit. Speakers make themselves understood by saying the same thing in different ways.

So, make sure the language of your presentation is easy to understand and clear to your audience. Make sure you are speaking (using spoken language) and not reading aloud (using written language) or repeating a written text (from memory).

Avoiding too much informal language

While spoken language is often simpler than written language in everyday situations, remember that university presentations are formal situations. Your colleagues and your lecturer will be there, so you should avoid using too much informal language. Your professor will mark you down and people will not take your ideas seriously. This may be a problem for you if you have learnt English informally at work or through spending a lot of time in an English-speaking country.

Look at the informal language that a student used in a presentation about health and safety rules in a restaurant. What should she have said instead? Check your answers at the end of the book.

Informal language	What should she have said?
Hi, guys. How's it going?	
If you've anything you wanna ask, keep it to yourself until the end.	

(Continued)

Informal language	What should she have said?
I'm going to give you the dirt on the dos and don'ts of working in a restaurant.	
That dude Richards – he had some sweet ideas about	
It's crazy not washing your hands. It is, like, so gross.	
Now that's it. We're outta here.	

Transitioning from one point to another

When writing, you need to signal to your readers when you move from one point to another. In presentations, using appropriate transitional signals is even more important because listeners cannot go back to listen to what you said before. Therefore, it is important to summarize the main ideas when you finish a major part of the presentation and tell the audience what you are going to cover next. These transitional signals are very similar to the ones lecturers use in lectures. We provide some examples in the 'Listening to lectures' chapter.

Learn from the best   TIP

Choose your best lecturer. Note down what they say when they move to a new topic in a presentation or lecture, such as, 'I'd like to talk about ... now.' Use the same expressions when you give a presentation.

Using visuals and other support materials

An image can say a thousand. Images give you something to point at and you can stop talking for a while so the audience has time to look. If pronunciation is not your strong point, images will help the audience understand you better. Research has shown that over 40% of people are 'visual learners', meaning that they depend on visual information more than on spoken words to get new information. So, including images in your presentation is a good idea.

PowerPoint is a popular tool, but there are a few things to keep in mind:

- **Don't read out every slide.** Each slide should summarize your key points or show something to illustrate what you have said, such as a picture. Some people put a lot of information on their slides because they are afraid they won't remember the information. If this is the case for you, then you have not practised your presentation enough.
- **Don't include too much text on a slide.** If you include too much text, people will focus on the text on your slide, not what you say. If you have a quote on a slide, give the audience a moment to read it.

- **Don't face the screen.** Look at your audience and point at the screen when necessary.
- **Make sure your font size is large enough.** Make sure the size of the letters on the screen is large enough for people to read from the back of the room (24 or larger is usually good). By making the font size big, you will be less likely to add too much text on your slide.
- **Be careful with colours and animation (things moving around the screen).** Usually they confuse the audience or take their attention away from the content of your presentation. You will sometimes hear people talking about the 'KISS' principle. KISS here stands for 'Keep It Simple, Stupid!' In other words, less is more. A successful presentation is when the audience listen to what you say.

Conclusion

How you close your presentation is just as important as how you open your presentation. Usually, it is a good idea to summarize the most important points you made in the presentation. You can also leave them with a question to think about. Just like in writing, the audience should have a sense of completeness after you finish your presentation.

Practise your presentation and improve your delivery

If you are nervous about doing a presentation, you are not alone. Most people find it difficult to speak in front of an audience. One study found that people are more afraid to give a presentation than they are of death!

Luckily, there are many things you can do to help you become more confident. Here are some of them.

Practise

Practising a lot so that you know the content really well will make you relax more on the day. Even the most experienced presenters spend a lot of time practising for an important presentation before giving it. Practise with a friend, in the mirror, with your dog – anything!

Practising doesn't mean you have to memorize every word. In fact, it is probably better not to. But practise giving your speech, and when you feel you know the content reasonably well, try to focus on ways of becoming more relaxed and speaking more naturally. When you practice, imagine yourself giving the real presentation. Imagine that you will be great as people listen to you attentively and applaud your ideas. Visualizing success will help you be more confident later in your presentation.

Breathe!

When we are nervous we usually breathe more quickly and our breathing is more shallow than normal. As a result our brains do not get enough oxygen and we can't concentrate well and we feel light-headed. Force yourself to take a few deep breaths and to breathe in a relaxed way. You should feel the difference almost immediately.

Trust yourself

It is incredible what we can do if we only believe in ourselves. People who get up and tell themselves, 'I can't do this; I can't talk in public,' usually don't do well. On the other hand, telling yourself you *can* do this, or even that you are good at it, miraculously, makes us better speakers! As you sound more confident, the audience will like your talk more.

Have a friend in the audience

Arrange for someone you know to sit at the front and put on a smile or a friendly face. If you get really nervous during the talk you can make eye contact with your friend to make you feel better.

Imagine you are talking to a friend

Related to the previous tip, imagine that you are giving your presentation to one or more friends over a coffee, rather than in a formal situation in a room full of people. When you talk to your friends you are likely to be relaxed and your tone will be more casual. As a result you will sound more natural and your audience will like your talk more. Some of the best speakers in the world say this is one of their greatest 'secrets'.

Keep your eye contact with all the audience

The key to a successful presentation is the connection you form with the audience. Keeping eye contact with the audience is one way of maintaining this connection. Students often forget to do this, but if you can keep eye contact and talk to your audience in a confident and relaxed manner, the audience will be more likely to pay attention to you.

Remind yourself to talk slowly

When people are nervous, they talk quickly, which makes the presentation less effective. Talking more slowly, emphasizing the important information with strong intonation and pausing after important information helps the audience to follow your ideas more easily. In giving a presentation, speed is not always a good thing.

Improve your presentation skills over time

Presentation feedback: what should these students work on?

If you would like to improve your presentation skills, apart from practising, you can also learn from the feedback that your lecturer gives you. Read the following feedback given to students after an oral presentation. First identify the problem. In what way do the students need to improve? Check your answers at the end of the book.

a. 'There were parts of your talk that I couldn't hear, which was a shame because I think you were making good points.'
b. 'Sometimes I found it difficult to understand you. Some of your language was very complex. Try to say things more simply and clearly.'

c. 'I had problems following your presentation. I wasn't sure where it was going and whether you were giving an example of something you had just said or whether you were moving on to a new point.'

d. 'It was difficult to understand your presentation because you were reading aloud.'

e. 'It just ended. I felt you needed to say something to round it off.'

f. 'When you described the structure of that company, I found it really hard to see how the different departments work together.'

g. 'I felt you looked at the screen more than at the audience.'

h. 'I wasn't sure what some of the things you talked about mean.'

Here are some possible solutions for the problems identified in the feedback. Read these solutions and match them to the feedback in the section above. Write the letter a) to h) next to the appropriate solution. Some solutions may work for more than one problem. Check your answers at the end of the book.

Problem	Solution
	Imagine you are talking to an old deaf man sitting at the far end of the room, then you will speak more loudly and more clearly.
	Try recording yourself when you are practising and then listen to yourself to determine if you are clear enough.
	Try talking from cue cards (small cards with three or four words only written on them).
	Pause more between sections.
	Use more repetition. e.g. 'Let me say that another way ....'
	Signal with your voice going down that you have ended one section of your talk.
	Signal with your voice going up that you are starting a new section.
	Use discourse markers more. e.g. 'Let me give you an example'; 'My next point is about...'; 'I'd like to move on to ... now.'
	Keep your sentences short and simple.
	Use more sentences to say the same thing.

Eye contact

TIP

Again, choose your best lecturer. Watch how they use eye contact to keep students interested. Do they look at everyone? How long do they look at one student before moving on? When you give a presentation, try to copy this.

Make an effort to work on your presentation skills

If you want to improve your presentation skills, here are some resources for you.

- Ted.com has many great presentations. As you watch a presentation, pay attention to what makes it great. Take notes of transitional language, body language and other techniques.
- In many parts of the world, you can join a club called Toastmasters. Club members meet regularly to listen to others' presentations and give each other feedback.
- There are videos on YouTube on useful presentation techniques.
- The language centre at your university may allow you to make appointments to practise your presentation with a language specialist, who will give you feedback on your presentation.
- Many universities offer public speaking courses. Enrol in a course to learn about presentation skills and other communication techniques.

If you plan to use English in your future career, you will likely have to make presentations to various audiences. It is a good investment of time to work on giving more effective presentations.

Summary: tips for successful presentations

Tick off the ones you already use. Try out the ones that are new.

Before

- Think about the purpose of the presentation.
- Think of the people (audience). Who are your audience?
- Plan how you will introduce yourself, your topic and your talk.
- Plan transitions between topics or sections in your presentation.
- Make sure your visuals are clear and easy to follow.
- If using technology, test it in the room you will use and have a back-up that does not rely on the technology.
- If you are working with a partner, practise together so you know who is doing what.
- Plan how you will conclude.
- Brainstorm a list of questions you think you will be asked.
- Practise your presentation.
- Time it before you do it.
- Record yourself and listen to it.

During

- Speak from notes. Don't read.
- Speak more slowly and loudly than you normally do.
- Pause between sections.
- Don't use slang.
- Talk about the points in your visuals, don't read them.
- Use markers to introduce new ideas / new sections e.g. 'My next point is about …' or 'Next, I want to talk about ….'

- Use body language and intonation to make things clear.
- Watch the time.

Dealing with questions

- Tell your audience when they should ask questions. For example, you can say, 'There will be time for questions at the end.'
- Allow time for questions.
- If you don't understand a question, ask the person to repeat it e.g. 'I'm sorry, I didn't catch that.'
- Use expressions like, 'Yes, that's an interesting question,' when you need time to think of a response!
- Don't be defensive! Say, 'Yes, that's a valid point.'
- Be prepared to open questions up to the audience. This means you say, 'Umm, that is an important issue. Would anyone else like to say something about that?'

Conclusion

As an academic assignment, a presentation has many similarities to a writing assignment, so you can generally follow some similar stages. However, because of the different mode of delivery, there are quite a few differences too. We have presented some differences between spoken language and written language in this chapter. The bigger difference lies in the fact that you are going to have an audience sitting in front of you and you may be inexperienced at giving presentations and nervous when talking in front of a big crowd. Keep in mind that the key to success is your diligent preparation and thorough practice.

Chapter

7

Academic Reading

Whatever course you do, you must read plenty. This takes time and in a second language can take over your life. Be smart about what and how you read.

This chapter will help you to:

- plan and keep track of your university reading
- find suitable texts
- read purposefully
- read a range of types of text efficiently
- learn about smart online reading
- become a critical reader.

Case studies: learning from other students' experiences

We interviewed many students to see what they had learnt about reading. For each reply underline the key problem. In the right-hand column make notes about these problems. See the first example. Check your answers at the end of the book.

Christophe	Your comments
At the start of most of my courses, the lecturer gives out a list of the topics of each lecture and a reading list. They usually have required reading, which is really important, and some suggested extra reading. I find it really helps me understand the lecture if I have done at least the required reading. The lecturer expects us to have read the required reading and so if I haven't, I can't understand the lecture. Often I don't have time to read the extra reading before the lecture. These texts are often more difficult than the required readings – often, though, if I just read the first two or three paragraphs or, if it's a research article, the abstract, then at least I know what the lecturer is talking about when he mentions them. I read them afterwards if I'm interested enough. Some lecturers put these reading lists online and I can download or print them.	Christophe needs either to find time somehow or to stop worrying about it. Christophe may be doing the best he can with the time available.

What did Christophe learn?

Marie	Your comments
At first I didn't understand the point of textbooks – especially introductory ones. They seemed boring and obvious. Then I realized how important they are – they define keywords for my course. Often the course is organized around that book. Books often explain key ideas so if I didn't understand something in a lecture, I could find an explanation in the textbook. Then at the end of my first semester we had an exam for 33% of the course mark and basically all the answers were in the textbook. We asked the tutor what would be in the exam. He said, 'What we have done in lectures and in the textbook.' If I hadn't read the textbook, I would have failed.	

What did Marie learn?

George says	Your comments
On my communication studies course we needed to read lots. Our lecturer used to comment on essays: 'You must read more widely.' At first I read everything the same way. I wasted a lot of time looking for library books, then photocopying and reading each article carefully with my dictionary. It was terrible. One student asked me to join a study group. This was great. The four of us got the reading list from the lecturer and divided up the reading. Each week, we read one article or book chapter and then met and talked about them. We had ten minutes each to summarize our article. We saved so much time and energy. When we listened we decided if we needed to read them ourselves. We also saved money. One person bought the book for each course and then we shared it.	

What did George learn?

Rose says	Your comments
My tutor's feedback said I needed to read more critically. I didn't know what this meant. He explained that I need to read and think things through for myself. I must challenge what is said and what is not said in each article. I found this very difficult. At first, I struggled to understand the words, but critical reading meant understanding and then measuring the message against everything else I knew and had read before and deciding for myself if it was right or made sense. I think I used to read very passively, just accepting everything – I had been successful in this way in my country. Now I needed to be a more active reader.	

What did Rose learn?

Andrea says	Your comments
When I did my master's I realized that I needed to read in different ways again. I had to understand other people's research in order to plan mine. My problem was that I couldn't see how one person's research fitted in with what others had said. Some things I had read were the result of more recent research findings than the article I was reading! I was reading 25 years of research, but ideas and theories were constantly changing so I had to keep the big picture in mind. The literature review in each article was important. One of my lecturers told me about 'state-of-the-art' articles. These were useful. They look at one research area and just review where the research is up to now. From these, I made a timeline in my head and fitted other reading and research onto this.	

What did Andrea learn?

Why university students read

Reasons for reading

Here are some reasons why students read. Think of something you have read recently for each purpose:

- to find out important course information
- to learn something new
- for pleasure
- to improve your English
- to prepare for an exam / assignment.

Whenever you are reading an article or book section, the first step is to ask yourself:

Why am I reading this?

If you can answer this question, then you can think about the best way to read it.

For example, if you are reading to learn words for your essays, then you would read like this:

1 Read to understand the main ideas.
2 Notice vocabulary that you can use when you are writing.
3 Read sections where those words are used in detail.
4 Check the meaning and use of these words in your dictionary.

What university students read

Types of academic text

It is also important to know what type of text you are reading. The task below will help you sort out some common academic text types.

Match the list of text types on the left to the descriptions on the right. Check your answers at the end of the book.

Text types	Description
Prescribed texts or recommended books	a) All the chapters in these books are written by the same writer(s). They often report that writer's work or summarize the work of many people.
Edited books	b) Conference presenters may be asked to write an article later. After editing, these are published so that people can read about the conference topics.
Single author books	c) These are journal articles summarizing current research. They are usually written by an established person and discuss the work of many researchers.
Journal articles	d) These books are chosen by the lecturer or department as really important for a particular course. All students should have a copy. They will usually be on a course reading list or your lecturer will mention them.
State-of-the-art articles	e) These appear in journals (academic magazines) that are important for your subject. They report current research. They come in hard copy and often on the internet annually or several times a year.
Research reports	f) While journal articles often have a word limit fixed by the journal, these will go into a lot more detail about the researcher's methodology (how the research was done). They may be written by a research company or a government department.
Theses	g) These books have chapters written by different authors on a similar topic. They are collected by an editor who usually also writes the introduction or final chapter. On the cover you will see *ed.* or *eds.* after the person's name, meaning *editor* or *editors*.
Conference proceedings	h) These are research reports written by students at your university and kept in your university's library.

Reading different types of academic text

The good thing about academic texts is that they are usually predictable in their format, and so when you understand how each text type is organized, reading other similar examples will be easier. For example, when you understand one thesis, you will find that others are organized similarly (although not necessarily theses in your language or in other subjects).

Understanding the organization will help you see the main point of each section and write different text types yourself. This section looks at one type of academic text – research articles. You can apply this kind of analysis to common text types in your subject. For example, if you are a science student and need to read laboratory reports, work out how they are commonly organized.

The organization of research articles

Usually research articles have these sections in this order:

- abstract
- introduction
- literature review
- method
- results
- discussions, recommendations and conclusion
- references and appendices.

You may find some variation between subjects. Find a research article for your subject   **TIP**
and compare it with the order given above. Are there any differences?

Find research reports on a topic you are interested in. To do this, go to a university library and look in some research journals or Google some keywords.

For example, to find a study about air pollution levels, type (for example) '2003 air pollution study'.

Now look at these questions and decide whereabouts to look for the answers. Then check the answers at the end of the book.

1 How was the study planned?
2 What do the results mean?
3 Who is interested in the results?
4 What was the study about?
5 Why is the topic important?
6 What did the researcher want to find out?
7 What was the main finding of the research?
8 Where was the research done?
9 What did the researchers find?
10 What research instruments were used?
11 Who else has studied this topic?
12 What have other researchers found out?
13 How does this research fit in with other researchers' findings?
14 Where are the full titles of the books and articles referred to here?

Planning your reading

Starting a new course or writing a research proposal can seem like facing a reading mountain. This can be depressing – especially in your second language! Here are two approaches:

1 Panic, go to the library, find as many books as you can on your reading list and frantically try to make progress.
2 Take a more strategic approach and plan your reading week by week.

Remember, you are looking at a whole semester's reading – or more if you are writing a thesis. Marathon trainers run many kilometres over the months beforehand. This would be difficult without a training schedule. The same is true with your university reading. If you step back and take a strategic approach, things become more manageable.

Keeping on top of your university reading

These three steps will help you plan and stay on top of your reading week by week.

Step 1: Get a list of reading for your course

You can usually get a course reading list from your lecturers. Sometimes these are published before the course starts or posted on the course webpage or handed out at the first lecture. They usually tie in with the lectures.

Alternatively, the course librarian in your library may be able to help you with particular reading. For writing a dissertation or thesis, you will have to find your own reading to a certain extent. Find a 'state-of-the-art article' or a book that summarizes many researchers' previous work on your research topic, and then make a provisional list and show this to your supervisor.

Step 2: Plan your weekly reading schedule

As soon as you get your timetable, work out when to do your weekly reading for each lecture. For example, a business student with marketing lectures on Mondays needs to read for this during the weekend at the latest, or earlier if they want to meet another student for a discussion. Likewise, before personnel management classes on Wednesdays, you need to finish reading on Tuesday at the latest. Many students plan to go to the library only once a week to find texts for all classes. This saves time. If you are in a study group, set a regular day each week to meet and discuss the reading.

Step 3: Staying on top of things

You will probably not have time to pre-read everything for every single course you are taking, so start with the essential texts and then read optional texts if you have time. Decide which are the most important by:

- checking the course reading list for notes such as 'essential', 'required' or 'extra reading'
- checking with last year's students
- looking at the course assessment schedule and seeing which texts feed directly into assignments and exams. Remember, exams often test topics of the set text, so make sure you read that!
- deciding which reading looks most interesting.

Lecturers often talk about important reading for the following week at the start or end of a lecture. They may confirm the information in the course outline or explain which piece of reading has a higher priority than others. Pay attention and adapt your plan if necessary.

Summary

Try to stagger your reading across the course. Don't leave it all until the week your assignment is due or when you are trying to revise for an exam. Early on in a course, there are usually fewer assessment dates so you should get most of your term's reading done then. Aim for a weekly pattern with regular reading slots for each subject and regular library time.

Finding reading texts

Once you have decided what you need to read, then find the texts. Some courses have one textbook that the lecturer refers to constantly. You could buy this. It can be really useful, even though expensive, to have your own copy. Here are the options.

Your campus bookstore

This is probably the most convenient option. It should have recommended booklists for each course. Remember you can always share the cost of a textbook with classmates.

Visit your campus bookstore. Find out about:

- new prices for prescribed texts or recommended course reading
- student discounts
- their buying back of textbooks later to sell second-hand. (If so, at what cost? and at what time of year?)

Other places to buy books

Ask current students how they found their textbooks. Find out about:

- a departmental noticeboard or union building where students advertise books for sale
- any good second-hand book store that sells university texts
- internet sites e.g. www.ebay.com or www.amazon.com for buying and selling books.

The university library

See the next section.

Using the library

Libraries are an important part of student life with large collections of books and resources plus digital collections of e-journals, e-books and databases of resources available worldwide from other universities. There could be significant differences between the way your university library operates and other libraries you have used. This section will help you get the most out of your library.

Getting the most out of your library orientation

At the start of each semester and maybe at other times, your library will run seminars and workshops. Make sure you go. Although they may not sound like much fun, one hour in a library seminar could save you a lot of time later. To keep things concrete take a list of books or references that you need to find. Then if the librarian starts talking about finding journal articles, you can ask about one you need to find.

Here is a checklist of questions for the seminar. Take it with you and tick information you find out.

Category	Questions	Tick here!
General services	opening hours	
	– during term time (incl. weekends)	
	– in holidays	
	rules e.g. no cell phones	
	library seminar times	
	extra services offered e.g. binding	
	study rooms you can book	
Finding your way around	number of sites	
	what's in each one	
	site that's most useful for you	
	what's on each floor	
	how the shelves are organized	
Finding books	how the catalogue works	
	who can help you	
	who your subject librarian is	
	which database will be useful	
	interlibrary loans	
Borrowing books	which books can be borrowed	
	which books can't be borrowed	
	which books are on short loan	
	how many books you can borrow	
	how long you can borrow them for	
	how much the fines are	
	where you take books	

(Continued)

Category	Questions	Tick here!
Photocopying	where the machines are	
	how the photocopy accounts work	
	how much photocopying costs	
Computer/ online resources	how to access the library catalogue from home	
	databases you can access	
	where you can print	
	internet access	
	e-books you can read	

A mini-glossary of library words

Libraries have their own technical terms. Here is a mini-glossary of library words.

author	The person who wrote the book.
binding	If you write a thesis or dissertation, you need to get it bound into a book. Your department or library will have information about this.
call number	The number or code that the library gives the book e.g. 664.805652.McD.
e-book	An electronic book that is stored on a library server and can be downloaded.
interlibrary loans	When your library doesn't have books, but other libraries do, you can request these, sometimes for a fee.
ISBN number	This is a number written just above the barcode on the back cover of a book. It is unique to that book e.g. ISBN 1-4039-0026-4 and is a common way of identifying books by librarians and bookshops.
keyword	An important word in the subject/title of a book, journal or journal article.
overdue notice	An overdue notice means your book is late. If you ignore this, you will probably be fined.
periodical	Another name for a journal.
recall notice	If a book you want to read is lent out to another student, you can request they bring it back. If you get a recall notice, you must return the book quickly e.g. within 24 hours, or pay a fine.
reference material	This includes dictionaries, atlases, etc. Usually these can't be borrowed.
short loan	These books may be borrowed for a short time (sometimes only two or three hours) from a short loan desk. You have to pay big fines if you are late returning them.
special collections	Your library may have a rare books section e.g. 16th-century poetry or early maps and records. You may have to make an appointment to see them.
subject librarian	This librarian has special knowledge to help you with a particular subject e.g. law, literature, history, agricultural studies.
title	The name of a book or journal. Sometimes you can search for journals separately.

Getting help in the library

It is important to ask for help. If you don't ask, librarians won't know that you need it.

Using your library catalogue

Your university library will give you access to its catalogue, which lists resources stored there. You can probably access the library catalogue off-campus, which saves time.
   You can search by:

Title (name of book or article)
Journal or serial title (name of journal)
Author (writer or writers)
Call number (the number the library gives the book)
Keyword (useful if you only know one word in the title)
Subject heading (your topic)

You can find out:

- if your library has the books you need
- which library site they are stored in
- whereabouts they are located (i.e. which shelf)
- if the books are there (or if they are loaned out)
- if the books can be borrowed.

Try out a library catalogue search

If you know the address of your library catalogue already, enter that in your web browser. Otherwise, choose a library from:
   https://libraries.psu.edu/
Try these searches.

Look up the **title** of this book **Studying in English: Strategies for Success in Higher Education** and find out if your library has a copy. Don't use **a / an / the** in title search.

SEARCH 1

Look up a **journal title** relevant to your subject to see if the library subscribes to it. Find out if you can access it online or not.
   TIP: To find a list of electronic journals for different subjects, go to:
   http://www.e-journals.org

SEARCH 2

Do a keyword search. These are useful if you don't know the full title. For this book, try **English study skills**.
   TIP: Use **AND, OR, NOT** to narrow your keyword search. For example, you can search for **English AND study AND skills OR strategies**.

SEARCH 3

Search for books by the **author**. You may know someone whose
books you want to search for. If not, try searching for books by one
of the authors of this book – **Lewis, Reinders or Phung**.
   TIP: Often if you search by authors with common names e.g. Smith you will
get thousands of results! Narrow your search by entering the author's initials e.g. M.N. or
combining the author search with a keyword search.

SEARCH 4

Try a subject search for resources on a topic you want to study. You could try the
title of one of your papers or the words **study skills**.
   TIP: Ask a librarian for suitable search terms.

TIP

Finding reading on the internet and in databases

The internet is a great place to start finding course reading. Sometimes you find
whole texts you can access free. Often you find references for articles and books
which you can search for in your library catalogue.
   You can find:

- research articles on particular topics
- articles that you can borrow
- people who are interested in the same subjects as you
- information to use in assignments.

Some essential searches to try out

1 Basic searches with a search engine such as www.google.com or www.bing.com.
   The advanced search function is really helpful as you can make your search as
   specific as you need.
2 Google scholar. This is a website that lets you search academic papers, theses and
   even full-text books. It is a great tool, especially if you can't access your university
   library.
3 Wikipedia: http://wikipedia.org/. This is an online encyclopaedia created by web
   users. Anyone can add an article to Wikipedia in any language. It is a great place
   to learn basic facts and definitions and is good for language learners because
   articles contain many explanations of common words. But be critical of the
   information you find. Because *anyone* can add and edit the information, it may
   not be accurate. Wikipedia is convenient for finding new information quickly, but
   other sources are more accurate. Make sure to ask your lecturers whether you can
   cite information from Wikipedia in your assignments.

Databases

In addition to the internet, many databases refer to new articles (often from
hundreds or even thousands of journals), abstracts of those articles, sometimes full

articles, conference proceedings, theses and much more. A *subject-specific* database contains information about one subject, and because it has so much and such carefully selected information, it can be one of your most powerful tools. Most libraries have a website with links to the different subject-specific databases they can access, so look under your faculty or subject for the most relevant.

You can search most databases in many ways: by keyword, by year of publication, by author, or by a combination of these. One of the difficulties students have is that they search for a certain word (using the 'keyword' option) without results. This does not mean that there really are no useful resources, but perhaps you need to use a different word. For example, the terms 'finance' and 'economy' are closely related, but searching for only one of them may not show the results for the other. In other words, think of synonyms!

So, if you find nothing for 'problems', try 'issues'. If you find nothing for 'elderly', try 'geriatric'.

> You can use a thesaurus to look up synonyms. Here is one of them: www.m-w.com   **TIP**
> Make sure you select 'thesaurus'. There are more tips in the chapter on vocabulary.

Another problem is that many students search for the wrong keywords. For example, if you are interested in Impressionism, the 19th-century art movement, you could look for 'painting', but the information would be too general. Similarly, you could look for 'Monet' or 'Renoir', two of its famous painters, but the results may be too specific. So, think about what terms are best. Let's look at an example.

Say you are interested in finding information on the topic 'care for the elderly in New Zealand in the 1950s'. This is a very specific search because you are looking not only for one particular topic (care for the elderly), but also for information limited to one country (New Zealand) and one period (the 1950s). Here's the best way to search:

1 Search for the exact information you want. Type in 'care for the elderly in New Zealand in the 1950s'. You never know, there may be a resource with that exact title or on that exact topic!
2 If that goes nowhere, try synonyms e.g. 'geriatric' instead of 'elderly' and 'healthcare' for 'care'.
3 If you still find nothing, try broadening your search. Perhaps you could leave out 'New Zealand' or '1950s'.
4 One way to make your searches more powerful is with operators. Operators are search terms such as AND, OR and NOT that make searches more specific. Or you could use '?' when searching for both 'woman' and 'women' by typing 'wom?n' and '*' which you can use to show results such as 'car', 'cars' and 'cardealer' by typing 'car*'. Not all databases and library catalogues use the same operators, but http://www.library.ubc.ca/hss/qso.html is frequently used. Similarly, http://www.googleguide.com/advanced_operators.html in Google is well worth practising to save time.

Once you find a text, read critically. Remember that everything on the internet has been written by someone with their own agenda and purpose. Question what you are reading as you would any other text. Ask yourself, for example:

- Is this true? Fact or opinion?
- Who wrote it? Who is paying them? Are they qualified to say that?
- Do conclusions fit in with other texts I have read or have heard in lectures?
- What are the problems with these claims?
- What evidence is given?
- Are there other ways of seeing this evidence?

Remember that an assignment needs to cite information from the internet so keep a record of your searches. Store searches in 'Favourites' on your computer or use services like Pinterest and Evernote. Also check out the section on 'Reading online' later in this chapter.

Becoming a more efficient reader

How not to read

Sometimes, when in the library looking for a reference, you find a book full of underlining, translations, notes in the margin and other signs that it has been analysed word by word. Please don't do this to library books. The book becomes impossible for other students to read and librarians will make you buy the book if they catch you!

Imagine the reading process this student used. What's the problem? Why do some students fall into this trap? Check your answers at the end of the book.

1 Open the book.
2 Start on page 1.
3 Get to the third word.
4 Get out your dictionary.
5 Check the translation of the word in the dictionary.
6 Write the translation in the margin.
7 Go back to the beginning. Read it again.
8 Underline difficulties.
9 Stop at the next difficult word.
10 Scratch your head.
11 Go back to step 5 and repeat for the next three hours.
12 Collapse exhausted.

Getting it right

Are you frustrated with all your reading? This section has ideas for getting on top again. One key first step is to be really clear about your reason for reading. Before beginning, ask yourself why you are reading the text and what you want to find out. Knowing this can show how to read and for how long.

Coming up with your own reading questions

Look at these situations and decide what text you need to read. Check your answers at the end of the book.

	Situation	Text
1	You are going to a conference on your subject at another university.	Conference programme
2	You are about to hand in your first written assignment.	Your department's submission guidelines for assignments
3	You need to design a practical science experiment to do yourself.	Experimental reports from similar experiments
4	You are doing background reading about the dangers of nuclear power for an essay.	Newspaper clippings of nuclear accidents
5	You are going to a lecture about public health policy in South Africa.	Three journal articles that report public health policy studies in South Africa

It's really important to have a clear plan when you approach a text so as to decide:

- if it is actually worth reading
- how long to allow for reading
- what to focus on and which sections to skip
- what information you need
- an effective reading process (see the next section)
- what notes to make.

Critical reading

In many English-speaking countries, critical thinking skills are highly valued; lecturers will often say that 'good' students think critically. It is important to understand the text's meaning and also its value. Is it fact or opinion? What is the writer's opinion? What is the purpose of the text: to inform, persuade, or raise questions? Is there supporting evidence? Do you trust that evidence? Is it possible to draw conclusions other than the writer's? Asking these questions while reading will help develop your own critical voice for university writing and speaking. This means questioning what people tell you and finding problems when things seem too simple. Of course, this is difficult when reading in a second language because you must go beyond the surface meaning, but you can train yourself to do this.

What does this mean? Looking beyond the text

A key first step in critical reading is to tell FACT from OPINION. Sometimes this is easy when the writer is explicitly giving her opinion. For example, in a magazine column, a writer argues against the law that makes helmets compulsory for cyclists.

> I will simply add my voice to those who think the law requiring all cyclists to wear helmets is draconian*.

* Draconian = harsh; related to Draco, a lawmaker from Athens in the 7th century who wrote a code of laws that prescribed death for almost every crime.

However, sometimes it is harder to spot differences, especially when the opinion is written as if it were fact.

Fact or opinion?

Look at the following statements about the artist Salvador Dalí and decide whether they are probably facts or opinions:

1 Salvador Dalí was a Spanish (Catalan) artist and one of the most important painters of the 20th century.
2 He completed his best known work, the Persistance of Memory, in 1931.
3 Dalí had an interesting life and liked doing unusual things to draw attention to himself.
4 Sometimes his behaviour caused more public recognition than his artwork.
5 Dalí should not have drunk so much.
6 Dalí experimented with Dada, which influenced his work throughout his life.
7 He met the poet Federico García Lorca and it was rumoured by some that they were lovers.
8 After the death of his wife, Gala, Dalí lost much of his will to live and deliberately dehydrated himself – possibly as a suicide attempt, possibly in an attempt to put himself into a state of suspended animation, as he had read that some microorganisms could do.
9 Dalí's work reflects his powerful imagination and idiosyncratic view of life.

Looking at these statements, you can see that they are all opinion to some extent. Even the second statement 'his best known work' is someone's interpretation and therefore opinion. When assessing the value of something, look out for the following:

general statements that you cannot check or are not supported by evidence	e.g. one of the most important painters of the 19th century, Dalí lost much of his will to live
words containing a value judgement	e.g. should not have drunk so much
words that sound good but are vague	e.g. rumoured by some
words that sound impressively complex but do not mean much	e.g. his powerful imagination and idiosyncratic view of life

Applying this to your university reading

Some students are criticized for accepting what they read and not working hard enough to understand the text's meaning critically. A critical reader asks questions, questions the evidence and evaluates the argument. Below are some questions to ask for critical reading.

The writer's purpose / world view / reason for writing?

Other things I know / have read? My purpose in reading? My ideas? My opinion? My experience?

How does it all fit together? How does this text fit with what I already understand?

Developing your critical reading: quest analysis

One useful way of putting this into practice and engaging with the ideas of the text rather than just the words' surface meaning is to try a QUEST analysis. Take an article or a chapter in a book on your course reading list and try it out. Compare your QUEST analysis with another student's. You will probably find that you have quite different responses to the same text.

Q	Questions	After reading, what questions do you still have? Are there parts where you need more information or that were not explained thoroughly enough? Does the article talk about concepts that you do not understand and so need to read more about?
U	Unhappy	Are you unhappy with anything? For example, was one opinion unsupported by evidence or does the writer take a position you do not agree with? Perhaps it seems badly written in places or difficult to read. You may simply feel confused by the article.
E	Excited	What excites you or makes you think differently about the themes? Maybe the article introduces some new research that helps you to understand a concept better. Maybe it summarizes an idea in a helpful way.
S	Strengths	What do you feel are the article's strengths? Is it well written and easy to read? Does it use helpful examples or definitions? Is there a useful literature review? Is its evidence supported?
T	Themes	What are the main themes and ideas? If someone asked you about it, how would you complete this sentence: 'It's an article / book / report that looks at ....'

Tips for doing a QUEST analysis   TIP

Read the article quickly first and identify the themes, then re-read it looking for the other parts.

As you read, use a different colour to highlight Questions, Unhappy, Excited, Strengths and Themes.

Try to identify at least one part for each section.

Other ways of developing your critical reading skills

Becoming a critical reader in a second language can be fun and challenging. Here are some ways of developing critical reading skills that will be useful before you apply to do your course. Remember that, when looking for the meaning beyond the text, first you do need to understand the words on the page.

Text types	What to look for and what to do
Magazine adverts	Look at a range of advertisements from magazines. First work out what product is being sold. Then, look at how the writer tries to persuade people to buy their product. You may find: – complex scientific-sounding language with evidence for why that product is the best – comparison with other products – statements that you cannot check – over-the-top language e.g. lots of adjectives that sound impressive
Song lyrics	Song lyrics are useful because often they are short and have an underlying 'message'. A critical reader must first understand the meaning of the words and second understand the message. What is the songwriter saying about themselves or their world? If there are any difficult cultural or musical references, look these up or ask someone.
News in brief	Often newspapers have a section that summarizes stories from around the world in short articles of about 50 words. This means that many details, facts and background points are left out. – First work out why the story is newsworthy. – Second, write the questions that you want answered. – You could go to a news site on the internet e.g. http://www.bbc.co.uk or http://cnn.com and find out what is missing.
Letters to the editor	Newspapers have a section where readers can write their opinions. They are great for analysing the writer's stance on an issue and spotting holes in the letter writer's logical argument. – First, work out whether the writer agrees or disagrees with the newspaper articles. – Decide how well the letter writer justifies their opinion. – Spot any holes in their argument or their logic.
Satire / comedy	In this kind of writing the author holds a mirror to society by making jokes about people or institutions in the news. Trying to understand why a story is funny is a good way to develop critical reading. The Onion (http://www.theonion.com/content/) is an American website that looks at stories about US celebrities, politicians and events. – First, understand the story. You may need to do some research if you are in another country looking at a site like The Onion. – Then decide why it is funny.

First task adapted from F. Grellet (1981) *Developing Reading Skills*, Cambridge University Press.

Ways of reading

Here are some different ways of doing university reading. Which of these are you good at?

reading for the big picture	reading something quickly to understand the main ideas
reading intensively	reading a section of text really carefully and understanding every word
scan reading	searching for a particular detail to find out more
skim reading	looking quickly over a text to decide on the topic
reading between the lines	reading critically to evaluate a text for yourself and working out the unwritten meaning

Which process you choose will depend on your reason for reading, the type of text and the questions you want answered. Look at these typical tasks and decide which processes you might use. Check your answers at the end of the book.

Reading tasks	Reading process?
1. Looking through the references section of an essay for the name of a particular text.	
2. Reading a research article to find out a study's topic and its main findings.	
3. Your lecturer tells you a particular book would be good background reading so you read it to get a quick idea of what it's about.	
4. Reading a literature review and deciding on the viewpoint of the writer.	

Improving your reading

This section has tasks to improve your reading for gist, scan reading and reading intensively.

Reading for gist

Reading for gist means reading quickly to get a rough idea about meaning. Make sure you know why you are reading. Predict the information you think will be in the text and then read quickly to see if your guesses were correct.

Tips for reading for gist

- Don't try to understand everything. Remember you can always read the text again if you want more information.
- Skim reading means getting an overview of the text. If you find yourself looking at individual words and trying to figure out their meaning, stop, because this is not gist reading. Move faster and think about the general meaning, not the meaning of individual words.

- The first line of every paragraph is often really important and explains what the paragraph is going to be about. Spend more time on these lines.
- Don't use your dictionary when reading for gist. It will slow you down. Skip over words you don't understand at this stage.

Read lots of fiction in English   TIP

Reading fiction is good practice for gist reading. There are many graded readers at different levels for language learners. They use only the most common English words so you can concentrate on the story without worrying about vocabulary.

Scan reading

Scan reading is looking at a text for particular words or numbers. It is a bit like the 'Ctrl + F' (FIND) function of a computer.

Scan reading is really useful when you know exactly which word you want to find – for example:

- you are looking up a word in the index of a book
- you get a page reference and then look at that page and look for the word
- you are looking for an idea in the contents page of the book
- you are writing an essay and need to check a fact or a quote
- you look for a name or date in an article.

Tips for scan reading

- Do it at speed.
- Have a number of search terms in mind e.g. don't just look for one word like **'earthmoving'** but also look for **'earth-shifting'**, **'landscaping'** and **'excavating'**.
- When you find one of these words, there's no need to read the others on the page.

Reading intensively

Reading intensively means reading to understand details. This is slow, so make sure the section is really worth reading intensively. An example of a text to read intensively is an exam essay question! You really need to understand it fully.

First read the passage for gist, then ask:

- Do I need to re-read this?
- If so, which parts?
- What information do I need?

If the answer to the first question is 'no', go on to the next text. If you need to understand something in the text in more detail, you may need to read it intensively.

Tips for reading intensively

- Read for gist first.
- Work out the meaning from word to word, but don't forget the whole meaning.
- It's slow and takes a lot of brain power, so don't do too much.

- Use a dictionary at this stage if necessary. You need the exact meaning of words.
- Read critically. Test the meaning against your previous knowledge and look for connections within the text.

Increasing your reading speed

Students often ask how they can read faster. There is no easy answer. The key to becoming an efficient reader is partly to read strategically, working out when to read for gist and when to read in more detail. You can also train your eyes and brain to process text more efficiently. This section has seven ideas that will help you to read faster. How many of these do you already do?

1. Set a time limit

Always set yourself an appropriate time limit. Look at how long the article is and think how important it is for your studies. Perhaps give yourself ten minutes. Then ask again: Do I still think it is important? Have I got enough out of the text? Should I keep going?

2. Be happy with good enough

Read well enough to answer your questions. You do not need (and don't have time!) to understand EVERYTHING. The next time you read something, aim to understand 60%. Set a time limit of half what you would normally allow for that length of text.

3. Read in a team

Form a study group to share reading.

4. Analyse your dictionary use

Some students are very dictionary-dependent. Looking up many words is slow and you may lose track of your reading. However, sometimes it can be important to look up the meaning of a few key words, for example in the abstract of an article. At other times, either skip over unknown words or try guessing their meaning from the context. You may not guess the meaning 100%, but probably well enough.

5. Chunk it

Read three or four words at a time rather than individual words.

   Don't read …

   THE + MOST + IMPORTANT + CONCEPT + IN + SPEED + READING + IS + ….

   but read …

   THE MOST IMPORTANT CONCEPT + IN SPEED READING IS + ….

   Train yourself by marking meaningful chunks of words together in one of your textbooks.

6. Read down, not along

Slow readers move their eyes along the line of text from left to right. More efficient readers move their eyes downwards. Focus on the middle of the line and place your finger there. Move your finger down and follow it with your eyes. This takes practice and is easiest for reading narrow columns like newspaper articles and magazine articles.

7. Notice the direction of the text

When you are reading, don't get bogged down in details. Look for signals showing the argument or direction. Look out for words such as these below.

In addition Moreover A further point in relation to X is ….	To add another point
Thus Therefore	To show a logical next step
However, …. On the other hand	To introduce a contrast
In order to illustrate X, take… Another example of this is ….	To introduce an example
To sum up In conclusion	To introduce a conclusion

Reading strategies

Many reading strategies can make you a more effective reader. This task will help you think about your current reading strategies and some worth trying.

A reading strategy checklist

Check your strategies against this checklist. Think about whether you would like to try new strategies.

Before reading

- Use a book's contents and index pages to find the most useful sections.
- Scan a chapter for relevant keywords.
- Recall what you know already from lectures and other reading.
- Make predictions about the content.
- Ask yourself questions that might be answered and then read to check these.
- Research the writer. Find out when they were writing and what their position was on the subject and who may have influenced their ideas.
- Use the title, abstract, introductory paragraph and illustrations to predict the content.
- Quickly look over the text and decide if it is worth reading on.

Text genre/organization

- Recall other texts you have read with the same aim as this one (e.g. other research articles or other introductory texts that define many technical terms) for clues to the text's organization.

- Look for general patterns such as claim–counterclaim, general–specific, and theory–example.
- Use these patterns to predict what is coming next.
- Notice signposting language such as, 'Another example of … is …' to think of the text as a map.
- Look for useful topic sentences as a clue to the content of each paragraph.

First reading

- Read for gist before reading for detail.
- Answer a gist question (e.g. what did the researcher discover?) when reading the first time.
- Set yourself a time limit.
- Live with a little confusion. Don't try to understand everything.
- Only use your dictionary for really key difficult words.
- Ignore unknown words. Try to make sense without them.
- Use skimming (looking over the whole text for main ideas) and scanning (looking for key words / numbers / dates).
- Note sections that look really important and think about questions for a second reading.
- Keep testing the ideas against your experiences and everything you have read / learnt.

Second reading

- Think carefully about your purpose in reading for detail. Why do you need a detailed understanding of certain parts?
- Set yourself detailed questions about sections of the text and answer them as you read.
- Set yourself a time limit.
- Use highlighter pens and Post-it notes for key areas.
- Test the text against your world knowledge and other texts that you have read.
- Make notes as you read using a note-taking summary sheet or your own system.
- Note questions about the text that you need to investigate further.

After reading

- Give someone who hasn't read the text a rough idea of the content.
- Talk the ideas through with someone who has read it.
- Cover the text and try writing a very short summary (one paragraph).
- Follow up key questions that you had when reading, with your lecturer or classmates, or through further reading.
- Make notes of useful expressions for your own writing.

Keeping track of your reading

It is frustrating when writing an essay or revising for an exam, when you need some information or a quote, and you are sure that you read something relevant, but you can't quite remember what it was or where you found it! Even more frustrating is to go searching for a reference in the library, find it and then realize that you've already read the article! It is amazingly easy over a year to waste a lot of time looking for things you have already read. The trick is to keep track of your reading and adopt some kind of system to store your notes, even of texts that you do not think are really relevant.

Different ways of keeping a record of your reading

There are many ways of recording your reading. Which you choose will depend on your own preference. Here are five ways to try:

- a paper record in a folder or notebook
- computer files
- OneNote (a Microsoft application)
- free note-taking software such as Evernote
- referencing programs such as Zotero or Mendeley.

Experiment with different storage strategies   TIP

Talk to other students about how they organize their notes and try different approaches until you find one that works for you and your course.

Reading online

Much of your university reading will be online. This section considers similarities and differences between online and paper-based reading and also some specific 'online' activities you will need for your course.

Reading online vs reading paper-based texts: same or different?

There are many similarities between online and reading paper-based reading. How true do you find these statements? Compare your ideas with the discussion in the answers at the end of the book.

1 You still need to read critically.
2 You can use the same strategies (skimming, scanning, reading intensively, etc.) when reading online.
3 It's easier to get distracted and waste time online.
4 It's worse for your eyes.
5 You find the same text types online.
6 It's better for the planet.

Some useful things about reading online

You can find many texts and information online and run advanced searches (see the section on finding reading on the internet). There are many more things to do with computers that make reading easier and save time, as you can find out below:

1 **Find on page:**
   Use CTRL+F to bring up this search box. This is a really useful tool for scanning a document or webpage. It can help you decide whether something is worth reading and then which parts are worth reading intensively. Imagine you are interested in air pollution from industry in the USA and you find an online article on it. Now find out how often the word 'industry' is mentioned. If it doesn't mention industry, then go to the next article. If it does, you probably don't need to read the whole article, only those sections where the word 'industry' is used.

2 **Save your favourites:**
   If you find useful articles, either download them and save them on your computer, or save the URL (internet address) as a 'favourite' or 'bookmark'. This means you can get back to it really quickly. Many students use online tools such as http://del. icio.us to share their bookmarks with other students and to find interesting new websites.

3 **Links to reference materials:**
   When reading online, you can open an online dictionary or subject glossary together to check word meanings. You can use 'extensions' in your browser to do things like click on a word for a translation or synonym.

4 **Tabs/windows:**
   Right-click on links you are not sure about and they open in a new window. This is useful because you do not navigate away from the first page. It's like opening a new book while keeping the one you are reading open.

5 **Copy and paste direct quotes:**
   You no longer need to copy out direct quotes to use in essays. While reading for an essay, keep a word document open for storing quotes, and copy and paste as you read. Remember also to keep a record of where the quotes are from so as to reference them properly in your essay including your bibliography. Remember to use quotation marks for direct quotes to avoid plagiarism. In addition, be careful about the number of direct quotes you use. Paraphrase some ideas instead of using quotes.

Conclusion

In this chapter we have tried to show that by thinking about why you are reading and by choosing appropriate techniques you can become a more active and efficient reader. Often students get feedback on their reading only when they write assignments, for example:

- 'Your writing shows that you are reading widely.'
- 'You have clearly researched this topic thoroughly.'
- 'You make good use of the sources you cite.'

This may be all the positive feedback you get about your reading. Keep track of these comments as well as more negative ones as they both indicate whether you are doing enough reading. For example:

- 'You have cited only two articles for this essay.'
- 'At this level you are expected to show that you have read more widely than this.'
- 'You need to read more critically and show in the essay what you think about the reading rather than just report it.'

It may be hard to work out how much you should be reading when your previous educational experiences were different; also subjects and lecturers may differ in requirements. If these expectations are not clear, talk to someone in your department or seek advice from an academic advisor.

Principles of Academic Writing

Many students who study in English have said that academic writing is one of the most difficult parts of their study. They say it is because lecturers usually expect more from a paper than, for example, an oral presentation. There are many types of academic writing, and this chapter and the next one will deal mostly with one of them, the argumentative essay (a type of writing in which the author tries to convince the reader to agree with his or her viewpoint). We also cover some general principles and processes that apply to all forms of academic writing.

This chapter will help you understand:

- some general elements of academic writing
- grading criteria
- essay questions
- how to start working on an essay
- some strategies for improving your writing over time.

General principles of academic writing

Audience, purpose and strategies

When you approach a writing assignment, you will need to ask yourself a few questions:

1 Who is the audience of my writing?
2 What do they already know about the topic?
3 What do they expect to learn more about?
4 What is the purpose of the writing?

In many cases, the audience of your writing in college is your own lecturers, who probably have more knowledge than you do about the topic. Therefore, you are not writing to inform them. Usually, you write to show them that you understand the materials taught in class and have the ability to analyse, interpret and evaluate what you have read and learned. Knowing this, what strategies should you use? The strategies really depend on the specific writing assignment, but consider the principles introduced below.

Organization

There are different types of writing with different organizational patterns. Examples of the types of writing that you encounter may include argumentative essays, summaries, research papers, proposals, lab reports, responses to case studies, text analyses and critiques. Each type of writing moves from one section or paragraph to another in a certain way. For example, in a research paper you may need to have an introduction, a literature review, a method section, a results section and a discussion and conclusion section. It is advisable to follow the patterns that are usually expected for each type of writing. The best way to learn about these organizational patterns is to read the instructions for the assignment carefully, ask your lecturer for advice and clarification, and read model papers. Sometimes, departments also prepare guidelines for students for specific types of writing and publish them on their websites or in their handbooks.

Choosing an appropriate style

What style is appropriate may depend on your subject, the type of writing and even the lecturer's preference. However, generally, in academic writing, consider the following simple tips:

- Whenever you use a phrasal verb such as 'find out' or 'look into', see if you can use a single verb such as 'discover' or 'investigate'.
- Whenever you have a prepositional phrase, see if you can use a formal adverb instead. For example, instead of saying 'describe the study in a few sentences', you may write 'briefly describe the study'. Notice the adverb 'briefly' is placed right before the verb.
- Do not use contractions, such as 'isn't'.
- Check with the professor to see if you can use pronouns such as 'I,' 'you' and 'we'. Usually, in academic writing you do not address the audience directly by using 'you'. Even when you express your opinions, you do not need to use 'I think' or 'In my opinion'.
- Whenever you have a direct question, see if you can turn it into a statement.

Pay attention to coherence / cohesion, accuracy and conciseness

Coherence / cohesion

When we talk we make connections with what has gone before. We say things like:

> *That reminds me ....*
> *Yes, but ....*
> *And another thing ....*

When we write formally we also join ideas up so that our writing is coherent and cohesive. This means that ideas flow smoothly from one sentence to another and from one paragraph to another to form one unified essay or paper. Below are three kinds of cohesion that you should aim to achieve in your writing.

Sentence-level cohesion

This means the sentence reads like one thought, not several thoughts just stuck together. Conjunctions like *and, or* and *but* are the most common links, but there are many more, such as *while, when, if, although, even though, whereas* and *because*. Pay attention to how punctuation is used with these conjunctions. More importantly, thoughts or ideas in different sentences should be logically connected. The connection could be made clear to the reader through the use of appropriate transition words and phrases such as *furthermore, for example, in contrast,* etc.

Essay-level cohesion

This refers to how the whole text fits together. Importantly, you have to make sure all your ideas support the thesis statement.

To improve cohesion in your writing, consider the following strategies:

- Whenever you use a pronoun such as *it, they, this* and *that,* make sure that the reader knows what you refer to.
- Use *this* and a summary noun, such as in this example:
  The number of international students attending US universities has increased significantly in the past five years. This increase can be explained by various factors.
- Use appropriate transition words and phrases such as the ones in the table below.

In the following table you will find some transition words and phrases. Decide which of the purposes in the right-hand column best matches these words. You can find the answers at the end of this book.

These words ...	Are used ...
Furthermore	To say the same thing another way
On the other hand	To refer to someone's published view
Conversely	To give an opposite view
Similarly	To make things clearer
As an example	To concede a point, but then rebut it
In other words	To illustrate a point
Even though	To say more of the same point
Despite the fact that	To agree slightly (to concede a point)
This is not the same as saying	
This point is also made by ...	

Accuracy

Accuracy has to do with whether your sentences are grammatically and stylistically correct. Errors in your writing may prevent the readers from understanding your ideas and sometimes make them stop reading. The paragraph below demonstrates the typical effects of errors on lecturers who read and grade students' writings.

How serious are errors?

Dr Lumley on linguistic errors:

> Language errors vary in severity. Sometimes they can be quite superficial and simply annoy me. Spelling mistakes often fall into this category (Type 1). At other times it causes me temporary confusion and I need to re-read a section of an essay to understand what you are trying to say (Type 2). However, errors may actually mean that I can't understand your writing at all and will give up in despair (Type 3). Even Type 1 errors will have a negative effect on me – especially if there are a lot of them and your essay is number 30 in a pile of 50 assignments that I have to grade. I very quickly become obsessed with language errors and stop taking the ideas in the essay seriously. Then my mind wanders and I start thinking about university entry requirements and how standards are slipping and how it was better in

the old days. On the other hand, when you do get an essay that reads well – it stands out. It's well worth taking the time to keep markers happy.

Strategies to improve the accuracy of your writing include careful proofreading after you finish your writing and possibly asking a tutor or a proficient English writer for feedback. The next chapter will help you to improve your proofreading skills and suggest ways to seek feedback and also provide feedback to others.

Conciseness

Conciseness means using fewer words to express the same ideas. By being concise, your writing may also become clearer to the readers.

Look at a few examples and notice how conciseness also makes the sentences clearer.

1a. In microeconomics, the field studies the behaviour of individuals or firms in making decisions on the allocation of limited resources.

1b. Microeconomics studies the behaviour of individuals or firms in making decisions on the allocation of limited resources.

2a. Charles Robert Darwin, who was quite a prominent person as a natural scientist in the world, is considered the first researcher of non-verbal communication.

2b. Charles Robert Darwin, a prominent natural scientist, is considered the first researcher of non-verbal communication.

3a. Almost everyone thinks that they know what translation is, but I assume that a lot of people think that translation is just the process of changing something that is written into another language.

3b. Many people assume that translation is simply changing written texts into another language.

Be cautious in your analysis and evaluation

In academic writing, being cautious means not stating something as a fact or saying something with absolute certainty. By being cautious, you acknowledge that there are situations in which what you or others observe may not be true. Usually, you do this by:

- distancing yourself
  - ○ citing sources, such as 'According to XYZ …'
  - ○ using structures, such as 'It is said that …', 'It is thought that …' and 'It appears that …'
- using modal verbs or verb phrases such as 'may', 'might', 'seem to' and 'tend to' instead of using verbs in the present tense without any qualifying language
- using adverbs such as 'certainly', 'probably', 'possibly' and 'apparently'.

http://www.phrasebank.manchester.ac.uk   **TIP**

This website provides you with many examples of academic phrases that you can use for different functions, such as being cautious, being critical, introducing sources, and others. It is a great resource that you should explore.

Pay attention to how you present your paper

Presentation in a paper is similar to how you present yourself to others through your appearance, your manner, your body language and other aspects of who you are. In academic writing lecturers may have very specific guidelines for the format of your paper. If so, follow them closely. If no guidelines are given, then it is important to be consistent. For example, if you begin a new paragraph with an indent (a few spaces before the first word), then do so throughout the entire text. There are some strategies for proofreading and editing your paper to improve its presentation in the later section of this chapter.

What bothers students?

Have a look at the list below of common problems that students report with writing. If any apply to you, read more about them below or in the next chapter.

1   *I often find it difficult to understand the essay question.*
    See the section below on 'Understanding essay questions'.
2   *I don't quite understand the grading criteria.*
    See the section below on 'Understanding grading criteria'.
3   *I don't know where to find the material I should be reading.*
    See the section below on 'Collecting ideas for your essay'.
4   *I keep hearing people talking about an 'argument' or an 'argumentative' essay, but for me an argument sounds like something confrontational. I feel much safer just reporting things.*
    See the section below on 'Arguing with a friend'.

Understanding grading criteria

The above section about general principles of academic writing provides you with some information on what your lecturer may look for in an essay. In addition, most of the time, your lecturer will provide you with the criteria they use to grade your paper. However, it is not always easy to understand what each criterion means. Understanding grading criteria usually means understanding what the lecturer thinks is important. In this section, we are going to give you an example of grading criteria for a research paper on an undergraduate course in the United States. This may provide you with some strategies to learn to understand them and 'read' the lecturer.

Look at how this lecturer presents the grading criteria of a research paper in the form of a checklist for students. In your own words, describe what the lecturer thinks is important.

Focus:

- Is my research question or thesis clearly stated?
- Does my paper provide new insight to make an original contribution? In other words, does my paper move beyond description to analysis?
- Does my paper build around one central idea, avoiding analysing the problem in multiple directions and trying to develop too many points?

Substance:

- Do I provide sufficient background information on the issue?
- Do I adequately try to integrate the core concepts, theories, political philosophies, ideologies and tenets of schools of thoughts that have been reviewed in the scope of the course?
- In my analysis, do I offer a good evaluation of the theories used in this specific context (topic of the paper)?
- Is the central point of my paper sufficiently supported by examples and evidence?
- Do major points receive sufficient attention?
- Are there any parts of my paper that digress from the main point by incorporating information that is tangential, irrelevant, or unimportant?
- Do I present the material in a persuasive manner?

Organization:

- Does my paper have an appropriate title and open with an engaging introduction?
- Are the ideas presented in a clear and logical order? Is the flow of my arguments easy to follow?
- Does each paragraph and section support the key objective of my paper?
- Does my paper end with a conclusion that provides closure by not simply repeating everything that has been stated but helping the reader make sense of what it ALL means?

Style/language:

- Does my paper conform to the standards of academic writing including correct spelling, punctuation and formatting, etc.?
- Do I write in clear, understandable language, or do I obfuscate/complicate the ideas through awkward language and overly abstract analyses?
- Are the voice and tone of my paper appropriate to my topic?
- Is my paper succinct, or is it long, tedious and repetitious?
- Is my writing style lively and full, portraying the interesting aspects of my subject, or has it drained the life out of the subject through dull and/or obtuse language?

This rubric was kindly provided by Professor Jean-Jacques Ngor Sène, Chatham University, Pittsburgh, PA, USA.

As you can see, the lecturer provides students with questions to analyse whether their paper meets the four major criteria: focus, substance, organization and language. You should spend time reading the criteria carefully, highlight the important points and think of steps you should take to address them. The steps you take may include reviewing lectures and reading previously covered in the course and reading more about the topic. It may also be a good idea to ask for a model of a good research paper from the lecturer and use the questions provided to analyse it.

Understanding essay questions

Simplifying the essay question

One reason why essay questions are often difficult to understand is because they use difficult language and are quite 'dense', meaning that there are a lot of important words in a small amount of text. In spoken English we usually use simpler language. So one tip is to try to 'translate' the essay question into spoken questions (including 'who, why, what, when, where and how'). Pay attention to the content words (words that carry most of the meaning in the text), as well as action verbs such as 'discuss' and 'describe'. Now try writing down spoken questions for each essay question. The first example has been done for you. The answers are at the end of the book.

Essay question	Simple spoken questions
Discuss, with reference to specific examples, the role of the messenger in ancient tragedies.	What did the messenger do? Which tragedies used messengers? How are they important to the plays' stories?
Describe how developments in management theory in the 1980s have affected management practice in the 21st century.	
Discuss the controversy over Iris Chang's interpretation of the Nanking Massacre, and account for the strength of the reaction to her work.	

If you are not sure you are accurately translating your essay question, ask your lecturer or seek support from an academic support centre at your university.

An A–Z of Words from Essay Questions

You may find this glossary useful when working out what essay questions are asking. The exact meaning of the words will depend on the subject you are studying, but this glossary will tell you what they normally mean.

Account for	Explain why something happened. This is not the same as 'give an account of', which asks for a detailed description.
Analyse	Write about something in depth – identifying, describing and criticizing in detail its main features.

Argue	Put forward an idea and support it. Discuss what the idea means and defend it against possible counter-arguments.
Assess	Examine something closely. Write about its strengths and weaknesses. Discuss the points for and against something. Finally, give your opinion.
Calculate	Work something out using maths.
Clarify	Simplify something and make it clear.
Comment	State clearly your opinions on something. Support your views with evidence or explanations.
Compare	Look for similarities **and** differences between two or more things.
Consider	Express your thoughts and observations about something.
Contrast	Identify and emphasize the **differences** between two or more things.
Criticize	Give your judgement about something. Explore what it means, discussing all the evidence available.
Define	Write down the precise meaning of something.
Demonstrate	Show how something works or operates and prove it by giving examples.
Describe	Give a detailed and full account of something.
Develop	Expand on something, taking it further.
Distinguish	Explain the differences between two or more things.
Discuss	Examine something by careful argument. Write about the advantages or disadvantages. Debate something and consider different ways of seeing it. This is probably the most common instruction term – you should say something interesting to answer the question. You can choose your own approach.
Elaborate	Add further details to something.
Enumerate	Make a list, giving the main features of something (leaving out details). Put the list in order.
Examine	Enquire into something, investigate, or look closely into it.
Expand	Go into more detail.
Explain	Make something clear. Account for it. Clarify, interpret and spell out a subject, giving reasons for its features.
Explore	Question an issue or idea, and consider it from a number of viewpoints.
Give an account of	Describe something in detail, and explain it fully.
How?	In what way, by what means or method, or to what extent does something happen, exist, or work?
How far ...?	Similar to questions that begin 'To what extent ...?' You should discuss the subject, and show any of its strengths or weaknesses.

(Continued)

Identify	Pick out the main features or the important points of something.
Illustrate	Make something clear by discussing examples of it.
Interpret	Explain the meaning of something. Make it clear, using your own judgement, experience, or opinion.
Justify	Show the reasons or the best arguments for something. Answer any objections likely to be made against it.
List	Make a list or catalogue of things.
Outline	Give the main features or the general principles of a subject. You can leave out minor details. Emphasize the structure or arrangement of its parts.
Prove	Show that something is true or false by presenting evidence.
Relate	Show how things are connected. Show how they affect, cause, or resemble each other.
Review	Make a survey of something. Examine the subject critically.
Show	Reveal something, in some form of logical sequence or explanation.
State	Present the main points of a subject in a brief, clear form.
Summarize	Give an account of the main points of a subject, leaving out any details and examples.
To what extent?	Similar to questions that begin 'How far …?' You are expected to discuss something, and show any of its strengths and weaknesses.
Trace	Follow the development or history of something. Explain the changes step by step.
Translate	Say something in a different way, or change it from one language to another.
Verify	Show that something is true, or confirm it.

Adapted from http://www.buzzin.net.

Making sense of question words

Look at the list of verbs above and group them into the appropriate boxes below. Check your answers at the end of the book.

analyse	argue	explain	develop	prove	compare	describe

Have a look at some of your previous assignment questions and check which of these question words are common in your subject. Look especially for any questions where the words themselves are not given and work out what you are supposed to do.

e.g. *The Victorians thought, 'Children should be seen but not heard.' Is this still true today?*

The question is asking you to compare an idea common in the past with modern ideas. The main issue here is changes in the way children are brought up and treated. The missing question words are 'discuss' and 'compare'.

Collecting ideas for your essay

Imagine you are asked to write an essay on this topic:

What services does the university have to help students learn English? How suitable are these services for someone of your language level and needs?

Step one: deciding what type of essay this is

Answer: Like many essay questions, this one is a mixture. It is mostly to explain the university's services, but you also need to evaluate the success of the services and argue to what extent they meet students' needs.

Step two: collecting your ideas

The main ways to collect ideas for your essay are:

- doing research on the topic and on the services provided
- brainstorming with your peers
- practising your arguments with a friend to hear other viewpoints.

We now look in detail at these ideas. Of course, there are other ways of getting ideas, such as using reference books, reading your lecture notes and textbooks and asking to borrow assignments from other students.

Doing research on the topic

Whenever you have to write about a topic, reading about it first will help you to better understand it and allow you to start forming your own opinion. The information you read and learn will also help you to support your position later. Doing research may involve consulting your lecturer on what you should read. Online resources, such as Google Scholar, and databases in the library will allow you to search for reading on the topic. You can also ask a librarian for help in finding reading materials.

Brainstorming to collect ideas

Another way to collect ideas is by brainstorming. These are the steps to follow:

1 Get a large piece of paper.
2 Write down everything you can think of related to the topic, even if it seems silly at first.
3 Do this as quickly as you can. Give yourself no more than a few minutes. Just write words / draw pictures, arrows, etc. Don't write full sentences at this stage – it's too slow.

Afterwards you can try to group ideas that seem related, for example by using colours.

A good way to help you in your brainstorming is to use the PPPPP system. In this system you try to come up with ideas by looking at different or opposite sides of a topic. Here are some examples:

Extend and sort your ideas out by looking at opposite sides of each topic	
Practical reasons	Abstract reasons
Personal reasons	Reasons affecting society
Permanent reasons	Short-term reasons
Proven reasons	Hypothetical (possible) reasons
People-related reasons	Financial reasons

Let's try these prompts with the following topic.

Learning a foreign language should be compulsory in all high schools.

Here are some notes you could brainstorm under each of the headings:

Practical reasons *helps trade*	**Abstract reasons** *any different type of learning develops the brain*
Personal reasons *students could travel, earn money and get better jobs*	**Reasons affecting society** *countries could understand one another better*
Permanent reasons *it will develop students' thinking skills*	**Short-term reasons** *it may motivate students*
Proven reasons *societies with multilingual populations are said to survive longer*	**Hypothetical (possible) reasons** *might help world peace*
People-related reasons *being able to understand another language helps us to develop better relationships*	**Financial reasons** *a multilingual society can trade more easily and be more successful financially*

Try out this next topic with the same PPPPP categories.

Cities would be better off if cars were banned.

Leave the list for a day and then come back to it. Can you think of new ideas to add?

Arguing with a friend

Here is a task we have called 'the tennis match' because you need to argue back and forth with someone who has a different opinion. The purpose is to collect three types of example that you need for an argument essay, namely:

- argument
- counter-argument
- rebuttal.

An **argument** is like an opinion, a **counter-argument** is an alternative to that opinion and a **rebuttal** is a response to the counter-argument.

Here are some examples to give you an idea of what these terms mean. In an essay addressing the statement that poverty in any country is the responsibility of all countries:

An argument

Today's world has been referred to as 'a global village'. Just as in a village everyone is responsible for caring for anyone who is poor, so in the world today richer countries must look after the poorer ones.

A counter-argument

The comparison with a village is an attractive one. However, we could argue that with better planning the poorer countries would not have become poor. In other words, it is their fault.

A rebuttal

Most belief systems around the world acknowledge that some people are better at looking after themselves than others and that the better organized are not necessarily better people. Neither are the poorer people necessarily to blame for their poverty. As in a family, we need to look after those who, for whatever reason, find it hard to look after their own needs.

Good essays don't just present one side of a topic, but usually also consider other viewpoints. This is a key aspect of critical thinking (see Chapter 12); being able to weigh up the benefits and drawbacks of different arguments. By doing the task below you will probably come up with a lot of ideas for your essay. You could do this task alone, but it works better if you do it with a friend. Your task is to find three types of statement: an argument, a counter-argument and a rebuttal.

Each counter-argument and rebuttal MUST refer to the previous statement. We have given an example above. Now you think of arguments, counter-arguments and rebuttals for the following essay questions:

This university should have better … for students.
People in country X have a better life today than they did a hundred years ago.
The elderly / the young are the worst car drivers.

We can't give you an answer without looking at your ideas. This is a task that you are best off doing with another student. If you can also find an 'umpire' (judge), as in a tennis match, you will get some good feedback on your points.

Improving your writing: advice from students

If you'd like to improve your grades for your writing assignments as well as become a better writer, you might want to follow some advice given by other students below.

Use the student learning centre, tutoring centre or writing centre

Many universities have support centres to help you with your study. Take advantage of them, like the student below.

> I learned some techniques and methods from a writing workshop at the Student Learning Centre. Now I get better grades for my assignments. I also made appointments with tutors from the centre. Their feedback was extremely helpful.

Talk with your lecturer about your draft copies

Professors may be willing to give you some feedback on a draft of your writing. They may mostly give you feedback on the content, not on the language. However, you need to plan ahead and give them time to get back to you.

Read the chapter on assessment for advice on making use of professors' feedback.

Practise writing

Some people who find writing difficult do as little writing as possible. Unfortunately, this makes it difficult to improve. By contrast, students who enjoy writing usually write more and get even better. As this student says, not all the writing you do needs to be for assignments.

I enjoy writing. Sometimes I write things even when I don't have to.

Learn from good writers

Students can learn how to write better if they see good examples of essays, as this student found.

I read aloud from good essays. That way I hear good language in my head.

One of the best ways to learn to write is to read and take notes of useful phrases and language. In other words, imitate respected writers in your field.

Talk about essay writing

This next student has a good idea.

I go around asking other people for advice. Sometimes they'll tell you how they prepared to write the essay and that's even better than seeing their actual essay. When I look at a good essay, I just think, 'I could never be that good,' but when they tell me how they got there, I think, 'I could do that.'

If you talk about essay writing with all the students in your class, you will collect plenty of ideas to try with your next essay.

Learn from textbooks

Some students find that having a textbook about academic writing is a help, even if they don't attend an actual writing class. You may even be able to find a book that tells you about essay writing in your own subject. At the end of the next chapter, we recommend some such books.

Conclusion

In this chapter we have presented some general principles of academic writing that you can apply to many types of writing. We have also presented a few ideas on how you can get started with a writing assignment, including understanding the essay question and collecting ideas for your essay. In the next chapter, you will learn about different strategies for each stage of your writing.

Essay Writing Processes

Chapter 8 helps you to understand general principles of academic writing as well as specific skills such as interpreting essay questions and collecting ideas for your essay.
    This chapter will help you understand and practise:

- writing the introduction and thesis statement
- organizing the body paragraphs
- expanding topic sentences to paragraphs
- referencing in an essay
- outlining your essay
- proofreading
- receiving and giving peer feedback.

Writing the introduction and the thesis statement

Many students have said that writing an introduction is one of the most difficult parts of an essay, but, once written, it will make drafting the rest much easier. The introduction of an essay introduces the topic and states the author's main point in what is usually called a thesis statement. The introduction often follows the general-to-specific pattern.

Parts of the Introduction

Let's look at one introduction to an essay on whether schooling should be compulsory. Notice how the sentences move from more general ideas to more specific ideas. The underlined sentence is the thesis statement of the essay.

Example of an essay introduction

(1) Ideas about when and whether children should have compulsory education have varied through the ages and from country to country. (2) In some countries the choice has been left to individuals and in others the government has made one rule for everyone. (3) Most countries of the world now have compulsory schooling between certain ages but the form of the schooling may vary between institutions. (4) Variety may sound like a democratic idea but in practice how does it work out? (5) In this essay the case will be made for national education to include certain fixed areas of learning. (6) The reasons will be explained in terms of equity for individuals and the good of the nation.

Let's look at another introduction in an essay about experiences of studying overseas. The sentences are in the wrong order. Organize the following sentences into the best order. Circle the thesis statement and check your answer at the end of the book.

a. While many people clearly benefit from the experience of studying at university in another country, for some students the experience is far less positive.
b. It is becoming increasingly important for individuals to experience life in another country to make them more employable in a world job market.
c. The case studies also suggest that, for some individuals, the sacrifice made for an overseas education may not ultimately be worth it.
d. By looking at a series of individual case studies, this essay will outline the ways in which young people can benefit from study overseas.
e. With the movement towards globalization in recent decades, both business and education have become more international.

Order: _____

Thesis Statement

You've seen two examples of thesis statements in the previous section. The thesis statement is probably the most important sentence in your essay. It states the main point of the essay as well as your critical stance towards the topic. You may only be able to form a critical stance after researching the topic, thinking about it from different angles and possibly talking to others about what you think. A thesis statement has been compared to an umbrella because it should cover everything you write afterwards. The thesis statement itself or the sentence after the thesis statement may also tell the audience how the essay is organized. Below are some examples of thesis statements. Are they good thesis statements? Why?

Topic 1: *Through the ages and from one society to another, views have varied on the extent to which children should be protected from the world around them. Discuss this issue with reference to two 21st-century societies.*

Thesis statement 1: Most societies agree that little children should be sheltered from some of the most frightening world events.

Topic 2: *'Companies selling tobacco products and marketing alcoholic drinks should not be allowed to sponsor sports events.' Discuss.*

Thesis statement 2: While it may seem illogical that companies selling products that are recognized to be harmful to health are allowed to market their products through sport, it would be impossible to limit sports sponsorship to 'healthy and ethical' companies for a number of reasons.

Topic 3: *Immunization against common diseases is a contentious issue in many countries. Looking at an illness you have studied, evaluate the arguments for and against mass immunization programmes.*

Thesis statement 3: Some immunization programmes have been highly successful; however, there are many reasons why immunization is not always the best way to fight disease.

Topic 4: *Describe the effects of tourism on an area that you have studied. Evaluate the extent to which it has benefited the area.*

Thesis statement 4: Although tourism is frequently reported in the media to benefit local people, in practice this is often overstated and any benefits tend to be at the expense of the environment.

Topic 5: *The standard of training of waiting staff in restaurants is critical to the success of a restaurant. Discuss with reference to case studies you have looked at.*

Thesis statement 5: For restaurants to be successful they need a combination of good staff, good food and a good location, amongst other factors.

Introduction Checklist

After you finish writing your introduction, you can use the checklist below to evaluate it to see if you can improve it.

	Questions	Okay or rewrite?
Topic introduction	Does it tell you what the topic of the essay is? Does it sound interesting?	
Thesis statement	Is your opinion clear? Is your critical stance on the topic clear? Is it clear how you will argue this?	
Signposting	Have you indicated how the essay is organized?	
Organization	Is the introduction organized in a logical way? Does it have a topic introduction, followed by a thesis statement?	

Organizing the body paragraphs

Many students move straight from the introduction to writing the body paragraphs of the essay. However, it is a good strategy to spend some time planning what you are going to write in them. List the main points for the body paragraphs, plan what you will write in each paragraph and then put everything together in an outline.

For example, your thesis statement in an essay on the challenges of competing in the Olympic Games is: 'Competing in the Olympic Games is a difficult challenge for many young people and may not be worth the time.' You may use the following stages to plan for the body of your essay:

Stage 1: List the Main Points

1 Takes a long time to get that good.
2 Necessary to sacrifice career, friends, family.
3 Need to have natural ability. Wrong genes?
4 Need expert coaching and facilities – not always available?
5 Need to care.
6 Need funding / sponsorship.

7 Need to meet qualification times / schedules.
8 Risks – sickness / lack of form / injury.
9 Need to peak at the right time. Olympics only every four years.

Stage 2: Reorganize the Points You Want to Make

At this stage, look at your list and decide which points are not necessary or could be combined.

Points 1 and 2 are about ambition and commitment.

Point 5 is about ambition.

Point 6 seems to follow on from sacrificing career (Point 2).

Points 3 and 4 – natural ability and coaching could go together.

Points 7, 8 and 9 are all linked. They are all about the selection process.

So you come up with this paragraph order: 1 then 2, then 5, then 6 then 3 and 4 and finally 7, 8, 9.

Stage 3: Write Each Point as a Topic Sentence

The topic sentence of a paragraph states the main idea of that paragraph. Everything else in the paragraph is related to and supports the topic sentence. It's like a mini thesis statement, but for a paragraph. The first topic sentence has been written for you. Now complete the others, using the order we decided on above.

1. It takes many years of training and competition for athletes to get to a standard where they can be considered for a country's Olympic team.
2.
5.
6.
3.
4.
7./8.
9.

Now check with our examples below.

2. For some champions the prize comes at a cost to friends and family.
5. Others miss out from lack of drive.
6. Many potential champions miss out because of lack of financial support.
3. Finally, nothing would bring results if a certain basic talent were not there.
4. To get to a standard where athletes can compete at the Games, they need specialist coaching and facilities.
7./ 8. In order to compete at the Games, athletes first need to qualify. There are many physical reasons why athletes may miss qualification.
9. Then there is the tricky matter of timing. People who peak between the four-year Olympic schedule will miss out on the prize.

From topic sentences to paragraphs

There are many ways to develop your topic sentence into a paragraph. The topic sentence starts the paragraph, but further sentences are needed to complete it.

Now you have your sentences. All of them are on the subject of becoming an Olympic champion. For each of the sentences you have chosen, try to develop it by adding one of the following.

Here are some examples.

- Add detail
- Compare or contrast
- Give examples
- Refer to a source
- Add a viewpoint at the end.

In this table we look closely at a paragraph on the topic *The world is a better place than it was a century ago.*

	What to write	Example
1.	A topic sentence	The options for entertainment in the early 21st century are enormous.
2.	More about the topic sentence	Performers from one country can travel by air to amuse audiences in a distant part of the world and be home again in a matter of days. We can flick on the television and be entertained by plays, musical events and of course sports matches from all over the world.
3.	Compare or contrast	All this is different from the standards of living of our great-grandparents.
4.	Give examples	In their day entertainment was more likely to be provided by people they knew.
5.	Refer to a source	According to … (2001) ….
6.	Add a viewpoint	It seems that the world of the 21st century is scarcely recognizable from the past.

Now you try. Find a topic you have been asked to write about in class. Write one paragraph about the topic by using some of the suggestions on what to write from the table above.

Referencing in an essay

As we mention more than once in this book, it is really, really important to let your readers know whether what you are writing is your own idea or whether you have used ideas from other sources. We call these other sources your references. If you use a reference, you will need to cite it both in your text and in the reference list. There are different citation styles, but you will need to ask your lecturer what style, such as APA or MLA, you should follow. This website gives you useful information on the abovementioned styles: https://owl.english.purdue.edu/owl/. You will learn useful phrases to introduce sources from this website: http://www.phrasebank.manchester. ac.uk. Failure to cite sources appropriately may result in charges of plagiarism, which is treated as a serious violation at many universities.

Find Out about Plagiarism

Go to this website:

URL

http://www.cite.auckland.ac.nz/
On this site you can watch videos of students and lecturers from different cultures talking about the importance of referencing by talking about their culture.

1 Find a definition of 'plagiarism'.
2 Watch the videos of the students and staff talking. Whose ideas match your own about plagiarism?
3 Find out how to reference electronic material correctly.
4 Read some of the postings from website users about plagiarism.
5 As you look at the website, note any differences between ideas about referencing and plagiarism in your country and on this website.

Is It or Isn't It?

Here are some scenarios where students describe how they presented material in their essays. You decided whether each one is or is not plagiarism. Then turn to the answers at the end.

I had good long quotes, sometimes half a page long, but I always acknowledged where they came from at the end of the essay.

Every time I used someone else's ideas, I used quotation marks and their name and date.

I take ideas from the textbook, but I always change the words.

If I take ideas from a book, I always say whose ideas they are. The internet is so huge, I can easily cut and paste and get away with it.

Find out about plagiarism in your university department.

If you are studying in another country or even at a different university, you need to check out the rules about plagiarism. At many universities, if you are caught plagiarizing, you will fail your assignment. You also risk failing your course or even being expelled from the university. Your department or faculty will have written guidelines for assignment submission. These may be in your syllabus or in a handbook or on the department website. Read them and find the answers to these questions:

1 What are the penalties for plagiarism?
2 Which referencing style (e.g. APA) does your department / faculty use?
3 How should you reference direct quotes in the text of your assignment?
4 How should you refer to other people's ideas?

5 What are the rules for referencing from internet sources?
6 How should you lay out your references section?

Putting it all together

When it comes to putting your essay together, it is a good idea to have an outline. An outline helps you organize your essay and your own thinking. Here is one example you can use for an argument essay.

The Whole Essay

Read the following argument essay. What *type* of information is missing at each point? Then look at the answers and see if you agree.

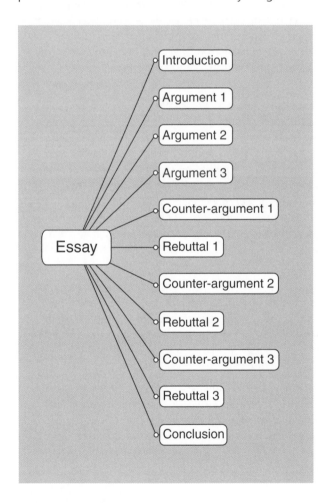

Figure 9.1 Essay structure

Is the world a better place today?

One hundred years ago the car and the aeroplane had recently been invented, world travel meant months at sea and the horizons of many people were the limits of their own village or town. Today, cars and aeroplanes are taken for granted as travellers cross the world for weddings and even for funerals, but has life really improved? It seems that despite technological advances the world is not a better place. This argument will be supported with examples from family life, entertainment, transport and health.

One hundred years ago families spent time together on shared tasks involved with maintaining the home and property. As they did these tasks there were chances to talk. By contrast, these days many household tasks are completed by machines. Furthermore, non-stop television and the ever-ringing telephone prevent people from having conversations with others even when they are in the same house. Some family members spend longer talking on the phone to people in other places than to those around them in the house. According to Smith (1999), national manager of a telephone company, [a] .... It could be argued, therefore, that [b]...

One hundred years ago entertainment meant [c]... ....

The options for entertainment in the early 21st century are enormous. Performers from one country can travel by air to amuse audiences in a distant part of the world and be home again in a matter of days. We can flick on the television and be entertained by plays, musical events and of course sports matches from all over the world. Does this make the world a better place? It could be argued that much of today's entertainment makes people more passive. This change seems more like a step backwards than forwards.

In the area of transport, it is true that these days [d]............................... ...., but these advances have brought extra pressures. For instance, people are expected to fly from all over the world to attend every momentous event in the lives of their families and friends. By contrast, a century ago when a relative was getting married in a different part of the world [e].. It seems that [f]..

Advances in public health are often given as examples of progress. People point to advances in surgery and to the fact that many former diseases such as tuberculosis and leprosy no longer occur on a large scale. This may be the case, but what has taken their place? Today people die just as frequently but of different causes such as [g].. If the only change is the cause of death, where is the progress?

In a word [h] despite ....
Perhaps we should define what we mean by 'better' before saying that everything in the world has improved. For many people 'better' could mean [i] ....

You have seen one example. Now use the same pattern to practise writing a real argument essay that you have to do for your course.

Proofreading

Sometimes, especially as deadlines approach and you have had a few late nights, you don't see the errors until after you have handed in your assignment, when it is too late. Therefore, it is extremely important to proofread your writing carefully before submitting your assignment. However, for second language writers, it is not always easy to detect errors. Below are some common errors that can be avoided by careful proofreading.

Types of Error

These are some common errors from second language writers. Try some of the strategies we introduce here to correct your own errors and avoid them in future writing.

Type	Example	Correction strategy
Spelling or typo	Programe	Use a spellchecker. Spelling errors may be understood as sloppiness and lack of effort. Remember your 'presentation' is important in academic writing.
Noun endings and articles	In Western part of the country, there are some village. (the Western part, villages)	When you proofread, underline all the countable nouns in your sentences and decide if the right form (singular or plural) and article (a, an, the, or the zero article) are used. Whenever you use 'the + noun' ask yourself if the reader knows what you're writing about.
Subject–verb agreement	The number of international students have increased. (has)	Underline the subject and the verb in a sentence to check for agreement.
Incomplete sentence	One stereotype is that international students are not motivated. Which is not true. (This is not true).	Try to identify the subject(s) and verb(s) in your sentences.
Run-on	Another dream I have is to work in Disney, I think this would be great.	Use a period to replace the comma or use a conjunction such as 'and'.
Punctuation	The rich get richer and the poor get poorer. (richer, and)	Check a writing handbook for rules in using punctuation.
Word choice	I am studying abroad to chase my goals. (pursue, achieve)	Check the dictionary when you're not sure. Use some tools introduced in the vocabulary chapter.
Word form	We choice to be independent. (choose)	Pay attention to the right word form: verb, noun, adjective, or adverb.
Verb tense	Although I have had many difficulties, I did not give up. (had had)	Make sure your verb tense is consistent.

Keep an Error Log

Read about the way this student monitored her written language. Do you think it could help you?

> I found at the beginning of my studies that I kept on making the same mistakes. I had a problem with word order especially with adverbs in English and also with punctuation. Every time I got feedback on my writing, I made notes of the errors in a notebook, and then, as I checked my next piece of writing, I checked all the things that I had had feedback on before. Soon I found I was able to cross things out of my notebook because I wasn't making those mistakes anymore.

Keep Paying Attention to Grammar

As a student of the English language, you probably own a grammar reference book. Use it! Don't stop improving your English. Look things up when you are unsure. Don't forget to turn on the spellchecker and the grammar checker in your word processor and always get someone else to proofread for you.

Peer feedback

In addition to checking your essay yourself or having a teacher or tutor check it for you, other students can also be helpful. By using the worksheet below you can give and receive feedback before handing in your work. Here are some reasons why this is a good idea:

1 Instead of getting feedback from just one person (your teacher), you get comments from several.
2 Dealing with feedback and learning from others' comments is a key skill you will need in the workplace.
3 By helping others with their writing, you have to read critically. This way you also learn to read your own work better.
4 By writing down your comments or talking about someone else's essay, you can improve the way you express yourself.

Working together with another student in this way is a win–win situation. Of course, you will not be able to find all the mistakes a teacher might, or get the same amount of feedback, but knowing if a non-expert can easily understand your essay and if not, why not, is very valuable.

How to Find a Good Proofreader

Write a list of everyone you can think of who might be able to proofread your work.
    Now, think about these questions and make notes on the people you have named. (You may wish to keep this secret).

What's their academic English like?

You don't need to be a native speaker to be an effective proofreader, but it is important that you trust the person's basic language proficiency. It might be a good idea to get someone who speaks a different first language for a different perspective.

Names	Notes (strengths and weaknesses)

e.g. Freda (ex-landlady)	+ Native speaker.
	+ University education.
	  • Finished university 20 years ago!
	  + Good at details but not so good at the big picture.
	  − Slow!
	  + I could babysit for her or help her fix her car.
	  + She's a good cook.

What's their subject knowledge like?

Sometimes when you get someone to proofread your work, it is helpful to find a person who knows about your subject (e.g. someone on your course) to give you feedback on your *ideas*. Sometimes it might be better to get someone with no knowledge of the subject and just get them to check your *language*.

What can you do for them?

Maybe you can do a deal with them and agree to proofread their essays too. Maybe you can help them in some other way.

How easy is it to provide them with your writing and receive feedback?

Maybe you'll be able to meet over a coffee. Maybe your proofreader is in another country and so you will need to email them and wait for feedback. This could be slower if you are working in different time zones, although it could work really well. Another option is to use a shared document like Google Documents and chat while your proofreader is correcting your writing.

How busy are they? How organized are they? What are their deadlines like? How much notice will they need? How much time do you have?

These practical considerations may be really important. If you are not sure about their schedule, make sure to ask them in advance.

Talk it through beforehand   TIP

It's really important to talk through the kind of feedback you want from a proofreader. You may have particular questions you want them to think about or you may be happy to accept anything from them, but remember, it's much easier to give feedback if you have an idea of what the other person wants.

Use a Peer-Feedback Worksheet

Peer feedback is most useful when you look at different aspects of the text, not just the language. Here are some ideas of what to look for:

PEER-FEEDBACK WORKSHEET	
Organization	Is the text organized well? Is it clear which part talks about what topic? Does the organization match the requirements for this type of writing? For example, a laboratory report looks very different from an essay. Ask your teacher for some examples.
Introduction	1. Does the introduction clearly state the topic? 2. Does it state the importance of the topic? 3. Is there any background or general information about the topic? 4. Does it look at what other people have said about the topic? 5. Does it clearly say what problem or questions related to the topic it will cover? 6. In case of an argumentative essay, are the two or more sides of the argument presented in the introduction? 7. Does the introduction present what will be covered in the rest of the text? 8. Does the introduction progress from general to specific?
Text structure	1. Is it clear what the main point of the text is? 2. Is the main point followed by supporting ideas? 3. Are the ideas presented in the text clear and meaningfully related to each other? 4. Are the ideas described clearly? 5. Do the ideas progress in a logical way (e.g. does the cause precede the effect – does the result of something come after what causes it)? 6. Does each paragraph focus on one point? Is it clear what that point is?
Conclusion	In academic writing, this part usually summarizes the whole article. That is, it repeats what has been said before. Ask yourself if the author has repeated the important points / findings from the text clearly and convincingly.
Relevance	1. Is the topic really important? 2. Is the text interesting? 3. Does it add anything to what you didn't know before, or does it talk about the topic in a new way? 4. Is the language used appropriate for the people it was written for? For example, if it is for people who are not likely to know much about the topic, then it shouldn't be too specific and technical.
Language	The other point to look out for is the language of the text. This covers areas you usually check such as grammar, vocabulary and spelling. You can use the separate worksheet at the end of this section if you want.

How to give feedback

When giving feedback to someone, there are some things to keep in mind to make your comments as helpful as possible.

1 Focus on strong points as well as on weak points. It is easier for others to accept your comments if you start on a positive note. Ask yourself: What do I like about this text? What is really good about it (e.g. good use of vocabulary, good sentences, logically presented argument).
2 Focus on the content first before moving on to the language. Focus on one point at a time.
3 Your feedback is on the writing, not on the right or wrong of the author's opinions. (However, if an argument is not logically presented, you should point that out.)
4 It usually takes more than one round to give feedback on a piece of writing. It is important to talk about the points that you didn't understand. Try to find out what the author meant and suggest ways to make it clearer.
5 Be patient and be careful with your comments. Even if the text is not perfect, it may have taken the author a long time and a lot of effort to write it.

How to receive feedback

When someone gives you feedback, keep the following points in mind:

1 Try to see why your proofreader gave you feedback on a particular point. You may disagree with him or her or maybe his or her feedback is simply wrong. But try to see their point and learn from it. Even if they misunderstood what you wrote, this could mean that you need to rewrite your text to be clearer.
2 If you don't understand why the proofreader commented on a certain point, then ask!
3 Don't forget: you don't have to agree with everything others say. Don't be put off if they have negative comments. You can learn from these as well!

Conclusion

In this chapter, we have presented the various stages of writing an essay. We may have made it sound as if there is just one order in which to go through these essay stages. That is not the case. Some students simply start writing and then rearrange the material later. This is, of course, much easier using a computer. The only problem with moving material around too much is that you can easily forget about cohesion (see Chapter 8). Other students say they like to write the conclusion first. Why not, if you know how your line of thought is likely to go. On the other hand, be prepared to change it later to fit what you have actually said in the body of the essay. Essay writing is like any other craft you may know, such as playing or even creating music. You cannot do it to a formula.

Book recommendations

Business

Ashley, A. (2003) *Oxford Handbook of Commercial Correspondence*, Oxford University Press. Covers practical business writing – reports, CVs, proposals, business letters, writing references – with lots of examples.

Manalo, E., Wong-Toi, G. and Bartlett-Trafford, J. (2002) *The Business of Writing: Written Communication Skills for Business Students*, North Shore, NZ: Pearson Education. Covers business assignments at university.

Science and technology

Kirkman, J. (2005) *Good Style: Writing for Science and Technology*, Routledge. A great book on vocabulary and grammar for people who have to write technical material.

Law

Krois-Lindner, A. and Translegal® (2011) *International Legal English*, 2nd edition Cambridge University Press. Designed for language students who need English for work (not study) but still a useful resource for legal students.

Medicine

Glendinnig, E.H. and Holmstrom, B.A.S. (2005) *English in Medicine*, 3rd edition, Cambridge University Press. Designed for language students who need English for medicine. Covers all four skills and has examples of medical writing – case notes, referral letters, etc.

Graduate Writing

Swales, J.M. and Feak, C.B. (2012) *Academic Writing for Graduate Students*, 3rd edition, University of Michigan Press. An excellent book for any graduate students studying in English.

Chapter 10

Small Group Learning

When you start attending lectures you will probably be given the outline of the course for the semester. In the outline you may notice that there are also some tutorials (also called seminars) listed. What are tutorials? What happens in them? Let's find out.

This chapter will help you to:

- understand the purpose of tutorials
- consider reasons why some people don't attend tutorials
- hear ideas from other students about how to act in tutorials
- plan for tutorials
- build up your vocabulary of phrases for participating in discussions
- note ways of getting a turn to talk.

Why have tutorials?

Tutorials or seminars are a really important part of university life. They are different from lectures in that the class size is much smaller (usually no more than 20 students) and students have different roles. In lectures, students are relatively passive. They listen and take notes. In tutorials students learn by talking about ideas, asking questions and doing tasks in small groups. So in tutorials, lecturers expect students to be more active and contribute much more than they do in lectures. Students are often unsure about their role in tutorials.

The purpose of tutorials

This section looks at the reasons why tutorials are a good idea. If you have already taken a tutorial, think about your experiences. To what extent do you agree with these ideas about tutorials? Add up your score and see what this says about your attitude to tutorials.

Reasons for not attending

We interviewed a number of students about their attitudes towards tutorials and the following themes came up to explain why they sometimes did not attend:

1 not understanding the point of tutorials
2 personal learning style
3 confidence about language
4 confidence about subject knowledge
5 feelings about the tutor
6 feelings about other students.

This next task will help you to analyse your own attitudes towards each of these themes. Place yourself on the scale according to how positively you feel about each one. For each theme, some suggestions are given.

	Strongly disagree	Disagree	Neutral	Agree	Strong agree
	1	2	3	4	5
1. Talking helps students clarify their own ideas.					
2. In tutorials you can learn about other students' ideas.					
3. Students make contact with students they can meet outside class.					
4. Tutorials give you a chance to use in context the new technical terms you have learned from the lectures or the coursebook.					
5. Students can find out what others think of their ideas.					
6. Tutorials often require students to contribute so everyone gets a chance to practise talking and thinking about the ideas.					

1. Understanding the point of tutorials		Suggestions from students
+	–	
I think they are useful. Talking about something is a good way to learn about it.	I can't see the point. I'd rather go to the lecture and get information from staff, not from other students.	- Keep trying. They will never be useful if you don't go. - Prepare well and go in with questions. (See next section.) - Try to say more each week. - Remember WIIFM (What's In It For Me?). - Talk to your tutor about how you feel.
YOUR ATTITUDE? ◄————————————►		

2. Personal learning style		Suggestions from students
+	–	
I learn well by talking and listening to other ideas on a subject. This helps me to think about something.	I learn best by reading or listening so they are a waste of time.	- Even if you are not learning a lot about the subject, they are great language practice. - I use tutorials to try out ideas I am not sure about. It's better to do this in tutorials than in assignments. - You can ask questions about things you don't understand.
YOUR ATTITUDE? ◄————————————►		

3. Confidence about language		Suggestions from students
+	−	
I've always enjoyed having a go at speaking other languages. Even as a child I'd try to talk with some of my parents' friends in their own languages.	I feel quite shy about how bad my English is.	- Try thinking about other students in the class who are also shy. - When you start speaking, look straight at the tutor and (we hope!) he or she will give you some encouragement.
YOUR ATTITUDE? ◄————————►		

4. Confidence about subject matter		Suggestions from students
+	−	
Some of the subjects I'm studying for my degree I studied to a high level at high school, so I feel reasonably confident that I know what people are talking about.	My only reason for taking this subject is that it's compulsory. I just know I'm not going to do well at it.	- Prepare for your tutorial by reading over the lecture notes. - Start by listening and then speak when you know even a little bit about the topic they are on at that moment.
YOUR ATTITUDE? ◄————————►		

5. Feelings about the tutor		Suggestions from students
+	−	
The tutor is the main reason I attend. She can make quite difficult ideas sound easy.	To be honest, nobody likes this tutor. I've heard lots of students say that's the reason they don't attend.	- My older brother started work last year after he graduated. He's told me that having to work with people you don't like is good preparation for the workplace. - I try not to think about my personal feelings for or against the tutor while I'm sitting there. I try to pretend she's someone else.
YOUR ATTITUDE? ◄————————►		

6. Feelings about other students		Suggestions from students
+	−	
Tutorials are a great place to meet other students socially.	Most of the people in my tutorial are as bad as I am at the subject. We are all there because we didn't fill in our names fast enough to get to a tutorial at a good time.	- Think of a tutorial as doing many things: it's a time for learning, and for socializing and (occasionally!) for relaxing and having fun! - Sit in a different spot each week so as to get to know more people.
YOUR ATTITUDE? ◄————————►		

Planning for tutorials

Sometimes it is difficult for native speakers to talk in tutorials. It can be even more difficult for non-native speakers. If you are finding it difficult to contribute in tutorials, then a good way to start is to be well prepared and go in with your own agenda.

Goal-Setting for Tutorials

Tutorial topics are predictable. Lecturers advertise them in advance. They have titles that tell you what they will be about. Often a tutorial follows on from a lecture, and is a chance for students to ask about issues that came up in the lecture. Sometimes tutors give reading that they expect students to complete before a tutorial. At other times they may use the tutorial to set up an assignment. If you want to participate in the tutorial, make sure you have done the reading, been to the lecture and thought about the assignment task beforehand! Bring your lecture notes and the reading texts to the tutorial.

Use this template to set your own goals for the tutorial each week.

Tutorial title:		
Tutorial date:		
Preparation:	What do I want to find out about / learn about in the tutorial? *(write your questions here)*	In the tutorial, did you find out what you wanted? *(if you did, tick in this column)*
Lecture title and date: Reading details: (author / text / pages)	I want to check my understanding of these points … I don't agree with these points … I would like some examples of these ideas …	
Assignment:	Check these points about the instructions for the assignment … Talk through my ideas about … Get more ideas from other students / the tutor about …	

Notes

- It is really important to make notes of what you want to find out and take these to the tutorial. This will help you keep track of what's happening if you feel lost.

- If you find out what you want from the tutorial, then great. If you don't, you may need to think about how you can ask extra questions (see later in the chapter).
- At the end of each tutorial, the tutor may say something to introduce what they are going to do in the next tutorial. She may say something like, 'Next week, we're going to discuss the question of ....' Or she may give out reading for the following week. Bring next week's template along and fill it in as she talks.

How to talk in tutorials

Having discussions in tutorials can be daunting. Often people speak fast and interrupt each other, and it can be difficult for second language speakers to get a word in. Remember, though, often lecturers set up group work or pair work, which can be easier than whole class discussions. By practising and memorizing the language below you will be able to participate better.

The Language of Discussions: Taking the Lead

Look at this list of useful phrases for joining in and being proactive in tutorials. These phrases will help you direct the discussion. Discussions are much easier to follow if you are in charge! Tick the phrases you would use already. Put a star [*] beside some that you could start to use.

Phrases for starting a conversation or discussion, and for asking someone's opinion	
	I'd like to know ....
	I'm interested in ....
	Could I ask ...? [formal]
	Could you tell me ...? [formal]
	Perhaps you could tell .... [formal]
	What do you think of ...?
Phrases for interrupting	
	Excuse me ....
	Sorry, but ....
	Excuse me for interrupting, but .... [formal]
	May I interrupt for a moment? [formal]
	Just a second .... [informal]
	Can I add something?
	Can I say something here?
	I'd like to say something, if I may. [formal]
	Can I ask a question?
	May I ask a question? [formal]

Phrases to use when you are explaining your opinion	
	First of all ….
	The main reason is ….
	The main thing is ….
	The most important thing is ….
	Secondly ….
	The other reason is ….
	Another reason is ….
	Besides that, ….
	And on top of that ….
	And, finally, ….
Phrases to use when you want to refer to a point in someone's argument	
	The trouble is ….
	The problem is ….
	The trouble with ….
	The problem with ….
	The point is ….
	Don't forget that ….
Phrases to use when you want to say something you think is new information	
	Do you realize that ….
	Believe it or not, ….
	You may not believe it, but ….
	It may sound strange, but ….
	The surprising thing is ….
	Surprisingly, ….
	Oddly enough, ….
	Funnily enough, …. [informal]
Phrases to use when what you are going to say may surprise or shock	
	Actually, ….
	The only thing is ….
	To tell you the truth, ….
	To be honest, ….
	Frankly, ….
Phrases to use when you want to change the subject	
	Talking of ….
	That reminds me ….
	By the way, …. [informal]
	Oh, before I forget, ….
	Why don't we move on to the next point ….

Phrases to use when giving your opinion, but when you are not certain	
	I think ….
	I suppose ….
	I suspect that ….
	I'm pretty sure that ….
	I'm fairly certain that ….
	I wonder if ….
Phrases to use when you are certain of your opinion	
	I'm certain that ….
	I'm sure that ….
	It's my opinion that ….
	I'm convinced that ….
	I honestly believe that ….
	I strongly believe that ….
	Without a doubt ….
	I'm positive ….
	I'm absolutely certain that ….
Phrases to use when you want to emphasize that what you are going to say is your own opinion	
	In my opinion, ….
	I personally believe ….
	I personally think …..
	I personally feel ….
	Not everyone will agree with me, but ….
	From my point of view, ….
	Well, personally, ….
	In my case ….

Trying out new expressions   TIP

Each time you go to a tutorial, set yourself the goal of trying out a few of these expressions. At the end of the tutorial, evaluate whether you used the expressions successfully.

Building discussions: reacting to what people say

Often non-native speakers find that group discussions are dominated by confident native speakers and they find themselves having to respond rather than lead. As well as agreeing or disagreeing, you can steer the discussion.

When you respond to something someone else has said, you have the choice of being able to:

1   check the meaning of what they have said
2   fully agree with them
3   draw conclusions from what they are saying
4   partly agree with them
5   disagree with them
6   add your opinion
7   say you are not sure / do not have an opinion yet
8   ask for other people's opinions
9   refocus the discussion.

Look at the following expressions. They are in groups that have a similar purpose. Give each group a heading from the above list. The first one has been done for you as an example. Check your answers at the end of the book.

8. Ask for other people's opinion

What do you think about ...?
How do you feel about ...?
Do you agree with ...?
You haven't said much about this. What do you think?
Are you opposed to ...?
I think .... What is your opinion?

What do you think / feel about ...?
Would you agree / say that ...?
John, what is your opinion on / about ...?

I'd just like to say (that) ...
I think / believe / feel that ...
It seems to me (that) ...
I am convinced (that) ...

I just don't know.
I don't feel strongly either way.
I'm not sure.
Actually I can see both points of view / both sides.
Maybe (who knows?).

In my opinion, the main thing is ....
As I see it, the most important point is ....
I feel that the most important consideration is ....
I believe that the highest priority here is ....
Let's move on to the next point.
Ok. We've talked about ..., what about ...?

Yes, I agree.
Yes, I see what you mean.
That's for sure.
That's a good point.
Absolutely!

I don't agree ....
I don't think so.
Yes, but I think ....
Yes, but don't you think ...?
I agree to some extent but ....
I'm afraid I must disagree with you.

It could be that ....
Maybe it is the case that ....
One option would be that ....
I partly agree ....
Probably you're right ....

Okay, so that means ....
That relates back to what we were saying about ....
The logical extension of that is that ....

I'm sorry, I didn't catch that.
Sorry, what was that again?
Do you mean that ...?
Are you saying that ...?
.... Is that what you mean?
In other words, ...
To put it another way, ...

Note all the ways of clarifying understanding   TIP

When you don't hear something or don't understand, it is really important to try to check your understanding. You can either get the speaker to say the same thing again or ask for confirmation by rephrasing what the speaker said. If you don't check the meaning, you will miss a learning opportunity.

Getting a turn

Accounting for this behaviour

If you understand how students and lecturers behave in tutorials, then you will find it easier to get a turn. This is a diagram showing a typical university tutorial. The tutor is sitting at the head and the 15 students are around the table.

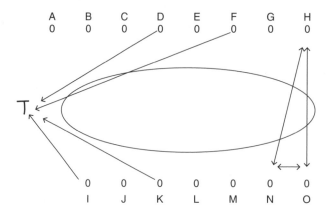

We'll look at the students' behaviour first. The following are descriptions of the way students typically behave in tutorial groups. Identify the students in the diagram that match the descriptions. There may be students that fit into more than one description. If you haven't been to a tutorial yet, then this will prepare you for what often happens in them. If you have experience of a tutorial group, then as you are reading the descriptions, think which people fit the descriptions in your tutorials.

1. Three students know one another very well. They are quite outgoing. If one of them puts forward an opinion, then the other two argue together. Who are they?
2. Four of the students never say anything unless the tutor asks them directly. Who are they?
3. Another four students like asking the tutor questions, but they are not very interested in what their fellow students say. Who are they?
4. Two of the students hardly ever say anything and even the tutor ignores them. Who are they?
5. Three students will speak occasionally to another student, but never seem to answer the tutor's questions. Who are they?

Now read the following explanations (a–e) of these students' behaviour and match them to the types of student (1–5) above.

a. For students like these, the teacher is the most important person in the room and the focus of their learning in the room. They may not see the point of talking to other students or the point of doing tasks in smaller groups because they want the right answer from the teacher.
b. These students may not feel confident and may be worried about speaking up in front of the whole class. They may be worried about their English language level or their subject knowledge.
c. These students do not seem to be participating actively in the class. They respond when they have to, but are not really involved.
d. These students are not actively involved. They may be interested in the tutorial, but are completely passive in the class. Maybe they are unfamiliar with this style of learning. Or maybe they are demotivated.
e. These students are fully involved in the ideas in the class, but communicate only with their friends.

Summary

All of these students are missing out in some way on the learning opportunities offered by the tutorial. They may be missing:

- the fact that tutorial learning should be active (i.e. you should be asking questions and testing out ideas)
- the fact that you can learn from talking to everyone in the group, not just the tutor or a couple of other students
- the point of groupwork.

The tutor's view

You may be interested to know that tutors, as well as students, give thought to interaction in small groups. For example, here is what one person said about her reasons for certain patterns:

> I use pair work if the group seems very shy. They talk about ideas with just one other person first and then they seem to find it easier to report to the whole group afterwards. As for the choice between group work versus whole class discussion, I find that often I will plan for one but then change to the other. I choose group work because it involves more people talking so it makes the class more active. I especially like using group work if each group has a different task. Maybe each group is looking at a different aspect of the same problem. This means that when groups report back, there is more interest. The biggest problem I have with group work is that often students don't seem to know how to work together. I sometimes give them roles in their groups – for example I might suggest that one person makes notes for the whole group and one person is the spokesperson who has to report back. The other problem with group work is that it can be slow and so sometimes I decide to go back to full class mode to speed things up.

Your participation: A reflection task

Try this reflection task after a tutorial if you found it difficult to participate. Use it to help you set goals for your next tutorial.

Tutorial date:		
Tutorial topic:		
Today, I was … *(mark yourself on the arrow below in terms of your participation)*		
active passive ←——————————————————————————→		
I was happy with the way I … *(tick the list below)*		
	understood the lecturer	
	understood other students	
	participated in pair work	
	participated in small group work	
	participated in whole class discussions	
	was understood by other students	

(Continued)

I was happy with the way I ... *(tick the list below)*
was understood by the lecturer
asked questions
answered questions
I want to improve the way I ... (choose an aspect of tutorial performance above that you want to improve)
To do this, I'm going to ... (here think about how you can solve the problem you have chosen above – what can you do differently?)

What Sort of Questions Can I Ask?

If you ask questions, try to make them interesting and think about how much discussion the question will generate.

Look at these two questions. Which will generate the most talk?

Don't you agree X is terrible?
Why do you think X is terrible?

The problem with the first question is that it really has only two possible answers:

EITHER: Yes I do.
OR: No I don't.

Although people often do say a lot more than yes or no (see the transcript below!), open questions, like the second one, ask for longer answers.

On the other hand, to answer the second question a person has to do more thinking.

Sometimes you may want to keep things simple and ask several closed questions. The answers to such questions are often predictable and short, making them easier to understand.

Look at this example of a tutor (T) talking to a student (S) about how the student has revised his writing. Notice how the tutor encourages the student to talk by using a combination of closed questions and open questions.

Transcript	Question types
T: Okay. So have you made many changes since we last met?	closed
S: Yes – a few. Mainly I have worked on the links between sections.	
T: Great. Like we talked about?	closed
S: Yes.	
T: Okay. And when you made changes, can you tell me about the process you went through? What were you trying to do differently?	closed open

Here are some more questions that would encourage more than just a short answer:

- Why do you think that?
- Can you explain that to me more clearly please?
- What proof can you put forward for that viewpoint?

Questions are also different depending on how much they make people think. We talk about this more in Chapter 11 on 'Assessment'.

Types of Question

First let's look at types of question, ranging from the simplest to those that make everyone think. In column one there are examples of students' questions. In the next column is a list of their functions. Match them up and check your answers at the end of the book.

Students' questions	Type of question
a) Could you please tell us what … means?	summarizing
b) What would happen if someone …?	predicting
c) What if … had been written in a different century?	evaluating
d) Is this similar to the point you made last week about …?	defining
e) Reading between the lines, is it true that the poet is trying to say …?	making an inference
f) Can we sum this up by saying …?	comparing and contrasting
g) In your opinion what would be the most likely cause of …?	hypothesizing

Try out different types of question … and check out the responses!   **TIP**

Culture and tutorials

We asked some experienced international students for advice about what surprised them about tutorials. This is what they came up with. Have you experienced this?

Sunny (from Korea): I was surprised when I started at university that different cultures have such different body language. At that time I found this strange. Students from some countries are very expressive in tutorials. They use eye contact and wave their hands around much more than Korean students, in particular to interrupt. I copied what they did and that helped, but I still find it difficult to keep eye contact through discussions.

Nikolay (from Russia): I enjoyed tutorials. In Russia, everybody is very serious in university tutorials. If you smile too much, people will think that you are strange. But here (Australia) I found that people made jokes and laughed – even the lecturer sometimes makes jokes.

Lu Lu (from Taiwan): I found it very difficult at first to give my opinion all the time. I was uncomfortable – especially when I had to give my opinion to older people. I got used to it. I couldn't believe how direct the native speaker students were with the tutor. To me it felt quite rude.

Ahmed (from UAE): I liked the oral learning style in tutorials. Sometimes the tutor gave us papers to read and this was good. I read them and could then talk about them with other students. And it was good you can ask any question you like. I also like the active learning style. It is more interesting for me than reading or lectures.

Before you start at university, talk to other students from your country who have experienced tutorials in an English-speaking university culture. Ask them what they noticed. When you start your tutorials, be aware that attitudes towards eye contact, body language, laughter, learning style and giving your opinion may be different from what you are used to.

Conclusion

We hope that, after reading this chapter, when you start tutorials in your university course, you will have a better idea of what you are getting into and can make the most of your opportunities. Like other aspects of university life, if you prepare well for them and have a clear idea of what you can get out of them, then you can participate and make them work for you.

Assessment

You may have been a very successful student in your own country and have passed all your examinations. Maybe you used to think that not getting an A grade was 'shameful'. The truth is, it is quite common for international students to fail some assessments, especially early on in a course. If it's any comfort, so do some local students!) This chapter answers the question: 'How can I do well in assessments?'

This chapter will help you to:

- understand various ways that universities assess students
- note some assessment criteria and ways of using them to your advantage
- learn from feedback
- prepare for exams
- succeed in building portfolios and other forms of assessment.

Understanding assessment for your course

Difficulties with language and adjusting to a new country, as well as to new ways of teaching and learning, are a few reasons why it is difficult to know what the university means by 'assessment'. One way to help yourself is by understanding as much as you can about how your course results are assessed.

Specifically, try to find out answers to these questions:

- How many 'points' do you need in total to get a certain grade?
- What is the pass mark for each assessment?
- Do you need to pass all assessments in order to pass the course – or can you fail one assignment and still pass overall?
- What happens if you are unwell during the course and miss an assessment?
- Can you retake failed exams?
- How many exams are you allowed to retake?
- Is there any penalty if you need to retake an exam? For example, will some points be subtracted? Do you need to attend summer school or extra catch-up classes? As an international student, will you need to pay more fees to do this?
- Can you resubmit assignments? If so, how many times and is there a penalty (e.g. a lower grade) if you do resubmit?

The answers to these questions will be written in a policy document (maybe on the department website or in your department's handbook). Information about assessments (also called the 'study guide' or 'course guide') can also be found on the syllabus handed to you at the beginning of each course. If you are not clear about assessments, ask your lecturer.

Types of assessment

Lecturers assess you to see if you are learning what they teach. There are many ways in which you can be assessed on university courses and some of these may be very different from how you have been assessed in the past. You can find out how you will be assessed when you choose a course or you may find out in the first lecture. It is important to understand how you are assessed when you start the course so you can plan how to prepare for the assessment.

Ways in which you may be assessed

Look at the ways of assessing students in the box below. How many have you done before? Match them to the definitions listed below. Check your answers at the end of this book.

a	continuous assessment / portfolios
b	essay exams
c	short answer tests
d	multiple-choice quizzes
e	practicals
f	oral presentations
g	open book exams
h	assignments
i	online discussions
j	learning journals
k	take home exams
l	exams – questions known

Definitions

	Students are observed doing something, such as teaching a class on a teaching course or making jewellery on a jewellery course, and are graded on their performance.
	Students are assessed throughout the course and have to prepare a folder of short pieces of work that shows what they have been learning throughout their course.
	Students need to write a reflective diary or series of stories to show that they are thinking about the content of the course and learning from it.
	Students have to do an exam in which they write answers of one or two paragraphs. These might be definitions or key ideas introduced during the course.
	This is an exam that students are allowed to do at home. They have a time limit of a week or two weeks from the time the exam is set. This is a common assessment for business courses as the deadline is realistic.
	This is an exam, but you are allowed to bring in your notes and some reference materials.

(Continued)

	In this type of exam you may be given a list of questions a week or two before the exam. During the exam you will be asked to answer only some of them.
	These are long essays that are set throughout the course. You do them at home. Each is set up by the lecturer and has a deadline.
	Students have to write a number of essays in a set time (e.g. three in three hours).
	Students have to give a short talk to other students on the course. They may have to lead a discussion after the talk.
	This is an exam. Students have to choose the best answer for each question. There may be up to 60 questions.
	This is common for distance courses. Students have to visit the course website and contribute to a discussion that is usually started by the lecturer.

In some courses you may be assessed by a combination of these methods. Find out how important each of these is for your course. For example, 10% of your overall mark may be an oral presentation, 30% may be coursework, and 60% may be a final exam. Use this information to decide how much time you are going to spend preparing for each assessment. If the oral presentation is only 10% of the course grades, do not spend too long preparing for it, especially if you are running short of time!

Put assessment dates in your calendar   TIP

When you find out how you are going to be assessed, write the deadlines or exam dates in your calendar and mark times when you can expect to be under more stress. This will help you plan your coursework and your social life around assessments.

Which assessment method is best for you?

Some courses will be compulsory (i.e. you have to do them) so you must complete the assessment chosen by the lecturer. Sometimes, however, you will have a choice of courses and you may choose one course over the other because you like the fact that it is continuously assessed (i.e. with coursework and assignments throughout the semester) rather than assessed with exams. For some students this decision may be very important. If you don't work well under stress or if you often find yourself with too little time left at the end of the semester, you may want to avoid the examination option, at least in the first year, until you get more control over your studies.

Look at the table below to see some of the differences between the requirements in exams and in assignments. Which ones suit you better?

Exams	Assignments
Short word limits.	Long word limits 1000+.
Large percentage of course marks in one day.	Often small percentage of course marks over several days or weeks.
Writing under intense time pressure.	Time to plan, write and edit your writing.

(Continued)

Exams	Assignments
High stress for a few days leading up to an exam.	Lower stress levels but over longer periods of time on the course. Deadlines can be extremely stressful.
Individual performance during exam (can't discuss with colleagues).	Can discuss assignments with other students, but final version still needs to be individual.
Often can't use dictionaries / reference books.	Can consult dictionaries / reference books.
Markers may be more understanding of inaccuracies if you are writing under time pressure.	High level of language accuracy expected.
You may only find out if you have passed after the exam.	You know how you are doing throughout the course.
You may never see your marked exam papers or find out what you did well and what not.	You get feedback on assignments which might help you to improve your writing.

Find out what it's really like

Here are some ways to find out what university assessment on your course is really like.

1. Interview another student who is studying or has studied your course

Ask that person:

- what types of assessment they have experienced
- how they prepared for the assessment
- how they coped with their English in exams
- if they have any advice for students starting out like yourself.

2. Check published information

There may be information on the department website. You may be able to see old exam papers in the library.

Understanding assessment criteria

When assignments are set, the lecturer will often hand out assessment criteria at the same time. Assessment criteria are statements that the lecturer uses to grade your assignment (see Chapter 6 and Chapter 8 for some examples). Make sure you understand the assessment criteria. If you don't, you may also ask the lecturer to:

- tell you what you have to write / speak about
- tell you what aspect of the question the lecturer sees as the most important and therefore carries the most marks
- give you a guide to use when you are writing – for each point in the criteria ask yourself if you have done it yet
- help you critically evaluate your work so that you can improve it before you hand it in
- help you understand your grade when you get feedback – you can look back at the criteria, and the lecturer's comments may make more sense.

Learning from feedback

When an assignment or an exam paper is returned to you, it will have a mark (e.g. 55%) or a grade (e.g. B-) on it. It usually has comments as well, although sometimes lecturers put all the comments together (anonymously) on one sheet for all the students. These comments will answer the following questions:

- How good is this assignment?
- Did you do what the lecturer wanted?
- How could you improve?

This section will help you understand grades and professors' written comments.

Understanding your mark

When you get your essay or assignment back, don't panic. The mark may be lower than you are used to. Take time to understand the lecturer's comments and think them through. Follow these steps.

1 Look at the grade and decide if you have passed or failed. Usually grades A to C are pass marks. Grades D or lower are fails. Check this against your department's assessment guidelines and the syllabus. You may have a percentage rather than a grade. Again, find out if this is a pass or a fail.
2 Check your grade with the class average. You may have a grade that you think is low, but this may be normal for the course or for your particular department. Your lecturer can't tell you the grades of other students, but some will be happy to tell you if you are open about your marks.
3 Read the comments the lecturer has made. Decide which ones are positive and which are negative. You may not understand the comments at this stage (see the next section).
4 Re-read the assignment and see if you can understand the comments now.
5 If you still don't understand, then make an appointment with your lecturer to ask them about your mark.
6 In your journal, make a note of useful feedback that will help you in future assignments or exams.

Understanding written comments: Decoding feedback

Hopefully, comments from lecturers will be clear (you can understand them) and relevant (you can see how they are useful). They may follow this pattern:

1 a general comment on your performance
2 detailed comments (may refer to keywords in the criteria) on how you did, including ways you could improve
3 a final comment that summarizes the main points.

In this way, 'negative' feedback may be 'sandwiched' between more positive general statements. Often teaching assistants use this strategy when they give oral feedback as well:

- something you've done well
- how to improve
- something else you've done well.

Task: Text patterns in essay feedback

1 Identify the positive comments, detailed comments with criticisms and final positive comment in the following essay feedback:

> You have presented a competent discussion of the article with an analytical approach that conveys aspects of the researcher's work in a systematic way. The section that needed more consideration was the final part in which I would have liked to see a fuller account of the practical implications of the study. Mostly the essay is well written; however, at times, I found it difficult to follow your argument and had to re-read sections to understand your logic. I felt that more signposting would have helped me with this. Overall, though, the assignment was a balanced critique of the issues that arose from the research and it was good to see that you mentioned many of the limitations of this kind of research that we have discussed in class. Well done.
>
> Grade B-

2 If you got the feedback given above, what are the two main areas you should try to improve in the next essay?
Check your answers at the end of the book.

Unclear feedback

In the example above, it is quite clear what the student did well and what they need to do to improve. Here are some reasons why comments on your work may be hard to understand and less useful than they could be:

1 The lecturer does not want to be rude and does not clearly explain what is wrong.
2 The lecturer may not be used to giving feedback to non-native speakers so may use indirect or confusing language.
3 They may only mention that there is a problem, but not tell you what the problem is or what caused the problem.
4 You may not be able to read their handwriting.
5 They may comment on the aspects that are easy to give feedback on (e.g. your ideas), but not on more difficult aspects of your language.

If you don't understand the feedback, then make an appointment with the lecturer and ask them about it.

Task: Spot the criticism

Read the examples of essay feedback below and work out what aspect of each assignment the lecturer is criticizing. Check your answers at the end of the book.

a. Your argument was clear in most parts of the essay. A statement that previews the structure of the assignment may have helped me navigate through the essay.
b. While you mostly followed the recommended referencing conventions, at times this was not the case and I was unsure whether you were referring to sources or claiming these ideas as your own.
c. This is a well-researched assignment; however, I feel it could have benefited from more time spent proofreading before submission.

d. Make sure that you answer all parts of the question.

e. This assignment is evidence that you have synthesized information from a number of sources. At times, though, I struggled to hear your voice coming through.

f. Your literature review is based almost entirely on two sources.

g. While parts of the essay read well and you make some valid points, the essay as a whole fails to read as a coherent whole.

h. This is an excellent description of the process. Your writing is clearly signposted and paragraphs flow seamlessly from one to the next. You follow academic conventions well and clearly have a good grasp of this topic.

A mini-glossary of common writing problems lecturers might signal

Sometimes the language that lecturers use when giving feedback on writing is quite specialized. This table will help you to work out what aspect of your writing lecturers are commenting on. Remember, if you don't understand their comments, you should ask them.

If lecturers use these words ...	they mean ...
awkward syntax	bad grammar
coherence	overall organization – introduction / paragraphs / conclusion
cohesion	the way one idea / sentence follows from the one before and leads to the next
inconsistent argument	your thesis statement does not match the conclusion that you have come to in your writing
inconsistent tone	writing sounds too 'spoken' – maybe you use too many idioms
lack of support	you need to give more evidence for your opinions
lack of sufficient development	you do not look at ideas in enough detail
need to develop your voice	not enough of your opinion or your analysis
need for further revision	you need to rewrite some sections
not managing the flow of information between paragraphs	you need to check that each paragraph leads on to the next
not managing the flow of information within a sentence	the main point you are making in a sentence is not clear
overdependence on sources	not enough of your opinion or your analysis
paragraph unity	you need to check that each paragraph follows a logical pattern – e.g. a topic sentence followed by evidence
referencing conventions	the way you quote other writers' words and ideas and the way you list references at the end of the essay
sentence fragments	some sentences are incomplete – e.g. 'Because of climate change.'
signposting language	e.g. 'firstly ..., in addition ..., therefore ...'
sources summarized but not synthesized	you report what writers you quote say, but don't build these quotes into your argument
too black and white – not tentative enough	if you give conclusions, these should be less general and definite
writing lacks control	bad grammar, spelling and punctuation

Oral feedback

Sometimes, when they hand back an assignment, lecturers will give oral feedback. In this case it could be helpful to take notes on what is said. Here is what one student reported.

> I decided to take notes when the lecturer talked to us about our assignment. Later I tried to ask myself why I had made certain mistakes. Often the answer had something to do with my English. Then I made a note to study that point.

In some university departments they hold tutorials, when small groups meet with a tutor to go over the assignments and also to prepare for the next one. This is a good time to ask questions. See Chapter 10 for more information and advice on participating in tutorials.

Examinations

Taking exams is still a common way you will be assessed at a university. Taking an exam in a second language can be stressful, but you can minimize stress and increase your chances of success through careful planning. This section has some general strategies that will help you succeed in university exams. Many will be similar to exams you have taken in your home country. Before you start this section, think about an exam in which you did well in your first language. What made you successful? Write your notes below.

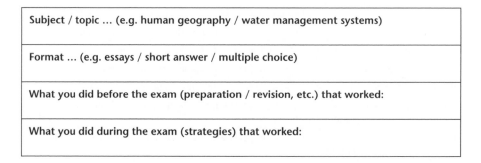

Subject / topic ... (e.g. human geography / water management systems)
Format ... (e.g. essays / short answer / multiple choice)
What you did before the exam (preparation / revision, etc.) that worked:
What you did during the exam (strategies) that worked:

There are, however, some key differences if you are taking an exam when you are studying in English at a university, namely:

- The format and procedure of the exam may be unfamiliar.
- The expectations of the marker may be different – for example, they want to see evidence of critical thinking skills.
- It will be harder to understand the questions.
- It will be harder to communicate your knowledge in a second language.
- The marker will not value long passages of text which you have memorized from textbooks and written out word for word.

This section will deal with these differences.

Finding out about an exam: A checklist

It is important to find out as much as you can about an exam well in advance of the exam date. You can find out about exams by:

- reading the section about assessment you are given when you start a course
- looking through past exam papers
- talking to students who took your paper the year before
- talking to other students on your course (to check that you have understood everything that may have been said about the course exams).

If you still can't complete the following checklist, then ask your lecturer. Lecturers may not want to spend class time answering lots of questions about assessment details so you could try emailing your lecturer between classes with a list of questions. He or she may choose to answer you directly or may decide to deal with everyone's questions together.

Topics	Check these ...	Notes
Exam day	date	
	start time	
	place (building/room)	
	length of exam	
	what you are allowed to bring: dictionaries, class notes, course materials, case study data?	
	any special rules if English is not your first language*	
Exam format	how many questions in total	
	how many questions you need to answer	
	what happens if you don't finish all the questions	
	how important the quality of your writing is	
	what type of questions (e.g. essay / short answer / multiple choice)	
	if you will be told the percentage mark for each question (so you can allocate more time to questions with more marks)	
Exam content	what topics will be covered	
	what lectures or reading will be most important for the exam	

* Note some universities in some countries on some courses allow extra time in an exam for students whose first language is not English. Find out early if this applies for your course and, if so, how you can apply for this extra time. You may need to apply for extra time a long time before your exam day.

Revising for exams

In some educational systems, you can pass exams by reproducing things that you have learnt in lectures and through reading. In many English-speaking universities, however, learning facts by heart is less important than using your own words and arguments. In the exam you are asked to show that you have understood what you have learnt and can apply it in exam tasks. If there is too much to revise, decide the important topics to focus on.

Revision is still important if you want to succeed in university exams, and the way you revise will depend in part on your preferred learning style.

Read the following revision tips and decide whether you think they will be useful revision strategies for you. When you have finished, check the answers and read what we think about these ways of revising.

Tip	Useful?	
	Yes	No
1. Start revising early. Don't leave it all until the last minute.		
2. Go back over all your lecture notes and copy them out again.		
3. Write out index cards with key points taken from your notes and reading.		
4. Get some past exam questions and write practice answers.		
5. Re-read all the key texts from your course before the exam.		
6. Learn essays that you think might come up in the exam by heart.		
7. Re-read texts from the course with reference to past exam questions.		
8. Form a study group and make a list of possible exam questions then talk about how you would answer them.		
9. Practise writing exam answers under time pressure.		

Smart revision   TIP

Working long hours in the library does not automatically get you more points in an exam. Make sure your revision is 'smart' – always think about the questions that you might be asked so that any reading you do or notes you make are purposeful. Allow frequent short breaks to stay fresh.

Exam Strategies

Use this page as a checklist. Read it again before you take your next exam.

Plan your time carefully	Allow equal time for questions as their marks. If one question is worth 25% of the total marks, allow 25% of your time for it.
	Spend five minutes reading the whole paper before you start answering questions. During this time, write down any ideas or key concepts that you think of for each question.
Choose questions carefully	If you have to choose which questions to answer, make the choice quickly. It is usually better to stick with the choice you make rather than change midway through the exam.
	If you have a choice, avoid questions you are not sure you understand. If you have no choice, then guess meaning from any examples given or any diagrams or notes provided.
	Take a critical stance in exams. Do not be afraid of taking an original position and supporting it with evidence.

Do it right	Read the rubric (exam instructions) carefully. The rubric may change from year to year.
	Invigilators (people who supervise exams) may announce changes or corrections at the start of the exam. If you do not understand what they say, ask for clarification.
	Do what you are supposed to do! This means if you have to answer three questions, make sure you answer three questions! Check with an invigilator if you are not sure what to do.
	Don't leave any questions blank. In multiple-choice questions, if you really don't know the answer, guess. For short answer questions, by writing something on the topic you may get a mark!
Dictionaries and reference books	If you are allowed to use a dictionary in an exam, do not overuse it. Looking words up in a dictionary takes time.
	Use it if there are words in an essay question you do not understand e.g. 'Lord Byron's earlier work has been described as the art of the capricious. Discuss.' If you do not know the word **capricious**, look it up. When you are writing, it may be quicker to think of another way to write the same meaning rather than look the word up.
Write well	You still need to write well-planned, coherent answers (see the next section).

Writing under time pressure

Even in exam conditions, remember that examiners are still keen to see how well you can structure your answer and make it relevant to the question, and how well you express your ideas. To meet examiners' criteria, you need to understand what is asked. Think about key ideas and organization even before you start writing, just as you would for your assignments. Here are some tips for you.

Planning your time in the exam

The chart below shows how you can manage these crucial steps in the writing process in the time allowed for each essay question, which is about 60 minutes in a three-hour exam.

Writing process	Time total (60 minutes)	
Understand the question	1–2 minutes	Allow for about one-quarter of the total time for these three steps (approx. 10–15 minutes).
Brainstorm main ideas	3–8 minutes	
Draw up an outline	8–9 minutes	
Start writing	40–45 minutes	
Edit and proofread	5 minutes	Make time for these two steps. A few minutes of careful editing and proofreading can improve your grade.

Now you try. Think of the last exam you did where you had to write a lot. How long did it last? How much time did you need? How much time did you spend on each part?

Writing process	Time spent
Understand the question	
Brainstorm main ideas	
Draw up an outline	
Start writing	
Edit and proofread	

Understanding the question

Quickly analyse the essay question to establish topic focus.

Look for topic or content words, which tell you WHAT you have to deal with in your essay. (Note: If there is a quotation, look for the content words in the question that follows the quotation). Look for the action verbs (e.g. discuss, compare and contrast, etc.) which tell you HOW you have to deal with the topic.

Here is an example. Can you find the 'what' and the 'how' here?

> *The revolution in mobile communication technology has blurred the boundaries between what is public and what is private.*

Discuss the impact of mobile phones on our public and private communications.

WHAT	
HOW	

Check your answer at the end of the book.

What exam questions mean

A simple technique for analysing exam questions is to turn the question or sentence into a real question starting with: How? Why? What? Which? In the section on 'Understanding essay questions' in Chapter 8 of this book, there is a task on this.

Here are the two complete essay questions again. Try to expand them and work out what topic you are writing about and what questions you would try to answer in your essay. Check your answers at the end of the book.

	Essay question	In an exam, answer these spoken questions
1.	*Describe how developments in management theory in the 1980s have affected management practice in the 21st century.*	
2.	*Discuss the controversy over Iris Chang's interpretation of the Nanking Massacre, and account for the strength of the reaction to her work.*	

Brainstorming main ideas

Here are some basic tips. See also Chapter 9 for more information on brainstorming.

- Jot down several important ideas and examples that help focus the answer on the question.
- Don't keep too many ideas. Confine yourself to three or four key points.
- Focus on what you DO know, not on what you DON'T know.

Drawing up an outline

Put ideas in order to fit the question type. Keep the structure simple – you are writing under time pressure. It's okay to have an obvious structure. Many essays follow a five-paragraph format, like this:

Paragraph 1: introduce topic and thesis
Paragraph 2: main point 1 and support details / examples
Paragraph 3: main point 2 and support details / examples
Paragraph 4: main point 3 and support details / examples
Paragraph 5: conclude with a restatement of your main thesis and the topic significance (keep this short and specific)

Remember: Your principle of organization should be drawn directly from the question. A common mistake is to write everything you know about a topic. Avoid this.

Starting to write

- Write quickly, with your outline at hand. As you move ahead with the writing, you may think of new ideas or sub-points to include in the essay.
- Stop briefly to make a note of these on your original outline.
- Write them neatly in the margin, on top of the page or on the last page, with arrows or marks to alert the reader to where they fit into your answer.
- Be clear. Signal clear relationships between paragraphs with appropriate transitions.
- Avoid irrelevancies and repetition.
- Write legibly.

The clock   TIP

Watch the clock carefully to ensure that you do not spend too much time on one question. If you run out of time, jot down remaining ideas from the outline to show that you know the material, but this is only a last option!

Editing and proofreading

Because you are writing under time pressure, your lecturers will not expect you to write as accurately as if you are writing an assignment, but it is still important to give yourself time to check your writing. When you check your writing, read the question again and check that you have answered it. See Chapters 8 and 9 for more information about proofreading your own writing.

Portfolio assessment

For some courses you may be asked to produce a portfolio of work that counts as your course assessment. Some lecturers like portfolio assessment as it can show your development over the whole semester. This means you have to write a collection of different kinds of text completed across the semester and this is what you will be marked on. For example, for a unit on a web design course, you may need to hand in:

Portfolio	<ul><li>a report of an interview with a client about a website design</li><li>a plan of the proposed functionality of the website you are designing</li><li>a budget plan detailing the programming work involved</li><li>layout screenshots to show a range of design options</li><li>a timesheet in which you outline your time on the project</li><li>a detailed project plan with milestones and deliverables laid out</li><li>a critical evaluation of your web project showing strengths and weaknesses</li></ul>

Students' experiences of portfolio assessment

These students were all assessed using portfolios. Read about their experiences and decide which students were positive, which were negative and which were neutral about portfolio assessment. Check your answers at the end of the book.

a. The word limits for each section were less and so, although I had to write lots of text, it was much easier than doing 3000 word assignments. And much better than taking an exam.

b. On my course, it wasn't clear how each part of the portfolio would be marked. I wasn't sure how important each part was and so I didn't know how much time to spend on each part. We had to include a journal over the course and it took me so long to write, but it was only 10% of the portfolio's overall mark.

c. At first, I had no idea what to do, but then I had a look at some previous students' portfolios and this was so useful. I could see what was expected of me and what I needed to do to get a good mark. In the end, it worked well.

d. I had only learnt how to write a discursive essay at school, but in this portfolio I had to write so many different types of text – a proposal, a report, a budget plan, a project timeline, etc. You have to get good at looking for these types of writing and working out how to organize them. Do you use headings? Do you put in diagrams? Do you need a conclusion? Our lecturer didn't offer much help with this, but I got advice from the Learning Centre.

e. There weren't any real deadlines – just suggested dates to complete work by. I missed a couple of deadlines at first and then I realized I was getting behind. Our lecturer wasn't very strict about this. When I realized it was my responsibility to get stuff done on time, I caught up okay.

f. Our lecturer was really clear about each part. She set up each section separately and introduced it well so we knew what to do.

Summary: A checklist for portfolios

These are things you should check when a lecturer sets up a portfolio assessment.

Deadlines

- Do you need to hand in parts of the portfolio as you go throughout the semester or do you hand it in all at once?
- When do you get feedback?
- If you hand it in section by section, when are the deadlines?

Marking

- How is each section weighted? Do you get one overall mark or is each part weighted differently?
- Is the portfolio the whole assessment for the course or do you need to do an exam as well?

Word limits

- Is there an overall word limit?
- How many words should you write for each section?
- How much time is each section supposed to take?

Text types

- Are there any examples of past students' portfolios to give you an idea of what to write?
- Are there guidelines and criteria for each section?
- Where can you find similar text types?

Conclusion

Assessment is an important part of life at university. As a student you may find it difficult if the rules are different from what you are used to. It is like playing a game. There are rules – and you may fail if you do not follow them. In order to win, you need to work out firstly what question the assignment or exam is asking and then how you are supposed to answer it. Like all games, you get better at working out what the lecturer wants you to do as the course goes on. It is important to try to take a critical stance in assessments at universities. Imagine how happy your lecturer would be if 100 assignments all said the same thing and then your assignment took an original or different view on the same subject.

12

Communicating with Lecturers

There will be times when you need to communicate with lecturers and other staff members to ask for information or make a request. This communication may take place through email, over the telephone, or face to face. This chapter reviews some of the reasons why you contact lecturers, tutors and staff members, and helps you think strategically about the best way to approach them to get what you want.

This chapter will help you to:

- decide how to communicate with lecturers and staff members
- use the right tone and language in making requests
- work with class representatives.

Why contact lecturers and staff members?

Why do students want to talk with their lecturer or other staff members? Look at the following list of common reasons why students make contact with academic staff and decide which of these purposes you would find hardest or easiest to face? You can look up some comments in the answers at the end of the book.

Reason	How hard is it to ask for this? (easy) 1 2 3 4 5 (hard)
You need an extension (more time) for an assignment.	
You want to get feedback on a draft that you have written.	
You want to change your appointment time.	
You want to find out about which courses to study next semester.	
You want to leave a class.	
You want to sit in on a class you have not enrolled for.	
You have a question about a lecture.	
You're not sure what to do for an assignment.	
You don't understand the mark you've been given.	
You want to complain about a course to the department chair.	

Now you have thought about WHY you might want to contact a lecturer or staff member. From here on you will think about HOW to make that contact. In the next section, we will look at the three main ways of contacting staff – using electronic communication, face to face and on the phone.

Electronic communication

In this age of advanced communication technology, instead of making phone calls and talking face to face, you may interact with your lecturers and other university employees through other means of communication. In a course, you may need to post your questions in a discussion forum on the course management system at your university. You may even ask questions on Facebook. Whatever the means of communication is, you need to follow the rules of communication for a particular context. The general advice is observe how others communicate in these media to understand the general rules. It is advisable to be clear, polite and respectful. The section on email below will address some basic considerations in making requests through email.

Email communication

Email is commonly used by students as a way of making appointments with lecturers. The good thing about email is that it is quick and convenient and lecturers don't need to respond immediately. You can also check your language before you send your message (turn on the built-in spellchecker for this). One of the problems with email is that, because you are not communicating face to face, it is easy to cause offence. Because emails are so quick to write, people sometimes forget that you should be as polite as if you are writing a letter, particularly if you are writing to people you are not close to.

Getting the tone right

Step 1

Look at the following email requesting an appointment. There are some problems with the tone of this email. How would the lecturer who got this email feel about making an appointment with this student? Check your answer below.

Subject: This is Miki :)

Hi Jim – I NEED to see you ASAP to check some stuff about the assignment. I've started but got stuck with. can I come tomorrow afternoon b4 4? I have a class then. Let me know if that's OK w/ u. BTW I enjoyed the class last week

cheers

Miki

He would probably feel that this student was inappropriate and disrespectful. The language was too informal. The student did not ask if the lecturer would be available. Instead, he/she dictated the schedule.

Step 2

Now think about what you would change to improve the tone. Rewrite the email so that it has a more positive effect on the lecturer.

Subject:

Step 3

Now compare the email you wrote with the one on the next page.
  What has changed from the original version?

Subject: Request for an appointment

Dear Jim
I'm having some problems with Assignment 2 and was wondering if it would be okay to come and talk to you about it later this week.
I am free tomorrow afternoon until about 4 o'clock if that is a good time for you. I am also free on Friday morning, if that works better for you.
Please let me know.
Many thanks
Miki

Did you notice?

- The subject line is more specific. It is not common to leave the subject line blank or to put your name in the subject line. Try to be as precise as possible. Many lecturers are very busy and will only read important messages quickly. If your message does not require an immediate reply, don't use the word 'urgent' or 'important' in the subject line.
- Avoid capitalization of whole words. It sounds as if you are angry.

- It is usually better to avoid abbreviations like BTW (by the way), ASAP (as soon as possible) and texting language e.g. b4 (before) when trying to sound professional.
- The tone of the original email was too personal and informal. Remember you are writing to a lecturer. In many English-speaking countries (e.g. Great Britain, New Zealand) it is fine to address your lecturer by their first name, but this differs between countries and even universities. Try to find out what other students are doing if you are not sure. Even if you call them by their first name face to face, writing is more formal so you should be more polite. If you are not sure, use their full name and title (e.g. Dear Dr Smith).
- The first email did not give an alternative time. The second lets the teacher choose their preferred option and is more polite.

Use the class representative TIP

Ask the class representative to find out what policy suits a particular staff member best.

Text messaging

Text messages (or SMS) are a popular way for students to contact each other. Most lecturers prefer to use email, but some do give out their mobile phone number. Check whether they are happy to receive class-related messages and take great care to follow the advice above about emails: it is even easier to sound impolite or unfriendly when using text messages. Always use your name in your text message as your teacher may not recognize you by your phone number!

Face-to-face requests

Of course, going to the office is not the only type of face-to-face request that lecturers get. At the end of a lecture there is often a queue of people waiting to ask a question. Even walking around the university grounds a lecturer might meet a student who wants to stop and talk about some personal concern. Students sometimes rush up and put a request to someone who is on the way to lunch. However, let's first look at the situation where you want to go to the lecturer's office.

Issues with face-to-face requests

Ideas about privacy, personal space and interrupting people when they are working are different in different countries and even in different universities. What is normal for some lecturers in some countries may be rude for lecturers in a different country.

Here are some issues about face-to-face requests. For each question choose the best answer and then read on.

Question 1: Is it okay to just turn up at any time with no appointment?
   A. Always
   B. Sometimes
   C. Never

For a few lecturers the answer is 'always'. They sit in their offices with the door open and always look welcoming when students come in. These are usually people who do not teach classes of 200 or more students.

For most lecturers, there are certain times when they make themselves available to students. These times are often called 'office hours', although the person might well be there at other times, sitting behind a closed door. Check when this person's office hours are in one of these ways:

- look at the notice on the door
- check the website
- ask the secretary
- email to ask for a time.

In a real emergency (and not everyone shares the same idea of what a real emergency is) then the rules can be broken and you can try knocking on the door. For most people, a real emergency includes the following:

- A situation where someone may be hurt.
- The examination is one hour away and suddenly you feel too ill to do it.
- You have just been told that a student has broken into the assignment box and stolen an assignment.
- You have just realized that the assignment you handed in yesterday was actually one you wrote for a different course.
- Your class of 150 students have been waiting for 30 minutes and the lecturer has not arrived.

Question 2: What sort of requests do lecturers look at favourably?
   A. Requests where the student looks distressed
   B. Last-minute requests
   C. Requests made early

This depends! Read on.

We asked some lecturers to comment on how willing they would be to say 'yes' to the following requests.

Before turning to the answers at the end of the book, decide whether each was likely to have a 'yes' or 'no' response.

There's a long waiting list in the library for the book you recommended. Do you mind if I borrow yours?   Yes / No

I know you are strict about dates for handing in assignments, but, as you can see, I've broken my leg. Yes / No

I just missed a bit of your lecture this morning. I wonder if you'd mind running through that last part again with me. Yes / No

Would you mind giving me your frank opinion on whether I should advance this subject next year? Yes / No

---

Try out your request with another student first TIP

You can find out if it will get a good reception and you can practise what you are going to say.

Lecturers expect to be asked about things they have not already explained in class or written on a handout. They expect that this request is special to a particular student. If the topic is more general, then ask your student representative to speak on behalf of the class. For instance, it may be that a group of students have three major assignments due for three different staff members on the same day. Then it's reasonable for the student representative to go and negotiate a different time with one of the lecturers.

The language of requests

The success of your request may also depend on the language you use and the way that you deliver the request. Your pronunciation (e.g. the way you use intonation) and body language (e.g. if you look stressed or smile) may create an instant positive effect on your lecturer or it may create a negative effect. Read the following student–teacher meetings. Both of the students have requests. What are they asking for? How successful are they? What words do they use to make their requests more polite? What is the effect of the students' choice of words on their relationships with their teachers?

Wen

T: Come in. How are you?
S: Good thanks. I just wanted to change my ... um ... tutorial time.
T: Oh okay, what time are you in at the moment?
S: I think I'm at ... um ... two o'clock on Tuesdays ... and I've got ... um ... clinic on that day for accounting.
T: You've got what?
S: Clinic. Accounting clinic ... so ...
T: Tuesday two o'clock (turns papers).
S: I'm sure it's at two o'clock.

Jane

T: Hello. Have a seat.
S: Thanks. Actually I have ... um ... written the short story for my assignment. I was wondering if you could give me some feedback and if I am on the right track.
T: Okay yeah. You've got it?
S: (finds and hands over story) That's my story.
T: Oh. Let's have a read ... um ... (19 seconds as T reads). Okay, yeah, that's what I mean, it's a story.
S: Mmm-hmm.
T: So what are you going to do with your story next?

Note: These extracts of meetings between students and teachers are taken from
E. Crandall (1999) 'Native speaker and non-native speaker requests in an academic
context', Occasional Paper No.12, Department of Applied Language Studies and
Linguistics, University of Auckland.

Wen wants to change his tutorial time. Jane wants feedback on a draft that she's
written. Both of them communicate what they want relatively successfully. Wen uses
the word 'just' to understate his request. This is very common amongst native
speakers and has the effect of making the request sound smaller and therefore easier
to say yes to. His choice of language shows that he is in control of the request, and
taking the initiative, again making it easier for the teacher to agree.

Jane uses the words 'I was wondering if you could'. This is a common way of
making a request polite and is a useful technique.

Now, let's look at language to make requests in a little more detail.

What's a good opening line?

If your English is very good then you can probably skip this part, although it's
surprising how many people rush in and ask for something without the usual phrases
that make their request sound polite. Look at these and decide why they are likely to
be successful. The first has been done for you. Check your answers at the end of the
book.

I was just wondering if …	'Just' – makes the request smaller and therefore easier to say yes to. 'Wondering' – again makes the request sound less serious and less threatening. There is less at stake than 'Can you …?'
Sorry to be a nuisance, but …	
Excuse me, is it possible …	
This is just a small request.	
Sorry I didn't make an appointment. Do you have a couple of minutes?	

Think about how your language will affect the lecturer TIP

Acknowledge that you are interrupting the lecturer / don't have an appointment / can come back later.

Get on with it! Don't waste time getting to the request. Practise first – work out what you will say.

Minimize the request using words like 'just' and 'small'

Impersonal requests using 'it' are easier to say yes to than personal ones using 'you' and 'me'.

How does the conversation end?

It is important to know when to leave. If you take up too much time, you will leave a negative impression on the lecturer and he/she will be less likely to listen to you next time. Listen for clues from the lecturer. Remember they can't leave – you are in their office!

Body language and actual words are the clues that the lecturer may expect the conversation to be over. Look out for any of these signs. The lecturer:

- looks down at the desk and starts shuffling papers
- summarizes an answer for the second time
- looks at his/her watch
- Says, 'Thanks for coming,' or, 'I hope that answers your questions.'

What if you are still unhappy with the answer?

This is where your student representative comes in. That person has the role of negotiating things between students and staff.

Troubleshooting lecturer–student dialogues

The following are transcripts of an actual visit by a student (S) to the lecturer's (T) office (Crandall, 1999). For each one, think about the dialogue and answer the question(s). Check your answers at the end of the book.

Dialogue 1: How many problems can you see in this?

T: Okay, what's up? What can I do for you today? (5 seconds of silence)
S: Yep.
T: What, oh just whatever you came to see me about. Yep?
S: Yep. Okay (taking out paper).
T: Oh. Exam script.
S: Yeah. I failed last semester.
T: Oh, okay.
S: Yep (laugh). You see, the mark is very low.
T: Yeah.

Dialogue 2: What does the student want? Why does the teacher get impatient?

T: What can I do for you today?

S: Ah. I've come about my assignment.

T: Assignment. Oh yes. Yep. You've been to the tutorial?

S: Yes.

T: Yep (9 seconds). Well, what is the problem with your ...?

S: Ah (9 seconds). I don't know how to write an essay at a university.

T: And why is it difficult for you?

S: I find it hard to get started.

T: And why is that?

S: I don't have much experience in writing and I make many mistakes.

T: Ah, I see. There is an excellent writing centre at the university where you can get help with writing ... etc.

Decide what you want to get out of the meeting and clearly explain to the teacher why you are there. Remember that the teacher doesn't know why you are there unless you tell him or her. Here is another way the student could have asked his question:

T: What can I do for you today?

S: I have come to talk about our next assignment. I am new to this country and find it very hard to write a good essay. How can I improve my writing skills?

Now look at the following situations. You have arranged an appointment with a teacher. How would you explain what you want? Compare your answers with our suggestions at the end of the book.

Reason	What would you say to the teacher?
You want to sit in on a class you have not enrolled for because you think it may be more interesting than the course you are taking.	
You have a question about a lecture that you didn't want to ask in front of the other students.	
You don't understand what to do for an assignment.	
You got a bad mark for an assignment, and you don't understand how it was marked.	

Telephone contact

Apart from the email and face-to-face contact we have already discussed, you can, of course, use the telephone. This is great when you do not have time or you are unable to travel to the department, for example when you are sick or overseas.

Problems of telephoning in a second language

As you will know if you have lived in another country, speaking on the phone in a second language is difficult. This is why.

- Speakers use lots of idioms on the phone and these are tricky if you are not used to them (e.g. ring up / call back /put you through / hang up / hold the line / hold on).
- Expectations of telephone conversations are different in different countries (who talks first / what they say / how long you should talk for / how to end the call, etc.).
- You can't use body language (e.g. eye contact, smiling, using your hands) to help you understand, show that you don't understand, or get your message across.
- Long pauses are not normal on the phone. You have very little time to understand what the other person is saying and say what you want to say.
- It's not always clear if the other person has stopped talking and it's your turn, or whether the other person has just paused mid-sentence.

Getting your message across

Here are some questions to consider before ringing. Check your answers at the end of the book.

---

1. What could you say if the staff member answers the phone immediately? Which of these options seems best to you?
   a. *Ask if this is a convenient time to talk.*
   b. *Give your name and state your problem.*
   c. *Say whether your call is urgent or not.*
2. What could you say if you hear an answerphone message? Which of these options seems best to you?
   a. *Ring off immediately.*
   b. *Ask the staff member to phone you back.*
   c. *Explain briefly why you have phoned.*

Becoming more confident on the phone

Here are some things you can do to help you become more confident on the phone:

1 Practise what you want to say into a voice recorder and play it back. This way you can hear what you sound like on the phone and check your pronunciation. Practise leaving answerphone messages.
2 Write out beforehand what you want to say. At the very least have a list with the main points you want to cover. You can also write down some difficult words (perhaps as you pronounce them rather than how you write them) and key phrases like your opening or closing sentences.
3 Role-play situations with a friend before you make the call.
4 Speak on the phone in English as much as possible – build up your confidence with more predictable requests.

5 Analyse the language of phone calls. When you are in a place where you can hear lots of phone calls, listen to the language that people use and analyse the way they introduce themselves and end conversations. Doctors' waiting rooms, cafes and train stations are great places to hear both formal and informal phone conversations. Try out the phrases you hear in your own phone conversations.

6 Study telephone language. Here are some references to check out:

In your university's self-access centre, you will find books on business English which will have sections on telephone language. One such is:

Naterop, B.J. and Revell, R. (2004) *Telephoning in English*, Cambridge University Press. It has a CD with dialogues you can listen to and exercises with useful language to use on the phone. It is suitable for upper-intermediate language students.

Class representatives

In many universities, one student will be an elected class representative ('class rep') for each class. Their job is to speak to the department or lecturer about issues that affect all the students in their class. They may have to go to training and will probably go to a formal meeting with a lecturer in the department once a semester. At the end of the semester, one of the duties in some universities is to organize a class party.

When to talk to your class rep

In which of these situations should you talk to the class rep? Check your answers at the end of the book.

Situation 1: You are really confused by an assignment and have spoken to other students on your course. They are just as confused as you.

Situation 2: It is impossible to get a really important book from the library because there are not enough copies.

Situation 3: You feel that a lecturer is giving you bad marks because he/she does not like you.

Situation 4: You fail an exam and don't understand why.

Situation 5: You feel that one lecturer's classes are really boring and think he/she doesn't care about the students.

Situation 6: You want to complain about a class. You feel that there is too much testing for that class.

Situation 7: You need extra tutoring with one of your assignments.

Conclusion

Personal communication is important in any setting because people will form an opinion about you based on the way you communicate. Although lecturers and other university employees are often open to your requests and willing to help you, you will need to communicate with them in a way that is clear, polite and respectful. This chapter has offered some specific advice and practice for you to learn to be a more effective communicator.

Dealing with Problems

As a student, expect to face problems and new challenges every day, especially when you study in another country, you live away from home, and you're cut off from old friends and family, in an unfamiliar country, dealing with an unfamiliar culture, speaking a second language and trying to pass a university course at the same time. It's not all bad, though. Coming up with innovative solutions can be fun, and experiences that are difficult at the time make great stories to tell people back home about later. How successful you are as a student will depend on how well you deal with these problems.

This chapter will help you to:

- learn about managing anxiety and staying motivated
- find out where to get help in your new university
- discover how to manage culture shock
- cope with academic issues
- live on a budget and make extra money.

Managing anxiety

One factor that stops students from doing well at university is their own negative feelings, in other words, anxiety. As teachers, we have seen examples like these:

- clever students who do well all through the semester, but become so anxious about examinations that they don't get the results they want
- students who are anxious because they are not studying, but can't make themselves start
- A+ grade students who are anxious in case they get a lower grade for their next assignment
- normally calm students who let themselves be infected by other people's worries
- failing students who feel no anxiety at all.

Do you recognize yourself in any of these descriptions?

Because motivation, personality type and anxiety are closely linked, we'll be talking about them all in this section.

What causes anxiety?

One way of thinking about anxiety is to see where you stand on the anxiety scale.

1. Being competitive

Do you find yourself comparing your results with other students' results?

a. Very rarely
b. Sometimes
c. Often

Comparing yourself too much with other students is one of the factors leading to anxiety.

2. Taking tests

When you think about a future test do you feel?

a. Not worried
b. Slightly anxious
c. Very anxious

In fact there is not much relationship between worrying and success. Some worriers do very well, some don't. The same can be said for students who hardly worry at all. For most students the answer is in actual readiness for the test, not in anxiety.

3. Your relationship with your teachers

When you think about your teachers, you:

a. Don't consider what they think
b. Feel encouraged
c. Feel very anxious

Anxiety can be heightened when learners are living as immigrants in the target culture and suffering culture shock. One reason is that teacher–student relationships can be very different from country to country.

4. Your feelings about managing your studies

When you are deciding what to do for an assignment, you feel:

a. Excited
b. A bit worried that you might not do well
c. Very anxious that you might not do well

You may find that you are expected to take much more responsibility for your studies in your new country than in the education system you are used to, especially if you are studying in a university for the first time. Finding that you have more educational freedom can be exciting for some students, but can leave other students feeling lost and extremely anxious. It often takes students time to realize how much responsibility they are expected to take for their studies.

Does motivation help?

Your motivation can go wrong (or right) at several stages of your course, starting with the choice of subject.

Why are you studying this subject?

For example, did you choose to study this subject? That might seem a strange question to ask, but students may be taking a particular subject for many reasons which have no connection with self-motivation. Check these out.

Who thought this would be a good course for you?

- your parents
- your teachers
- you
- people offering you a scholarship
- nobody.

If the answer is 'nobody' there may be other reasons why you are studying it such as:

- This is a compulsory subject.
- It fitted your timetable.
- Your first choice (course) was scheduled too early in the morning for you to get out of bed.

As you can see, negative reasons for taking a course can make it difficult to be motivated. Still, if you want to pass, you need to try motivating yourself in other ways.

Examine your attitude to the subject

You can do something to improve your motivation. One way is to start thinking positively about your course. Try this:

- How many reasons can you find for the importance in the world of the subject you are studying?
- How many different future options could this subject give you?

Thinking about time can help too. If you are eight weeks into a 13-week term and you are not motivated, divide up the rest of the time available, look at the lecture topics each week and ask yourself:

- What's one thing I want to get out of each week remaining on the course?

Monitor your motivation levels over time

The motivation questionnaire on the next page will help you measure your current motivation levels (if you answer it truthfully!). 'Intrinsic' motivation is internal motivation – how meaningful things feel to you. 'Extrinsic' motivation is external – from other people and society. Some people will have stronger 'intrinsic' motivation than 'extrinsic' motivation. On the other hand, some people will have much stronger 'extrinsic' motivation. This is not better or worse.

'Synergy' is about connections – in your case between you and your course and with people on the course.

You should try this questionnaire at different stages of your course and keep track of your scores. For each question, place yourself on a scale of 1 to 5.

It is normal for motivation levels to go up and down over a course, or even a semester, but if you are aware that your motivation levels are slipping, you can try to change this or talk to someone about it.

Write down your scores here.

Date	Score out of 60
1.	
2.	
3.	
4.	

Category	Key questions	Your motivation level
Energy		
Level of activity	How much work are you putting in?	a little .... a lot 1 2 3 4 5
Achievement	To what extent do you feel like you are making progress?	going backwards .... good progress 1 2 3 4 5
Fear of failure	How much do you feel your hard work is being recognized?	not at all .... well 1 2 3 4 5
Synergy		
Personal growth	To what extent do you feel that your course is helping you grow as a person?	not at all ....a lot 1 2 3 4 5
Course	To what extent do you feel the course is right for you?	not right ....100% right 1 2 3 4 5
Relationships	To what extent do you feel you are working well with other people on your course – the other students and your lecturers?	not at all .... working well 1 2 3 4 5
Intrinsic		
Interest	How interested are you in your lectures, tutorials and reading at the moment?	bored .... very interested 1 2 3 4 5
Enjoyment	How much are you enjoying your course at the moment?	hate it ....love it 1 2 3 4 5
Autonomy	How much control and choice do you feel you have over your studies?	no control .... full control 1 2 3 4 5
Extrinsic		
Progress	How important are the grades you get to you?	don't care .... care a lot 1 2 3 4 5
Accountability	How important is your progress on the course to your family, friends or company	doesn't matter .... very important 1 2 3 4 5
Future hopes	How important is your performance on the course to your future career?	not important .... very important 1 2 3 4 5

How important is personality?

Personality is one more factor affecting how anxious a student is. If you are working in ways that do not fit your personality, you could get bored or turned off study. Take this two-minute personality test and then read about the best way for someone with your personality to study. It is based around some typical decisions that international students make. For each question, decide which of the answers sounds most like you. The one that sounds most like you gets score '1'. The next closest answer gets score '2', and so on.

1 The country you decided to study in. When you chose a country to go to, what was the most important factor in your decision?

   a. It was the most logical place for me to go and study.
   b. It fitted in with my friends and family.
   c. It was the most practical – this was the place I could get the results I wanted.
   d. I liked the idea of it. It seemed the most exciting.

2 Your career choice. Which of these sounds most like you?

   a. I want a job where I can analyse things and see what makes them work.
   b. I'm interested in jobs with lots of contact with people.
   c. I want to do something where I can solve problems and make a difference.
   d. I want to do something where I can be creative.

3 Your ideal teacher. Which of these sounds closest to your ideal?

   a. Teachers should know their subject, give me the facts and get to the point.
   b. Teachers should care about their students.
   c. I like teachers to be practical and give me real world learning tasks.
   d. I like teachers who give me the freedom to take things my own way.

4 Working in groups. Which one sounds like you?

   a. I prefer to think about the issues myself first and then come together with others.
   b. I think it's really important that everyone has their say.
   c. The key thing is that we make a decision and get the task done.
   d. I like to challenge others and ask questions like, 'What if?'

5 Your subject choice. How did you decide what subject to take?

   a. I like working things out in a systematic way. Accuracy is important. I like to be able to understand how things work.
   b. I am interested in people and feelings. I want to take a subject where I can explore and understand why people behave in the ways they do.
   c. I like solving problems and seeing how things work in practice. I like applying ideas and getting results.
   d. I like creating things and seeing new possibilities.

6 Going out. How do you choose a movie to go and see?

   a. I look at all the available information – reviews, listings, etc. – and choose the best one.
   b. I talk it through with my friends and we go and see something that suits everyone.

    c. I choose one that is on at the right time and fits my schedule.

    d. If it looks interesting, I'll give it a try.

7 Handing in assignments. When you have to check your piece of work before you hand it in, which of these sounds like you?

    a. I want it to be accurate, so I take a lot of care to make sure it is.

    b. I end up spending so much time helping my friend that I don't really check mine properly.

    c. I check it well enough to get a pass, but don't waste time on it because I have other things to get on with.

    d. I am not really interested in checking it. If I know some sections are great, I'd rather move on to a more interesting project.

8 Getting help and advice. When you get stuck with something, how do you decide when to ask for help?

    a. I like to figure it all out myself before asking for help.

    b. I like to share my problems and talk it through with someone.

    c. I will do whatever it takes to solve the problem efficiently.

    d. I am open to suggestions. Sometimes people say things that help me see the problem in a totally different way.

Now add up your score for each letter:

Total score for a =
Total score for b =
Total score for c =
Total score for d =

The lowest score is your dominant personality type. Read this table to find out how people with this personality type approach study. The right-hand column has some tips for avoiding anxiety.

	How you naturally learn	How to avoid anxiety
a = Analyser	You learn by thinking deeply about things. You are logical and technical. You like rules and precision. You are better with concepts than people.	At times you may get stressed because you have to make decisions without understanding everything. You are too cautious and need to go with the flow a bit more. You also need to remember that other people's ideas can be useful too!
b = Supporter	You learn by watching people, sharing ideas and talking about feelings. You are emotional and sensitive and good with people. You are sociable and understanding.	You are sometimes too worried about what everyone thinks to get things done. This may cause you anxiety. Sometimes you need to focus more on the result and be more decisive.
c = Director	You learn by putting things into practice. You like getting results. You are good at problem-solving. You are good at planning and organizing people and things to get the best result in the situation.	People get frustrated with you because you organize them too much. Remember the end result is not everything – you also need to keep everyone happy.

(Continued)

	How you naturally learn	How to avoid anxiety
d = Creator	You like action and learn by trying things out. You are a free spirit and are creative. You don't plan, but do things spontaneously.	At times, remember you need to concentrate more on things that seem boring – like details. You also need to be more consistent and work hard over time.

Note: This questionnaire is adapted from one that can be accessed at the link given below. If you are interested in finding out more about personality, you should take the full test:

Learning and personality styles test: http://www.engr.utexas.edu/eoe/PeerLeaders/ Resources/Learning&PersonalityStyles.pdf

At this stage, it could be a good idea to look back at the learning styles questionnaires that you took back in Chapter 2. Again, if you are trying to learn in ways that do not suit your natural learning style, you may be causing yourself anxiety.

Anxiety summary: make a plan

Finally, let's see how many of the following tips are relevant to you.

1 Consider trying to compete with yourself rather than others.
2 Remind yourself of the support that is available to you, such as counsellors, tutors and staff members from different offices on campus such as Health Services, Student Affairs, International Student Services, etc. (see the next section).
3 Taking action helps, even if it's only drawing up a plan of what you will start studying tomorrow.
4 Evaluate your learning. Remind yourself of signs of progress.
5 Talk with a friend about the benefits of studying in the course you are enrolled on in.
6 Give yourself a reasonable amount of time before considering changing courses.
7 Plan some rewards for yourself when you have done a certain amount of study.
8 Monitor your feelings. Don't let yourself be too sad for too long.
9 Remember that other people think and learn differently from the way you do. Don't let their difference stress you out.
10 Be realistic. Even if you are doing really well, you can expect some anxious days! If you are never anxious about your progress, you should be worried!

Sources of help

Most universities have well-established support services set up for domestic and international students. These can give you help and advice when you are facing all sorts of problems. This section introduces the different agencies in a university and gives you some ideas of where you can turn for help and advice. Don't worry about going to the wrong person. If they can't help you, they will know who can. The important thing is that if you have a problem, you take action and talk to **someone**.

Who can help?

On the left is the type of problem. On the right are some of the people who might be able to help. The names of the people will change between universities, but there will be people who can help with these problems.

Type of problem	Examples	Who can help?
academic	need study advice	an academic advisor / your lecturer / learning centre advisor
	complain about a class	your class rep / your lecturer / an academic advisor
	appeal against a grade / decision	an academic advisor
	problem with a lecturer	your class rep / an academic advisor
	need help in the library	a librarian / your subject librarian
	need help improving English	learning centre / tutoring centre / English language department
	have questions about plagiarism	learning centre advisor / academic advisor
	are not sure which courses to take	an academic advisor in your department
accommodation	complain about a landlord	Student Union Accommodation Office / International Student Office
	need help finding a flat	
	can't pay the rent	student financial counsellor
health	feel sick	university health centre
	need advice about pregnancy	
	need to register with a doctor	
	need advice about contraception	
	want a female doctor	
mental health	feel depressed	student counselling service / university health centre
	have an eating problem (e.g. anorexia)	
	have worries about your sexuality	
	have a question about drugs or alcohol	
	want to stop smoking	
	need help with stress	
money	need to find a job	student financial counsellor
	run out of money	
	need help budgeting	
	have a question about tax	
international	have a problem with your immigration status or visa	International Student Office
	need a translator	
	feel homesick	
religion	need somewhere to pray	university chaplaincy service / International Student Office

Get help early

As you can see, there is help available for every kind of problem you can possibly have while at university. The most important thing is to tell someone you have a problem early so you can get advice before your problem gets too big. No problem is too small, too simple, or too terrible for a university counsellor. Remember, they talk to thousands of students every year, all with similar problems.

A note about counsellors

In some cultures, it is not common to seek counselling services. In an international university situation this is not the case. Getting help from a counsellor is considered normal and a positive thing to do. Counsellors will give you advice, but they will not tell you what to do – that is your decision.

If you go and see a counsellor for whatever problem, the counsellor will:

FIRST	try to understand your problem by asking you questions
THEN	talk through choices with you
SO THAT	you have enough information and understanding to make decisions for yourself.

In your orientation week at university, make a note of where you can go to get help with:

● academic issues
● health issues
● financial advice.

Culture shock

Culture shock is a series of feelings that many people go through when they move to a new country. If you have lived in another country before, you may have already experienced culture shock. If you haven't, then this section will make you aware of it so that you can prevent it from becoming a problem at university.

What are the stages of culture shock?

There are generally thought to be four stages that people go through when they arrive in a new country.

Stage 1	**The discovery stage.** You feel like you are just on holiday. Everything is new and fun and exciting. You do lots in the first few weeks and find everything interesting – there are new parts of the university and city to explore and it's all a bit unreal. Even catching a bus is fun and exciting.
Stage 2	**Things go flat.** Life's okay, but you realize that you are going to be in this country for a long time. You get into a routine – lectures, assignments, etc. You may find it difficult to make friends. You realize that people in the host country don't understand you that well. You have some bad days, but at this stage you can live with them.
Stage 3	**The complaining stage.** You start getting angry when things go wrong. You may worry about your health. You have negative feelings about people in the host country. Why is the bus always late? Why is the food so horrible? How do these people put up with it all? You see problems everywhere and find yourself comparing things in your new country with things in your old country, all the time. Sometimes it feels as if everyone in your new country is trying to make things difficult for you. You may find yourself getting depressed at this stage or very tired or just angry.
Stage 4	And finally … By now your language is better and living is easier. Gradually you are getting over the culture shock. Sure, the new country is different, but it's okay. And when things go wrong you can laugh about it and about your negative reaction. The university is different from the one you have previously studied at, but there are good things and bad things about this. You still miss people at home and some of the things about your country, but that's okay.

A culture shock survival kit

Try these things before you leave for your new country.

1 Tell one of your friends at home about culture shock. Explain about the four stages and give them examples of things that people say in stage 3:

- 'The shops shut so early in this country. It's crazy. Life is much better at home where ….'
- 'There's nothing to do here in the evenings. People are so boring in ….'
- 'The internet connection is so slow. How do people live like this? In my country, we had better internet connection five years ago.'
- 'There's so much bureaucracy in this university. Everything takes so long. I'm sure they just make it difficult for students.'

Ask your friend to ring you every week and ask you how you are doing. If you say things that sound like you have stage 3 culture shock, they should tell you and help you to lighten up.

2 Make a list of all the things that you want to do in the country you are going to e.g.

- spend a weekend in …
- catch the ferry to …
- spend the afternoon on … beach.
- camp in the mountains near …
- go to the opera in …

- find yourself a conversation partner … (see the next section)
- go to the art gallery in ….

    If you find yourself in stage 2, you should revisit your list and do one of the things on it. This way you stay in the discovery stage.

3   If you have a hobby, then make sure you take any equipment you need to your new country. Having a hobby outside your studies will help you feel less culture shocked.

And once you are studying in your new country …

1   Meet a friend from your home country regularly e.g. once every two weeks. Allow yourselves to say what you miss about your country, but also reflect on how you are adapting to the change. Set yourselves goals that you can evaluate when you next meet e.g. 'By the time we next meet, I'll have joined a university society and tried out the local swimming pool.'
2   Keep a diary. Note down how you are feeling about your move / the new country / the local people / the change of university. Also write down any successes you have (friends you make / positive experiences, etc.). If you find yourself in stage 2 or stage 3, go back through your diary and see how far you have come.

Some common areas of cultural misunderstanding

This is a task you could try in your first few weeks in a new country. Here are some topics that can cause cultural misunderstanding. They will not be a problem if you are aware of them. First read through the list and think about whether they are okay in your country and in your new country. Then find someone from the new country and talk about them.

	Okay in your country?	Okay in your new country?
1. Arriving 10 minutes late to meet a friend.		
2. Arriving 20 minutes late to meet a friend.		
3. Kissing when you meet someone for the first time.		
4. Kissing when you meet good friends.		
5. Wearing shoes inside someone's house.		
6. Touching someone on the arm when you are talking to them.		
7. Calling a lecturer by their first name.		
8. Calling someone older by their first name.		
9. Arriving at someone's house for dinner with no gift.		
10. Giving your teacher a really expensive gift – like a new phone.		
11. Asking questions about someone's age or how much they earn on a first meeting.		
12. Asking a woman if she is married when you first meet her.		

(Continued)

	Okay in your country?	Okay in your new country?
13. Standing less than 1 metre from someone you don't know very well at a party		
14. Making direct eye contact with a teacher in class.		
15. Laughing and smiling when talking to a teacher.		
16. Making jokes about old people / women / sex. Comparing people from a particular part of the country with people you don't know well.		
17. Making jokes about the royal family or the president.		
18. Talking loudly with a friend on the train.		
19. Using a cell phone in the library.		
20. Getting drunk.		
21. Driving home after two or three beers.		
22. Inviting someone out and insisting on paying the full bill.		

Summary: some things that help students overcome culture shock

1	Knowing about it (see the notes above).
2	Making sure you keep some contact with people from your own country studying in the university and also with people at home.
3	Exercising. This stops most people worrying about things and makes most people feel more positive about life.
4	Getting involved with people in the host country both in the university and outside. For example, you could take up dance classes or join a football team.
5	Focusing on your studies. Get busy – you really don't have time to worry about culture shock.
6	Setting yourself goals e.g. 'Next week, I'm going to get out to the mountains,' or 'This week, I'm going to go out for a drink with people from my class.'
7	Continuing to learn about your new country – discovering new places and people.
8	Finding someone else who has experienced culture shock and having a joke about it with them.
9	Remembering it's okay to miss your family, friends and country.
10	Talking to a counsellor if you are getting depressed.
11	Remembering you will probably not be living there forever.

Academic issues: what would you do? A quiz

So far, we have looked at anxiety and the sources of help available to you at university. In this section we will deal with academic problems. Take this quiz and decide what you would do in each case.

Are you a proactive problem-solver?

1 You get an email saying that you owe the library $65 in fines and cannot use the library again until this fine is paid. Your own records suggest that you may have some fines owing, but you don't think you owe that much. Do you:

   a. Do nothing and keep working on your assignment – there's no time to lose.
   b. Phone the library and ask them about the fine.
   c. Pay it straight away so that you can borrow books again.

2 You get a new assignment in class. You are not sure what the assignment asks you to do. What should you do first?

   a. Write what you think it's about and hand that in.
   b. Make an appointment to ask your lecturer what it's all about.
   c. Talk to other students on the course and see if they can explain it.

3 You are struggling to meet a deadline. You have three essays due in the same week (three weeks away) and you don't think you are going to be able to get them all in on time. Do you:

   a. Stay up every night, work really hard and try to get them all in – you can hand one in late – it doesn't matter that much if it's a couple of days late.
   b. Ask one of your lecturers for an extension now.
   c. Do your best and then plan to ask for an extension the day before it has to be handed in.

4 You get an assignment back and you have failed, but you don't know why. You thought you did the assignment well and you don't understand the lecturer's comments. Do you:

   a. Make an appointment to ask your lecturer why you failed.
   b. Make an official complaint about the lecturer.
   c. Try to read the assignment of a student who did okay first.

5 You are trying to find a book for your course in the library. You have found it on the computer, but can't find it on the shelf. Do you:

   a. Go for a drink and come back later for another look.
   b. Decide to spend the rest of the day figuring out how the library's shelves are organized.
   c. Ask a librarian to help you locate the book.

6 You are worried that you don't understand much of the lectures on one of your courses. Do you:

   a. Make an appointment with your lecturer and tell him or her.
   b. Record all the lectures so you can listen back to them later.
   c. Seek help at the English language self-access centre in the university.

7 You are having trouble finding somewhere quiet to study. Your flatmates are too noisy and watch television all the time. Do you:

   a. Buy ear plugs.
   b. Watch television with them.
   c. Ask someone in your department about available study spaces.

8 You are struggling with your course – you have exams in a couple of weeks and you don't know where to start. You think you might fail. Do you:

a. Make an appointment with your lecturer and tell him or her how you feel.

b. Start studying even harder. Spend all weekend in the library.

c. Pack your bags and go home.

9 You have a problem with your course. You don't think the assessment is fair. Do you:

a. Talk to your class representative (the person in the class who you voted for to talk to your department about issues within the class).

b. Do nothing – it's probably no big deal.

c. Complain to the head of department about the lecturer.

Finished? Now check your answers at the end of the book and then read the advice for your personality type. See if you agree with the advice.

Critical thinking

Lecturers in English-speaking universities often complain that students are not able to think critically, and may give them bad marks because of this. In the chapters on reading and writing in this book, we have already talked a bit about critical thinking, but in this section we look at this topic in more detail.

So, what do lecturers mean by critical thinking?

You may know the word 'criticize' with its everyday meaning of 'make negative comments about someone or something'. However, when talking about 'critical thinking' that is not the meaning your lecturers have in mind. There is not one definition of critical thinking, but here are some examples. Critical thinkers:

- think logically
- put things into categories
- decide whether something is a fact or an opinion
- evaluate arguments using a wide range of evidence
- weigh up evidence and come to their own conclusion
- make connections between different ideas
- apply theories to practical situations
- ask questions like 'why?' and 'what if?'
- ask questions and see problems in the 'normal' way things happen.

So, critical thinking is about *ways* of thinking, and the ability to analyse ideas and arguments.

Why is critical thinking important at English-speaking universities?

In Anglo-Saxon (British and American) culture the individual's personal development is seen as very important. Students must show that they can read, think, question, analyse and come to their own conclusions. Teachers may expect and encourage learners to discover things for themselves. They may ask questions like:

- What do you think?
- How did you come to that conclusion?
- To what extent do you think …?

For this reason, remembering a lot of facts and simply working very hard may not be enough, and will most likely not get you very good grades. This may be different from your own country where hard work may be more rewarded.

What sort of problems might I have with critical thinking?

The idea of critical thinking is important in lots of areas at university. For example, you will find that:

- There is an expectation that you should learn in an active / questioning / discovering way and find things out for yourself.
- The way the course is structured is different– with tutorials where you need to discuss and evaluate ideas.
- Assignments often have a critical element where you need to evaluate and argue.
- The sort of feedback the lecturer gives you is different from what you are used to.
- How you speak in lectures and tutorials and the questions you ask are different.
- How you are supposed to read and question what you read are different.
- How you plan and write assignments is different.
- How you cite sources in assignments is considered very important.
- How you answer exam questions and how these are marked is different.

How does it feel when you are struggling with critical thinking?

It can be really hard! Read what these first-year students said about it:

> I am not a lazy student – I'm working harder and harder, but my marks don't get better.

> It is like playing a sport that you know you are good at, but with new and different rules that you don't really understand.

> I just feel lost. I don't know how to start this assignment / answer this question.

> I'm always being asked for my opinion. I don't have one and even if I did I am just a beginner in the subject so, compared to the people who wrote the books, my opinion is not really important.

How are plagiarism and critical thinking connected?

If students do not understand about critical thinking, they can have problems with plagiarism. Here is an example of plagiarism from Umut and the chain of events leading to her problem with plagiarism. As you read, think about how her problem is related to critical thinking, and how you can avoid this situation.

1 A lecturer sets an assignment asking students to report and evaluate some research articles on a topic. She wants the students to show they have thought critically about the research and come to their own conclusions. The question reads:

> With reference to the work of X, Y and Z [three important researchers on the topic], to what extent do you agree with the idea that …?

2 Umut doesn't really understand the question but focuses on the bit she does understand, the first part, and starts work. She doesn't understand that she needs to give her conclusions about the research.

3 Umut reads the articles in detail and writes her assignment. She tries to report and summarize what the writers say, but this is really hard. She is anxious about her English.
4 Before she hands her work in, Umut checks her essay. She is unsatisfied with her work. Her words are not nearly as good as the original articles she read and she feels very uncomfortable about changing the meaning of the original writers. So she uses some of the same sentences from the original articles.
5 Umut hands in her work. The lecturer reads it and highlights all the bits that have been copied and writes feedback using words like: 'PLAGIARISM ... SERIOUS OFFENCE ... THIS UNIVERSITY ... INTELLECTUAL PROPERTY ... URGENT APPOINTMENT', etc.

Now look at the diagram to see how Umut should have answered the question.

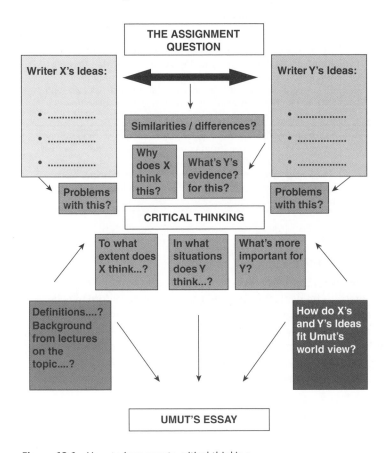

Figure 13.1   How to incorporate critical thinking

So, how do you get better at critical thinking, get better marks and avoid problems with plagiarism?

This is a big question – if you have read this section and our other references to critical thinking in the chapters about reading and writing, then you have made a good start. But there's more you can do.

What to do	How to do this
Find out more about critical thinking	Many universities or departments have courses that teach more about critical thinking. Your department may make all students take one. Even if they don't, there may be seminars or workshops you can go to in your department, in the library, or in the self-access centre. Ask at the International Student Office or in your department.
Think about your past success	Make a list of things that you have done that have made you a successful student in the past. For each one, decide how useful it will be in a learning situation based on critical thinking.
Find out how to make changes	Talk to other students from your country who have studied in the university you are going to. Learn from their mistakes! Ask them about critical thinking. Find out what problems they had and how they got better at thinking critically. If you have a mentor, ask them about critical thinking.
Get help from your lecturers	This is especially important when they set up assignments or talk about exams. Tell them if you don't understand what they are asking you to do. Ask to see examples of other students' assignments so you can see what you have to do. Ask to see how they will mark the assessment so that they can explain how important the parts of your answer are.
Find out how to reference properly and get better at it	Go to any available workshops on referencing and using other people's ideas. Get help from your department or the self-access centre in the university. If you have problems or are not sure about referencing, make an appointment with your lecturer or an academic counsellor and take your writing with you.

Academic issues: summary

Many of the academic issues touched on in this quiz are dealt with in more depth in other chapters in the book. Be aware that the university culture may be different from what you have experienced before, and it is fine to ask about your responsibilities as a student and what is expected of you. You will need to be proactive – if you sense a problem, do something about it and talk to someone or a range of people – a fellow student, advisors in the university's self-access centre, academic advisors, or your lecturers – so that you understand the issue before taking action.

Money

Most students face money worries from time to time. Being an international student is extremely expensive – your course fees are higher than for local students, you may not be able to get a study grant or a student loan, you have to pay for regular flights and you may be on a visa that does not let you take a job. Money worries cause stress and anxiety. This section will help you work out a budget plan and give some ideas of ways to raise money while you are studying.

Three case studies

Read these three case studies and make sure you don't make the same mistakes.

Cindy, 23 (from Taiwan): I planned the academic part of my studies in Montreal really carefully – but I guess I never thought about money. My parents had made all my financial decisions for me. Well, anyway, I arrived in Canada with a large amount of cash in Taiwanese dollars that was supposed to last me for the whole semester. I changed a bit at the change office down the road from my department and just hid the rest of it in my flat. About three weeks before the end of the semester, we got broken into and we got home to find the whole flat turned upside down and my money was gone. By then, there wasn't much left – it could have been much worse. I went straight into town and put everything I had in my wallet into a bank account – it was really easy. There was even someone there who spoke Chinese.

Kenshiro, 21 (from Japan): My parents paid for my studies in Australia so I arrived with enough in my bank account for living expenses for a whole year. I had never had that much money before, so it went to my head. I bought lots of stuff when I arrived – things I was used to in Japan. A Nissan Skyline, a stereo and a new laptop. Of course it was stupid. I got into debt, had to sell the car and live off nothing but rice for months. In my second year, I learnt to budget.

Hamed, 23 (from Saudi Arabia): In my culture, you lose face if you say you can't afford to go out with your friends because you have no money, so I went out a lot with people at my university ... and ran out of money. I couldn't believe how much I spent and I don't even drink! I learnt that it is okay to say 'no, sorry, got no money,' and suggest an evening in playing cards and telling stories instead of hitting the town.

Work out your budget

Use this plan to help you work out how much money you've got to live off each week. Fill in the amounts and work out **total a** and **total b**.

Income (write down all your income for the semester)		Spending (write down all your predictable spending for the semester)	
Item	Amount	Item	Amount
Study grant		Course fees	
Scholarship		Exam fees	
Savings		Union fees	
Money from other sources (e.g. family)		Health insurance (essential for international students)	
Wages		Accommodation (rent etc.)	
Other		Other	
total a =		total b =	

Now, work this out.

   total a - total b = **c** _____ (This is the amount of money you have for living expenses for the semester.)

   Next, work out how much you have to spend each week.

   Let **x** = number of weeks in the semester. (e.g. 14) + the number of weeks' holiday (e.g. inter-semester break = 2).

   c / x = **y** _____ (This is the amount of money you have for living expenses per week.)

   These are some of the things you will need to buy with **y:**

- bills – power, phone, etc.
- food
- transport
- clothes
- going out
- books
- library fines
- other.

Keeping track of your expenses   TIP

It is easy to spend more than you can afford, especially in another country where the currency is different and you may not know where to get the best prices for products and services. There are many free 'expense trackers'. These apps allow you to type in what you spend and at the end of the month show you how much the total is and what you spent it on. They can also warn you if you spend too much.

Ways to save money as a student

Here are some strategies for cutting your expenses. Read them through and tick the ones you already use:

- Write down everything you spend in a notebook or an online expense tracker (see above).
- Share a flat rather than renting one for yourself.
- Reduce transport costs by living close to the university.
- Take advantage of 'student specials' at the cinema, pubs, hairdresser's, etc.
- Cook your own food rather than buying takeaways.
- Buy second-hand books and clothes.
- Buy pre-paid phone cards for international calls or use voice or video chatting on your phone or computer.
- Share the cost of study books between friends.

A treasure hunt: find the best deals in your new city

People who are new to a city or country often don't know where to find the best deals. In the orientation week when you start your course, businesses in the city will advertise to new students, but it's a good idea to spend a day or so finding out ways of living cheaply in your new city.

Find these things in the city you have chosen to study in:

1 The name of a cinema that has 'student nights': _____ which night: _____
2 The location of a market that sells cheap food and clothes: _____ which day:_____
3 The name of a suburb that is close to university but has cheap rent:_____
4 The place where students advertise textbooks they want to sell: _____
5 A name of a second-hand bookstore: _____
6 The address of a website where you can buy second-hand furniture (e.g. ebay. com): ____
7 The name and location of a second-hand bike shop: _____ where: _____
8 The name of a pre-paid international phone card: _____ and where you can get it: _____
9 A shop that sells discount bus passes for students: _____
10 A hairdresser's that does cheap haircuts for students: _____

Ways to earn money while you are studying

Check the terms of your visa. You may be able to take a part-time job while you are studying. Some visas allow you to work for a limited number of hours per week e.g. up to ten hours per week. The first place to try is the Student Union. They may have a noticeboard where companies place advertisements when they have jobs that students could do.

Here are some ways that international students earned money while at university. They may give you some ideas of how you could earn money while you are studying. Decide which ones you could do on your visa. Then rank them in terms of best to worst for you.

- **Use your area of study**: I was majoring in computer programming and was desperate for some money. I used to go to a gym and got talking to the manager one day. He needed a website – so I designed one for him. It was pretty simple and looked good on my CV.
- **Use your talent**: Although I studied drama, I did a lot of music at university. I formed a small band and we used to play at university parties – student balls, graduation parties, etc. We used to play in a pizza restaurant and that led to some weddings. It was well-paid and easy work, and we could do it whenever we wanted.
- **Use your department**: I was studying chemistry and saw an advert for lab assistants. I worked every evening for two hours just clearing up and getting things ready for the next day's classes. I then became a lab assistant helping first-year students doing experiments.
- **Use your first language**: I got a job teaching my language to kids studying for their high school exams. I had never taught before, but that didn't seem to matter. I also got work translating documents for schools.
- **Use your ethnicity**: I am Japanese and got work easily in a Japanese restaurant. The pay was not good, but I was feeling a bit homesick so it helped me meet some Japanese people.

- **Use your study skills**: In my third year, I started running workshops in the Language Learning Centre for other international students starting their studies. I also got paid to be a student mentor for new students.
- **Use your holidays**: Rather than go home in the holidays, I used to go and live on a farm and pick fruit. I made a bit of money and they gave you accommodation too so I didn't spend too much.
- **Use your library skills**: I never thought I'd become a librarian, but I saw an advert and applied. I met lots of people and got to know the university library very well.
- **Take part in an experiment**: My lecturer was looking for participants in a psychology experiment. It was quite interesting and well paid. Easy money. I don't think I'd do medical experiments, though.

Now, look back at the list and decide which you could fit in around your study and which would take too much time.

Balancing work and study

The problem with getting a job is that it can take up too much valuable study time. However, it might be fun, you will definitely meet people, it could be a good break from study and it may help you fit in with life in another country. If you do take a part-time job, you might decide to organize your working hours so that you work fewer hours around exam times or times when you have lots of assignments to hand in.

Grants, scholarships, loans and other sources of funding

Often students don't know about funding that they may be able to get. In some cultures, it is embarrassing to ask for extra funding. As a student, it is always better to ask than go short.

Here are seven places to look for extra funding. Once again, tick any that you may be able to apply for.

1. An extra grant

If you already have a grant from a government or some other source, go back to them. Explain that you need more money to finish your studies, explain what has happened (e.g. your housing costs have gone up) and ask if they can give you more help.

2. Special grants

You may be doing a special subject that needs expensive equipment and you may be eligible for a grant for that equipment.

3. Photocopying or textbook allowance

Some departments offer help with photocopying costs and/or the cost of buying course materials. You may need to apply for this, so make sure you find out about it.

4. A scholarship

Some scholarships are awarded by a department or faculty and given to the students who get the best marks across the year, but you may be able to apply for others. Have a look on your university website or ask your department secretary.

5. A research grant

If you are doing research, you may be able to apply for a grant to cover the cost of hiring a research assistant or for some other expense e.g. translation costs. Ask your supervisor.

6. Hardship grants

Often student unions have 'hardship grants' – this is money they keep for emergencies. For example, if you have to spend a lot of money to find new accommodation and find you don't have enough money to buy food, you should ask your student organization. They may be able to help.

7. A bank loan

Most banks offer overdrafts with low interest rates for students. You may be able to apply. It's worth checking the terms and conditions.

Summary

See Chapter 3 for more advice on how to apply for a scholarship.

Running out of money is a serious concern for many international students, but you can reduce stress by taking action:

1 Make a budget plan
2 Minimize your expenses
3 Earn some money
4 Apply for all the help you can get

Also remember – you can get help on budgeting from university counsellors. Universities are very worried about people (especially international students) not finishing their studies, so it is definitely a good idea to talk to financial counsellors about money problems.

Conclusion

As a student, especially an international student, you can expect to have to deal with some of the problems mentioned in this chapter (and maybe some different ones). We have tried to show some creative solutions to these problems and encourage you to be proactive. We have also tried to encourage you to find someone to listen to your problem. Whatever your problem, if you talk to someone about it, it will feel more manageable and you can reduce your anxiety. There are lots of people you can talk to at university about study, money or personal problems – your friends, the international student advisor, learning centre advisors, university counsellors, your supervisor or your lecturer, so don't suffer in silence.

Life beyond the Classroom

So far this book has been mainly about your studies. This final chapter is about other things you need to know when you start university, especially when you study abroad. This chapter discusses aspects of university culture, including student–lecturer roles and expectations, activities, student organizations and clubs. There are also suggestions for contacting other students and making new friends.

This chapter answers the following questions:

- What's different about university culture?
- How do students get to know one another?
- How can students meet people outside the university?

University culture: what's different?

This section starts by talking about culture in general. We then discuss ways that universities are different from other places of study, such as schools. In this section you will find answers to these questions:

- What is culture?
- How is a university culture different from a school culture?
- How might English-language universities differ from universities in your country?

In the English-speaking world, universities have many traditions which are the same from one country to another. However, detailed answers to the questions listed above change from one university to another and even from one part of the university to another. For example, lectures and tutorials could have different forms in science, architecture, English literature or language, law, medicine and so on. In one department students may take plenty of notes during lectures, while in another the lecturer might give full notes at the end. In one department the custom may be that students prepare for tutorials, but in another the discussion topic might not be given until the tutorial starts.

What is culture?

We talk about belonging to a particular culture, but what does the word mean? 'Culture' can refer to any of these:

- old buildings which tourists love to photograph
- people dancing in traditional clothes
- religious beliefs that go back hundreds of years
- books and music that belong to particular language groups.

One meaning of 'culture' is a group of people with the same language, beliefs and history, but the word can also mean a group of people who belong together in some way. That second meaning is the one we use in this chapter. Let's start by thinking of smaller cultural groups that you know already. How many of these cultural groups do you feel you belong to:

- people who like the same type of music
- speakers of your language or your dialect
- people who play the same sport as you?

When you are with these people you act like them in various ways, such as:

- the way you talk to one another
- the jokes you enjoy
- the things you do in your spare time.

When we talk about the culture of the university, we mean the things that make universities different from other places of learning such as schools and from other groups of people such as colleagues at a place of work.

Comparing school and university cultures

Let's start by comparing the cultures of universities and high schools. Here are some differences you will find.

Differences	High school	University
Students' independence	School responsible for students Teachers supervise activities Attendance noted Teachers guide homework	Students independent Students organize clubs Attendance not noted Students plan own assignments
Teaching styles	Vary from class to class	Lectures, tutorials, labs, etc.
Assignments	Shorter	Longer
Students' ages	Similar ages in one class	All ages in one class

Let's see what some of these differences mean in detail.

Teachers and students

At high school teachers notice if students are late to class or absent and want to know a reason. In fact, they often take attendance, particularly in junior classes. If you are absent at university you will probably not be missed in the big first-year classes. However, if you are on a student visa, regular attendance may be required for your visa status. Lecturers might notice people walking in late, but usually they don't say anything. There are only a few times when the lecturer might say something about students' behaviour. Probably the most frequent one is asking students to turn off their cell phones, especially after one has rung in the middle of a lecture. Another time is if some students talk noisily during the lecture. Otherwise students are in charge of their own behaviour and will sometimes ask other students to keep quiet.

Teaching styles

In high school there are great differences in the way teachers teach, but generally they take time to check if students have understood by asking questions. At university the lecturers do their best to make new ideas clear, but they don't say the same thing over and over until everyone understands.

Assignments

In high school you had homework after every class and this may or may not have counted towards your end-of-year results. In contrast, in most universities today every assignment you do counts towards your final results. That is why it is important to have a medical certificate if you are ill and miss an assignment, or have to hand work in late. Also, it is important to follow the deadlines of all the assignments.

Outside class

High school teachers are interested in out-of-class activities like sports and drama. At university, once you walk out of the lecture or tutorial, your time is your own. You can go to the library and study, you can go to the cafeteria and meet friends, or you can lie on the grass and go to sleep. You have freedom to choose what you do outside the classroom.

The age of students

School students are usually about the same age in each class, but at university you will notice that students are of all ages. Many students start a degree or return to university later in life.

One student's story

As well as differences between school and university, there are differences between university cultures from one country to another. The student who tells the story below found many differences between studying in his own country (Holland) and studying in Syria. After each part of his story, there is a chance for you to make your own comparison. For those who study in 'Western' English-speaking countries, we give some information about practices at universities in those countries, and then there is a space for you to think about a system you are accustomed to.

1 Some students were an hour early to get a seat close to the lecturer. When I came in people looked surprised. Kindly they made room for me at one of the tables close to the lecturer's stand.

'Western' university	Your school or university
Students arrive at the last minute. They sit wherever they want.	

2 When the lecturer came in everybody got up and greeted him.

'Western' university	Your school or university
Nobody stands for the lecturer. The lecturer might say 'Good morning', but students don't usually answer.	

3 Once the lecturer started his lecture, he never stopped. There was no introduction about what was going to be covered, no summary of what the previous lecture had been about. He mainly told in his own words what could be found in the coursebook.

'Western' university	Your school or university
Lecturers say at the beginning what they will be talking about. They usually pause from time to time. The lecture covers more than just the textbook.	

4 Some students asked questions about the lecturer's opinion about a certain topic, something that wouldn't happen often in my country where the lecturer is usually expected to be objective and not share his personal opinions too much, at least not in lectures. Some of the questions were obviously intended to allow the lecturer to show off his/her vast knowledge of the topic.

'Western' university	Your school or university
Students usually ask about opinions in tutorials, not in lectures. If students do ask questions it is because they really want an answer.	

5 Occasionally a student would get up and start what seemed like a short presentation on the topic, almost repeating what the lecturer had just said.

'Western' university	Your school or university
Only lecturers stand at the front and talk. Students present their ideas in seminars, not in lectures.	

6 No one ever disagreed with the lecturer, which also was quite different from what I was used to.

'Western' university	Your school or university
People don't usually disagree with the lecturer in the middle of a lecture, but they might have a discussion later in the tutorial or even one to one.	

7 I found out that many students used the lectures to avoid having to read the book, as a sort of human audio cassette. Memorization was very important, and some students remembered whole pages of text.

'Western' university	Your school or university
Students need to read the textbook as well as attend lectures. Students would find it very difficult to learn pages of the textbook by heart.	

Students talk about their own countries

Readers from different countries will recognize some things about this student's story, but they will also notice differences. Here are questions and answers from students of many nationalities who were asked about the culture of their countries. Thinking about your own culture will help prepare you for similarities and differences.

1 What do people think about teachers in your country?
  Teachers are important people in society.
  Teachers know the answers to all students' questions.
  The job of a teacher is to make students learn.
2 In your country, how do students pass their courses?
  They go to all the classes.
  They learn information by heart.
  They have one examination at the end of the year.
3 What happens during lectures?
  The lecturer give students all the information about the subject.
  Lecturers speak slowly like a dictation.
  Students write down everything the lecturer says.
4 Apart from lectures, what do students learn from?
  One textbook has everything for each course.
  The lecturer hands out notes for students to learn from.
  We copy the notes of the best students in the class.
  We can't borrow library books. We take notes from them in the library.

Comparisons with 'Western' universities

Now let's make more comparisons between your answers and answers you could hear if you asked the same questions about English-speaking universities.

What do people think about teachers?

Teachers in English-speaking universities are usually called professors, lecturers, or teaching assistants, but students often call them by their first names. In society they are usually seen as no better or worse than anyone else. Western students certainly do not believe that university lecturers know all the answers.

We asked some university staff and students to say what they thought the teacher's role was. Here are their answers, starting with the staff:

Lecturer 1: When I started out I was a teaching assistant and then I thought my job was to make clear what the lecturers had said in their lectures. Then when I became a lecturer myself I thought it was really for me to make myself clear the first time without leaving it to teaching assistants later in the week.

Lecturer 2: My work is making the subject interesting for the people who want to learn. My sister's a secondary school teacher, and she says her work includes making people learn, but I think at university it's more up to the students. They have paid their fees. If they want to learn that's good, and I'm there to help them, but if they fall asleep in class I never wake them up.

This is what two students said:

Student 1: Our teaching assistants say they are there to teach us how to find answers to questions ourselves.

Student 2: I come to a lecture for a purpose. I want to learn more about that topic. It all depends on what I have learned before and where I'm going in the future. The lecturer doesn't know what subjects I'll be specializing in next year and doesn't have to. I see him/ her as someone who can guide me to the information that I need.

How do students pass their courses?

In English-speaking universities attending lectures every week and doing the final examination is not enough. You must also do assignments, whatever form they take. There will usually be in-class tests as well. In general, you need to show that you understand the subjects and, on some professional courses, that you can apply that understanding. In other words, you can use your knowledge in a new situation.

Lecturers introduce a subject and then tell students where to find more information by themselves. Students take notes but don't write down everything that is said.

What happens during lectures?

See Chapter 5 for information about what happens during lectures.

What do students learn from?

Students learn in various ways. They go to the library to find information, use the internet and borrow resources to take home and study further. As well as the lectures and assignments that we have already talked about, they go to tutorials where they learn in small groups. Out-of-class discussions with other students are also an important part of learning.

The university culture is not only about studying. As you will see in this next section, making friends is one important way of starting to feel at home in a new place.

Friends

Meeting people can seem scary at first, but remember it's the same for everyone. You do need to get out of the library, though, and look for opportunities to find people with similar interests. The good thing is that with email, chat software and free internet calls, although you may be a long way from home, you can still communicate with old friends all day and all night so you do not need to feel alone.

A university can seem a very unfriendly place. Students hurry along with their books and papers, looking busy, or sit for hours talking to their friends. Although it is easy to think that everyone else is happy and in groups, that may not be the case. The students you see hurrying to their lectures or tutorials or the library could be feeling quite lonely.

Even students who study in their own country can feel very lonely in their first few weeks at university. They too ask questions like these:

- Will I be able to make friends?
- Do people talk to strangers at university?

The answer to these questions is 'yes', but making real friends can take time. The good thing is that everyone else will be keen to form friendships as well, especially in your first term. Below are some great ways to meet people and make friends at your new university. Read the following suggestions for some ideas. Tick three that you will try.

Ways to make friends

1. Move into shared accommodation

University halls are great places to meet people, and they are often the easiest accommodation option for international students new to a city. If you can't face living with so many other people, move into a flat with three or four others.

2. Form a study group with other students on your course

Meet for coffees and a chat about lectures or assignments and gossip about your lecturers.

3. Start a language exchange

A language exchange is when you meet someone who speaks the language you want to learn and is learning the language that you speak. You speak for half the time in your language and half the time in their language. There may be a language exchange set up in your university somewhere – the International Student Office will know about it. If not, set one up for yourself. Find the modern languages department in your university and put a notice up with your contact details, or try online.

4. Join a university society

Universities have societies (clubs) for all interests you can imagine. Hill-walking, politics, debating, drinking, engineering, computer gaming, religion, chess, chamber music, the environment, drama, dancing, poetry, etc. To join a society, look for contact details on a poster. Often societies try to get new members in orientation week, so look out for a society that you are interested in. Even if you are not interested, you could go along anyway – you might meet some different people.

5. Join an orchestra or a sports team

If you are good (or even just okay) at something like music or sports, join a group either at university or in the city.

6. Get a part-time job

Earn money and meet people at the same time. Have a look in the Student Union for advertisements from companies who need students to work for them.

7. Become a class rep

A class rep (short for 'representative') is the person in each class who goes to meetings in the department and brings up problems from each class. It is a great way into all parts of university life. You need to get elected, but that is usually easy as most students are happy for someone else to be class rep. First, you introduce yourself to the class and tell everyone that if they have any problems they should tell you. You then get emails from people in your class who want answers to their questions. Then you go to a meeting with the department and finally pass on the answers to your class. Sometimes class reps have to organize the class party too. You might even find out that your department will subsidize the food!

8. Look out for events for international students

Check out the noticeboard in the International Student Office for news of any events organized for international students. It's a great way to meet people in exactly the same situation as you.

Culture and politeness

Rules of politeness differ from one culture to another. Listen to conversations around the university and think about these questions:

1 In a conversation between students, which is more common?
   - People wait a few seconds between speakers.
   - Everyone speaks quickly one after the other.
2 When students want to refuse something, which is more common?
   - They say 'no thank you' clearly.
   - They find an excuse for saying 'no'.
3 In groups of students, who usually speaks first?
   - The older person or the younger person?
   - Males or females?
   - The senior student or the junior student?

These are just a few examples; there are no fixed ways of behaving. When you are studying with people from many different countries you will become accustomed to many different ways of doing things and many different ways of speaking.

Friends and spending money

You will find big differences in how much money students can spend on food and entertainment. If someone says 'No thanks' when you ask them to join your friends for a meal, maybe they are worried about how much it will cost. If you are the one who is being careful with your money then you could suggest other activities such as:

- going to the beach to go swimming or surfing
- going for a walk away from the city
- having a picnic
- visiting a museum
- meeting in a coffee shop.

Finally, one way to start talking is to meet the person who has been voted as the class representative (class rep for short). Speak to the rep if you have problems with the course, and this person can then talk to the staff for all the students in the class. For example, here are the things that one group of class reps mentioned at a meeting with staff.

1 Does this class have to be at that time of day? We would rather have a different time.
2 We have a problem finding the set books in the library.
3 Can we have a different classroom? That one's not comfortable.

Finally, don't keep only to the people who are like you. Think of all the groups you could be meeting:

- science students, arts students, architecture students, etc.
- international students, local students
- mature students who are older than you
- first-, second-, third-year students.

In your lectures and tutorials you will meet all of these students in your courses or in other parts of university life.

Life outside university

So far we have discussed life inside the university. To finish this chapter and book we talk about non-university life. Although some people spend their whole lives with other students, others who have made an effort to join the wider community say they have found fresh interests and people there.

Finding somewhere to live

You have a number of choices for accommodation. Here are five ideas.

1. Dormitory (dorm)

A dormitory (dorm) is often run by the university you attend. It is often located on campus. Sometimes undergraduate students are required to live in the dorm for the first year so that they can be immersed in the university environment. In a dorm each student has a bedroom, but shares the kitchen and bathroom with a number of others. If students want to, they can talk with one another, but if they prefer to be alone that is easy too. The advantages of living in the dorm include easy access to your classrooms, campus facilities and activities. Usually, you will need to contact the Housing Office at the university so that they can make an arrangement for you before you arrive on campus.

2. Homestays

A homestay means living with a family. People choose a homestay in an English-speaking country if they want to use English every day and improve their speaking and listening or if they want to meet local families. Being in a homestay means sharing the house with at least one adult and sometimes children as well. Homestay students eat with the family and sometimes share in the household tasks. The arrangements are usually made by a company which is part of the university or by an agent in your own country. Ask the International Student Office at your university if you are interested.

Homestays can work very well, as shown by these comments from two students:

Student 1: To me it was an excellent way to see how people in that country lived. I was lucky because they were very kind to me and took me around and showed me places, especially in the first few weeks when I didn't know anyone yet.

Student 2: It really helped me to improve my English! In the beginning I felt quite shy and it was easier to talk to my homestay family than to strangers. Also, I learned a lot of English that I hadn't heard before, like local expressions etc.

The host families have their opinions too.

Example 1: We really enjoyed the Japanese student who stayed with us. She was willing to join in our family life and we often invited her to go out with us at the weekends.

Occasionally, though, the student and family do not seem to enjoy the arrangement. Here is a comment from the same host mother.

Example 2: Unfortunately the last student we had shut herself in her room all the time except for meals. She wouldn't join in activities with us and she didn't seem to have any student friends either. We felt she would have been better mixing with other people.

Think about a homestay. If you would rather spend your time alone studying, then you can find a cheaper arrangement. It may not be too difficult to change the arrangement if you are not happy, but you should talk about whether this is possible before you sign on.

3. Hostels

In a hostel you have your own bedroom, but someone else prepares your meals and these are served at fixed times. Hostels are usually more expensive, but if they are close to the university you will save money on public transport. The cost of the hostel usually includes all your meals, or perhaps just breakfast and the evening meal. You may be able to cut down the cost by doing extra duties such as cleaning or answering the telephone at fixed times. Because hostels are quite popular, you would probably need to book your place before arriving in the country.

4. Sharing a flat or apartment

The house may be an old one divided into flats or a building specially built for flats. Flats are owned by landlords, and they like a regular arrangement for paying, such as having automatic payments from your bank account to theirs.

Finding other students to share a flat with is difficult when you have just arrived, but you will probably find a few other students to share with before long. One way of doing this is by looking at the noticeboard in the Students Union building. You can also ask the International Student Office of your university for information on how to find a flat or a roommate.

Once you have found people to share a flat with, the arrangements vary enormously. Here are some questions that students usually talk about beforehand:

- Do we cook meals together or separately?
- If we prepare meals together, do we take turns?
- Do people with bigger rooms pay more rent than others?
- How do we divide the housework, such as cleaning and taking the trash out?
- Does the landlord want the rent together or separately?
- If the landlord wants the rent together, who is responsible for collecting it?

5. Living alone

To live alone means that you have enough money to rent your own flat, apartment, or house. This can, of course, be more expensive than sharing a flat with others, but it suits people who have enough money and who are very independent. The way to find a flat is to look in one of these places:

- newspaper
- Students Union noticeboard
- real estate agent's office or website.

Travelling to university

When you think about where to live, at the same time you could think about how you will get from your living place to the university. Here are some questions to help you to decide.

- Is there good, frequent transport at all hours?
- How expensive is transport?
- Do students have special rates?
- Is it easy to walk to the university?
- What about walking around the streets at night?

Some students in English-speaking countries buy their own cars. Of course, whether you choose to do this depends on a number of things, including parking. Does the university have free student car parks? A car is expensive to run. Check the price of petrol and repairs before you buy your own car. A cheap old car may not be cheap if you are always paying for repairs because in most English-speaking countries the people who repair cars have quite a good income.

Joining the wider community

In your own country you were part of many groups of people. First there was your family and then there were your school friends. You were probably also part of wider groups that covered all age groups. Here are some groups you could be interested in outside the university.

Sports and hobbies

If you have a sport or hobby interest that could help you be part of the wider community, look in the newspaper, especially smaller local newspapers, to find out where these groups meet. Music and chess groups, to name just two, are part of most local communities.

Voluntary groups

In every community there are groups of people who offer their time free to others. One overseas student found herself pouring cups of tea one morning a week for people with disabilities. Through that work she came to know many of the other volunteers.

Places of worship

If you usually attend a mosque, temple, synagogue or church then have a look in the paper to see advertisements for these. As well as being places where you can continue with your faith, these places could have families who are very welcoming to overseas students. Here is what one student found.

> At home I always went to the … once a week. When I got to … I went to the nearest … but I saw that it was full of other international students. I didn't want that. I wanted to meet local people. Anyway, I asked a few people and they said, 'You should go to ….' It was only one

bus ride away so I went there and found some friendly people. Especially people with little children were good to me. I played with the children and they didn't mind about my English.

Be like this student. If at first you don't find the right place, try again.

Conclusion

In this chapter we have tried to show a picture of university life outside the classroom, and we have given you some examples from students' experiences. If you go straight from school in your own country to university somewhere else, then of course there will be many, many unusual things to find out about. As we have seen, there is no short way of saying exactly how one university will seem to you. We hope that this chapter has been a help to you in finding out about differences and being ready for them. There may be difficulties, but there is also support for you. The most common answer to what makes the difference between feeling lonely and feeling happy is 'communication'.

A Mini-Dictionary of University Words

Here is a list of words that have been used in this book, with their meanings. When you first arrive at a new university you will hear many new words and phrases. Some of them refer to people, some to places and some to parts of your courses. The terms in the following list are particularly common in universities that follow the British tradition. You will find differences in places where they use American terms.

Word	Meaning
Active listening	Thinking about what the lecturer is saying rather than just copying everything down.
Additional or recommended reading	Extra books and articles suggested by the lecturer for your course reading.
Aegrotat pass	An examination pass for someone who is too ill to take the examination. Aegrotat passes may be given to students who have done well through the rest of the course.
Assessment	The way students' work is measured (assignments, tests, examinations).
Assignments	Students' essays, projects, etc. which count towards the course grade.
Attachment	A file that comes with an email.
Body of the lecture	The main part of the lecture, between the introduction and the conclusion.
Boolean operators	Words you can use to make your internet search more specific.
Brainstorming	Thinking of many ideas for a piece of writing.
Breaks (mid- or inter-semester breaks)	The weeks when there are no lectures.
Calendar	The book that lists all official university information.

Word	Meaning *(Continued)*
Campus	All the university buildings and grounds.
Catalogue, online catalogue	A list of all the books in the library.
CEO (chief executive officer)	The leader of a university or polytechnic. (Most universities use the term 'vice chancellor'.)
Certified copy	A signed piece of paper which says the paper is a true copy of the original.
Chaplaincy	The people who are interested in students' spiritual life.
Conditional admission	Admission to a programme with some additional requirements students need to meet during a certain period of time.
Conjoint degree	A degree from two different university faculties. It takes longer than one degree, but not as long as two.
Co-requisites	Two different courses which must be taken at the same time are called co-requisites.
Counsellors	Staff who listen to students' problems.
Course reader	Articles and/or chapters on the topic, photocopied and bound together for students on a course.
Credit	Points towards a degree for a course you have taken at another university.
Criteria (singular: criterion)	What you need before you can do something else e.g. 'There are three criteria for getting on to this course.'
Database	A collection of information, usually on a computer.
Dean	The head of the faculty.
Degree	A BSc, a BA, a BCom, etc.
Degree programme	All the courses you take to make up your degree.
Department	One part of the university e.g. the history department.
Deputy vice-chancellor	The person who works with the vice-chancellor but at a slightly lower level.
Diagnostic test	A test to tell students what they are good and not so good at.
Draft	A copy you write of an assignment or an article before the final copy.
Edited book	A book with chapters from more than one author.
E-journals	Electronic journals that you can find and read on a computer.

Word	Meaning *(Continued)*
Eligible	Able to do something e.g. eligible for a course.
Emoticon	Little face-pictures like these: ☺ or ;-).
Exchange programme	Students from two countries who do some study in each other's country.
Exemptions / exempt	Permission not to take a compulsory subject. If you know a language very well you may be exempt from the first-year course.
Facilities	Places (libraries, computer rooms) and things (photocopiers) that students can use.
Faculty	A large part of a university where similar types of subject are taught. A faculty is a larger grouping than a department.
Foundation programme	A course for students who are not yet ready to enter the university.
GPA	The marks you have already got for your previous study.
Graduation ceremony	The time when you receive your degree.
Handouts	Pages of information used in a course.
Harassment	Harassment is unacceptable behaviour between university staff and students. Sexual harassment is a serious offence. If you suffer from harassment contact your university counsellor.
HOD	Head of department.
IELTS	International English Language Testing System.
Index	An alphabetical list of words and their pages at the end of a book.
International baccalaureate	A school leaving examination which is recognized all over the world.
International Student Office	The place where staff look after overseas students.
Intonation	The way a speaker's voice rises and falls to change the meaning.
Justice of the Peace	A person who is legally allowed to sign documents.
Keyword	A word you use on a computer to search for the topic you want.

Word	Meaning *(Continued)*
Language exchange	You teach your language; the other student teaches you his/her language.
Learning journals	A book where you write about your studies.
Lecturing styles	Differences in the way individual lecturers speak in public.
Literature	1. The novels, plays, poems, etc. of a country or language. 2. Books and articles on a particular academic subject.
Mailing list	A list that people subscribe to where they exchange messages with anyone on the list, usually about a certain topic.
Major	A main subject.
Mentor	A mentor is an experienced student who is paired with a new student to help them with aspects of study and university life.
Minor	A subject studied for only one or two years.
Moderated discussion list	A computer address list where messages are first read by one or more people before they are sent to everyone on the list.
Needs analysis	A way of finding out what your weaknesses are and what you need to improve first.
Non-verbal information	Everything you find out about a message apart from the words (e.g. the speaker's hand movements).
Orientation day	The time at the beginning of the year when students are welcomed to the university.
PhD	The highest degree at a university.
Portfolio	A collection of work in one subject as part of the course assessment e.g. an art portfolio.
Predict	Work out what is coming next when listening to a lecture or when reading
Prefix	The first part of a word which has a meaning of its own e.g. pre-departure.
Prerequisites	Courses you must study before you can enrol on a course or programme.
Prescribed / required reading, reading list	Books and articles that you must read for your course.
Proficiency	Being good at something.

Word	Meaning *(Continued)*
Provisional entrance	Permission to start university study without the right qualifications. Students with provisional entrance who do well continue to study at the university.
Reference books	Books which students may read in the library but not take away.
References	A list of everything read and used in a book, article or essay.
Research article	A piece of writing in a journal about some original work.
Research assistant	Someone employed in a department to help staff and senior students with their research.
Scholarship	Money to help students with their study.
Semesters	The two or three parts of the university year.
Seminars	Times when students present their work orally.
Short-loan collection	Books which may be borrowed for a short time only.
Spellchecker	A function of a computer program that checks your documents for spelling and grammar mistakes.
State-of-the-art or review articles	An article which sums up what other people have written on a topic.
Study break	Time without lectures when students prepare for examinations.
Supervisor	The lecturer who guides you as you write your thesis or dissertation.
Style	The way one person does something which may be different from other people's styles. Lecturers have different styles (ways of speaking).
Teaching assistants (TAs)	(Mostly postgraduate) students who teach (part of) a course.
Thesaurus	A book which lists words of similar meaning.
Thesis	Original work by one student for a postgraduate degree.
Thread	Messages about one topic on a discussion board.
Tips	Suggestions or ideas for doing something better.
TOEFL	Test of English as a Foreign Language.
Truncate	To shorten e.g. very long emails may be truncated.

Word	Meaning *(Continued)*
Tutors	People who organize tutorials (see below).
Tutorials	Times when small groups of students and their tutor talk about the course content.
(Under)graduate advisor	Someone who helps students plan their first degree.
Undergraduates	Students who have not yet received a diploma or a degree.
Vice-chancellor	The leader (or 'head') of a university.
Voicemail	A telephone answering machine. You can leave a message on someone's voicemail.

Answer Key

Chapter 2: How to Become a Better Language Learner

What kind of learner are you?

To find out your total score:

1 Take your answers to questions A–H and add up the total: _____

2 Take your answers to questions I–P but reverse the points by counting 1 point if you scored 3 and 3 points if you scored 1. For 0 and 2 you can keep the same score. _____

3 Now add up the total and look up your score below. _____

0–12 **Not sure?**	Your score does not mean you are not a good language learner. Perhaps this is the first time you have thought about how you learn English. It is good to find out more about your preferences as this will help you choose the most efficient way for you. Read this chapter carefully and next time you study English, take some time to think about how you do it.
13–24 **Risk-taker**	You like to take risks in learning English and you have lots of confidence. Probably your speaking skills will develop quite quickly. But do also pay attention to accuracy, both in speaking and in writing.
25–36 **All-round**	You like to know the rules of English and be accurate, but you are not afraid to speak and practise fluency. This is a good overall approach as long as you make sure to use different approaches at different times.
37–48 **Careful learner**	You think it is important to speak English with as few errors as possible. You don't like to make mistakes or take too many risks when using the language. You will probably become quite accurate in your English, but don't forget that language is a skill that needs to become automatic and that you can use without thinking. Maybe you can set aside some time to practise free speaking, or try writing a text under time pressure.

Chapter 4: Academic and Technical Vocabulary

Types of vocabulary

Type	Examples
Everyday vocabulary	three / the / other / is / has / as / years
Non-technical academic vocabulary	review / outline / research / interpret
Technical subject specific vocabulary	integrative motivation / integrativeness / instrumental motivation

Formal and informal language

A. The more academic words in the list are the following:

consider
summarize
investigate
establish
describe
minute.

B. Of the different words shown, kill is the least emotive, and butchered the most.
In order, from less to more emotive:

growth / big increase / explosion
successful outcome / huge success / victory
good / great / fantastic
embarrassed / insulted / trashed

C. Here are some possible ways to rewrite the sentences in a more academic way:

Original: The argument is over the top.
Revision: The argument is made too strongly.
Original: That is nonsense.
Revision: These findings do not appear to be supported by the evidence.
Original: The great article.
Revision: The well-written article.
Original: I don't like this.
Revision: My preference would be ….
Original: This is a bad research project.
Revision: This study does not seem have been constructed carefully because ….

Work out the meanings of new words

Prefix	English meaning	Example
ante- & pre-	= before	pre-war period
anti-	= against	anti-war protestors
auto-	= alone, self	autonomous, autocrat
inter-	= between	interaction = action between people
intra-	= inside	intraregional = within a region
bi-	= two	bicycle
mis-	= wrong	misinterpreting = interpreting the wrong way
mono-	= one	monotone = one tone, i.e. boring

Prefix	English meaning	Example *(Continued)*
multi-	= many	multinational = for many nations
neo-	= new	neo-colonialism = new colonizing
pan-	= all	pan-Pacific = all the Pacific
tele-	= far away	telephone, television

What information does a dictionary give?

1 The pronunciation in IPA (international phonetic alphabet). If you don't know how to read this, have a look in the front of your dictionary.
2 The meaning or definition.
3 An example of how the word is used.
4 The verb can be used both transitively (x accentuates y) or intransitively (x is accentuated by y).
5 We learn that 'accentuate' can be used with both people and things.
6 We can see its frequency.
7 Vn means that the word is a verb that is followed by a noun.
8 = intensify is a synonym of the main word.

What information does a dictionary give? (Part 2)

1 Yes. 'To call a meeting' means to organize a meeting.
2 No.
3 Not really. It is a less harsh word for 'damn', which is more offensive.
4 'Break out' means (among others) 'to escape', in a literal sense. 'To break away' can have the same meaning, but is used in a metaphoric sense.
5 On the first syllable.
6 Shocking.

Using a thesaurus successfully

a. Meaning 7: the means or procedure for doing something (figured out the best *way* to accomplish the task). See the entry 'method' in the thesaurus.
b. The following words have a meaning that could work in this sentence (although you would need to change the words around so that the sentence works):

approach
strategy
system
technique.

c. Notice how the grammar of the sentences has to change:

approach: One of the best approaches to learning new words is using vocabulary cards.
strategy: One of the best strategies for learning new words is using vocabulary cards.

system: One of the best systems for learning new words is vocabulary cards.
technique: One of the best techniques for learning new words is using vocabulary cards.

d. Approach, strategy and technique are all words that are in the Academic Word List so will make the sentence sound more academic.

Approach is closest to the general meaning of way.
Strategy puts more emphasis on a process for success – something you do in order to be successful.
System emphasizes the organizational aspect of making vocabulary cards.
Technique emphasizes the practical aspect of making vocabulary cards.

Using a corpus

1 'Scared of' seems to be the most common.
2 Yes, this is common. Another way of saying this is that to scare is both a transitive and an intransitive verb.
3 This is a difficult one. It seems you can use afraid in the same contexts where you would use scared. But the word afraid is also used more 'lightly', as in this example: 'I'm **afraid** I can't give you a good guide because ...' The meaning here is close to 'I'm sorry'. 'Scared' thus seems to have a more intense meaning.

Checking collocation

The three prepositions are:

1 Of
2 With
3 On.

Chapter 5: Listening to Lectures

The purpose of a lecture

1 **Make sure that students are serious about their studies.** How would going to lectures check seriousness? Some students sit in the back row and check their text messages. Just being in the room doesn't say anything about mental attitudes.
2 **Check attendance.** Some lecturers do pass around the roll during lectures and attendance counts as part of the course. Check how many lectures you can miss before having to do extra work. It is also important to attend classes to maintain your visa status if you study in a foreign country.
3 **Give information that can't be found anywhere else.** The information may be found somewhere else, but more likely it is scattered in several different sources (see 6 below).
4 **Make university learning interesting.** Yes, when the lecturer is a good communicator he or she does make the learning more enjoyable.

5 **Let students ask questions.** Sometimes there are questions in lectures and sometimes these are asked in smaller groups, such as tutorials. This is probably not the main point of the lecture.

6 **Bring together information from many sources.** Yes (see 3 above).

7 **Let students get to know one another.** Lectures are certainly a good time to meet other students, although that is not really their main point.

8 **Present information in a new form from the textbook.** Yes, the material in lectures won't contradict anything in the textbook but it might present it in a different order or with different examples or in different words.

Linear notes

Good points include:

- use of bullet points
- underlining section headings
- examples of each point easy to see – indented
- use of punctuation – ? marks indicate interesting issues raised in lecture
- brackets indicate lecturers' asides – interesting ones!
- use of abbreviations and symbols – e.g. / etc. / celeb. (= celebrity) / $ = money / $$$ = lots of money / v = very / < = less than.
- use of arrows to show logical connection / result.

Seminar on note-taking

Okay. Thank you all for coming. Today our seminar is about good note-taking practice.

At the beginning of last year, I did a small study of the note-taking habits of successful students looking at the techniques they use when taking notes in lectures and then I asked them for their advice to students who wanted to improve their note-taking. I will present some of the findings of this study and then at the end of this presentation, there will be an opportunity for you to talk about the note-taking strategies that you found the most effective.

First of all, let's look at what you should make notes on – I mean the paper – not the topics! Now, lots of students use notebooks for their lecture notes. This is fine but some students find it easier to use a loose-lead notebook – that means one that you can take the pages out of – rather than one with fixed pages. This means that you can take the pages out and put them into a folder with your course notes. Then you can collect notes and course reading for each course in one place, in a separate notebook or section of a notebook – write the name and date of the lecture. Sometimes lecturers give out a handout with the main points from the lectures. You could find it useful to make notes on the handout in the margins – this will help you organize the notes you make. Also, some lecturers put their own notes on the course website after a lecture. You can print these out and put them in your folder next to your notes. The appearance of your notes is really important too because you will need to refer to them later. If you find yourself making doodles or writing notes to your partner on your lecture notes, remember that not only is this manual activity stopping you from concentrating, but it will also be annoying and confusing when you look back at your notes – i.e. when you are using them to revise for an exam.

It is worth losing a bit of speed in order to write legibly – this saves time in the long run. If you find you don't have time to write neatly, then you are probably writing too much. Note only key words, not every word – and think critically about what you write down. If it is not going to be useful later – don't write it! The other thing you can do if you can't keep up is to leave gaps [ ] when the speaker is moving too fast. You can always check with a friend later if you see a gap in your notes.

In fact, it's a really good idea to review your notes as soon as possible. You could do this with another student. Read through and improve the organization as necessary. Look at the layout – some students make the mistake of writing all their notes in the top quarter of the page. Leave space between points. Indent. Spread it out. Mark ideas that the lecturer emphasizes with an arrow or some special symbol. Put a box around assignments and suggested books so you can identify them quickly.

In terms of developing your listening skills, pay attention to signals for the end of an idea and the beginning of another. If you hear these, they will help you follow the flow of a lecture and lay out your notes logically. Transitions such as 'therefore', 'finally' and 'furthermore' usually signal an important idea. Also, pay attention to the lecturer's voice. It will often go down in pitch at the end of a section and then up at the start of a new section.

As a final point, often the most interesting and useful things you can gain from lectures are the examples, sketches and illustrations that the lecturer presents. Lecturers often talk about their research in relation to points they make or tell stories from their experience. You can get the theory from a textbook, but often this experience is unpublished and cannot be got from books. These stories are often the most interesting parts of lectures and you can use them in your assignments and exams – so although stories may seem off the point, they may be worth noting down.

Okay. Now, I'd like you to look back over your notes and ....

What is the lecturer saying?

These words ...	Mean
I'd like to talk about ... What we're doing today is ... This morning we'll start by looking at ...	Announcing the topic
In other words ... So the question is ... So ... / What I'm saying is ...	Explaining something he or she has just said in a different way
That's not the same as ... The catch here is ... That's not what we really mean by ...	This is different from something else
And that leads to ... We now come to look at ... Right. Well, if we move on ...	A new sub-topic is coming

These words ...	Mean *(Continued)*
For instance ... For example ... One of the ways this works out is ... Let me give you an illustration ...	Giving an illustration of something that's just been said
According to ... I'm a great believer in ... X would have us believe ... The most interesting point here is ...	These are opinions rather than facts
By the way ... / I might say here ... As a sidelight ... But I'm getting a little ahead of myself ... So where was I? Well anyway ... To get back on track ...	This is not part of the main lecture
That would go for X as well as for Y ... Along the same lines ...	This is the same as something

A lecture transcript

The lecturer's words	The purpose of the words
Today we are going to have some information about how students can help themselves learn a language. In other words, I'll be talking about what we call language learning strategies. One definition of these strategies is on your handout. Cohen (1998:4) defined them as 'processes which are consciously selected by learners ....' In today's lecture I'll be starting by discussing the need for strategies and some definitions of them. I'll be passing on some theories as well as providing you with some examples. Finally there will be some general points about how you might apply the ideas from today's lecture. Let's start with a question. Why is this topic important to you? We have various categories of learning strategies. These are social strategies, cognitive strategies, organizational strategies and metacognitive strategies. Now let's turn to some examples of cognitive strategies for learning vocabulary. You have probably used some of these yourselves. Let's see, how many of you try to remember a word by linking it to another word you know in any language?	To announce today's topic To introduce a technical term To remind students that they needn't write it down. To define a technical term To outline (signpost) the order of the lecture To signal the 'real' start of the lecture To try to make the topic relevant to the students To introduce a section about the theory of learning strategies To move on to a section giving examples To involve the students in what is being said To move on to the next topic To explain a technical term

The lecturer's words	The purpose of the words *(Continued)*
Another aspect that students say they need to learn better is listening. Think of all the contexts where you need to listen: on the telephone, in a social conversation, at a public place and of course in a lecture like this one. In some of these places you have to practise selective listening. What we mean by this term is that a person decides to block out much of what is said and listen just for some information that they need. Some of the occasions when you might practise selective listening are .... Etc.	

Ranking questions for usefulness

1 Is it okay if we email you about changing the time of handing in the next assignment? C
2 Excuse me, what was that point again? B
3 I have a problem with reading your handwriting on the board. My eyesight isn't great. A
4 Will you be telling us more about that shortly? D
5 How does this point compare with what you said earlier about ...? A GOOD QUESTION

Chapter 6: Academic Presentations

Speaking and Writing: What Are the Differences?

1 Which one uses more words to say the same thing? *Speaking*
2 Which one uses more complex sentences? *Writing*
3 Which one uses shorter and more frequent sentences? *Speaking*
4 Which one uses the most complicated vocabulary? *Writing*
5 Which one has more repetition? *Speaking*
6 In which one do you need to be the most accurate? *Writing*

Avoiding too much informal language

Informal language	What should she have said?
Hi, guys. How's it going?	Thank you all for coming.
If you've anything you wanna ask keep it to yourself until the end.	There will be time to ask questions at the end.
I'm going to give you the dirt on the dos and don'ts of working in a restaurant.	I'm going to talk about some health and safety rules for people working in restaurants

Informal language	What should she have said? *(Continued)*
Now that dude Richards – he had some sweet ideas about	Richards (1992) made some good points about ....
It's crazy not washing your hands. It is, like, so gross.	Not washing your hands is both disgusting and dangerous.
Now that's it. We're outa here.	Thank you for listening. If there are no further questions, then we'll finish.

Presentation feedback: what should these students work on?

a. This student needs to work on pronunciation – speaking more loudly and clearly than when they are speaking normally.

b. This student needs to remember that spoken language is simpler than written language.

c. This student needs to work on how they introduce their presentation and use signposting language.

d. Reading aloud is boring and difficult to understand.

e. There was no conclusion.

f. The speaker could have used an image to show the structure of the company.

g. Be careful not to read from the screen when using PowerPoint. Keep eye contact.

h. Think about the 'who' of your presentation. Who are you speaking to? How much do they know about the topic?

Some solutions

Problem	Solution
a.	Imagine you are talking to an old deaf man sitting at the far end of the room, then you will speak more loudly and more clearly.
a.	Try recording yourself when you are practising and listening to yourself speaking to see if you are clear enough.
d.	Try talking from cue cards (small cards with three or four words only written on them).
c.	Pause more between sections.
b., d.	Use more repetition e.g. 'Let me say that another way ....'
c.	Signal with your voice going down that you have ended one section of your talk.
c.	Signal with your voice going up that you are starting a new section.
c.	Use discourse markers more e.g. 'Let me give you an example'; 'My next point is about'; 'I'd like to move on to ... now.'
b., d.	Keep your sentences short and simple.

Problem	Solution *(Continued)*
b., d.	Use more sentences to say the same thing.
c.	Give a really clear introduction at the beginning. Say what you are going to say before you say it e.g. 'In this talk, I'm going to describe ....'
e.	Give a clear summary at the end. Say what you have just said in another way e.g. 'So, to conclude, I've told you ... and I'd like to finish by saying ....'

Chapter 7: Academic Reading

Case studies: learning from other students' experiences

Christophe learnt how to integrate his reading into the course as a whole – reading to prepare for a lecture and then afterwards to find out more about some of the topics in a lecture. He also learnt that even if he doesn't get time to read a whole article, it's still useful. See the sections on 'Planning your university reading' and 'Increasing your reading speed'.

Marie realized that textbooks were actually really helpful because they taught her the technical meaning of words on her course. See the section on 'Types of academic text'.

George learnt that reading could be something that he shared with other people and this was a good way of saving time. See the section on 'Increasing your reading speed'.

Rose struggled to become a critical reader and eventually understood that she was expected to question everything and not just accept it. This was different from her previous studies in her own country. See the section on 'Critical reading'.

Andrea realized that she needed to position each text and piece of research in relation to each other and herself – to work out how her field had changed over the years. See the section on 'Critical reading'.

Types of academic text you will need to read

- prescribed texts or recommended books d)
- edited books g)
- single author books a)
- journal articles e)
- state-of-the-art articles c)
- research reports f)
- theses h)
- conference proceedings. b)

Understanding the sections of a research article task

- How was the study planned? (methods)
- What do the results mean? (discussion, recommendations, conclusions)

- Who is interested in the results? (discussion, recommendations, conclusions)
- What was the study about? (abstract)
- Why is the topic important? (introduction)
- What did the researcher want to find out? (introduction)
- What was the main finding of the research? (abstract)
- Where was the research carried out? (methods)
- What did the researchers find out? (results)
- What research instruments were used? (methods)
- Who else has studied this topic? (literature review)
- What have other researchers found out about this topic? (literature review)
- How does this piece of research fit in with what other researchers have previously found out? (discussion, recommendations and conclusions)
- Where are the full titles of the books and articles referred to in the article? (references)

How not to read

There are two main problems with the way this student is reading. First, they are not taking a critical approach to their reading. This means that they are not actually thinking when they are reading, but are trying to soak up the information. They need to take a more active approach to their reading. They must also think more carefully about the reading techniques they need to use to get the most out of the text more quickly. Both these issues are dealt with in the next few sections of the chapter. You can waste a lot of time reading like this. But it is easy to fall into this way of reading when you are using a second language because:

1 The vocabulary is difficult.
2 The subject is complicated.
3 The structure or organization of the text may be unfamiliar.
4 You don't want to miss important stuff!

Coming up with a reading question

Situation 1: Which presentations look the most interesting at each session? What time are they? Which room are they in? I need to do some shopping at some stage during the conference. When's the best time to do this so that I don't miss something good? How do I get to the conference location from the station? Etc.

Situation 2: What font should I use? What line-spacing is required? Have I met the referencing conventions? Who do I hand the assignment in to? Do I need a cover sheet? If so, where do I get it from? Will I need to sign anything when I hand it in? What time is the office open until?

Situation 3: How similar were these experiments to what I have to do? What were the strengths and weaknesses of their methods? What results did they get? What results should I expect?

Situation 4: What happened in each story? What were the probable causes of the accidents? What were the consequences of each accident?

Situation 5: What aspect of health policy was each looking at? What were the major findings of each study? What questions do I want answered in the lecture?

How do students read?

Reading tasks	Reading process?
1. Looking through the references section of an essay for the name of a particular text.	scan reading
2. Reading a research article to find out what a research study was about and the main findings.	gist reading
3. Your lecturer tells you a particular book would be good background reading so you have a look to get a quick idea of what it's about.	skim reading
4. Reading an exam question before you start an essay.	reading intensively
5. Reading a literature review and deciding on the viewpoint of the writer.	reading between the lines

Reading online vs reading paper-based texts: same or different?

1 You still need to read critically.

Definitely! The internet allows everyone a chance to express their views. Writers no longer need to go through a publishing company! This is very democratic; however, as a reader, you need to be just as critical about texts you find online as you would texts in books.

- Who wrote the text? What do you know about them? Are they cited in journal articles you have read?
- What organization are they from?
- Are they trying to sell something? Or defend a particular opinion?
- Where is the evidence for their conclusions? How did they find this evidence?
- What evidence is not discussed?
- If they are citing an opinion, how widely accepted is this view or is it actually just the opinion of a few people?

2 You can use the same reading strategies (skimming, scanning, reading intensively, etc.) when reading online.

Yes. You still need to read efficiently and need to avoid too much slow 'bottom-up' processing. Scanning is much easier with a computer. Look at the next section for advice.

3 It's easier to get distracted and waste time when reading online.

Possibly. If you are clear about what you need to read and have clear questions you want answered when you are reading, it is easy to evaluate pages that you open. If you are not clear about why you are reading something and what you need to find out, you can easily get distracted and waste time. Sometimes online links can take you somewhere useful. Often they take you somewhere you don't need to go and you can lose track of why you wanted to read that particular page. For example, you may be reading about early car designs on http://www.Wikipedia.com and the article mentions 'steam engines'. You click on the link and find yourself on a page about steam engines which is very interesting but not what you went online for.

4 It's worse for your eyes.
5 You find the same text types online.

A lot of the same text types e.g. book reviews, research reports, journal articles are accessed online plus a few new ones: online discussions, e-lists and of course websites, etc.

6 It's better for the planet.

Maybe. You may use less paper; however, lots of pages are printed that are never read. And e-waste (rubbish from old computer parts) is an increasing environmental problem.

Chapter 8: Principles of Academic Writing

Simplifying the essay question

- What were some developments in management theory in the 1980s?
- How have these developments affected management practice in the 21st century?
- What are the examples of effects?
- What was the controversy over Iris Chang's interpretation of the Nanking Massacre?
- What was / has been the reaction to her work?
- Why was the reaction so strong?

Making sense of question words

analyse	argue	explain	develop	prove	compare	describe
criticize assess review examine explore	justify discuss comment	interpret give an account of relate	extend elaborate expand	verify show illustrate demonstrate	distinguish contrast compare	give an account of show

Coherence and cohesion

Furthermore = To say more of the same point
On the other hand / Conversely = To give an opposite view
Similarly = To say more of the same point
As an example = To illustrate a point
In other words = To say the same thing another way
Even though = To concede a point but then rebut it
Despite the fact that = To agree slightly (to concede a point)
This is not the same as saying = To make things clearer
This point is also made by ... = To refer to someone's published view

Chapter 9: Processes of Essay Writing

Parts of the introduction

Order: e, b, a, c, d.

Thesis statement: d.

Is it or isn't it?

I had good long quotes, sometimes half a page long, but I always acknowledged where they came from at the end of the essay.

This is not clear. It depends on whether the student used quotation marks and put the author's name in the text or in footnotes. Although it is acceptable to use quotes, using quotes that are too long or too many quotes in an essay is often discouraged.

Every time I used someone else's ideas, I used quotation marks and their name and date.

Not plagiarism, but you only use quotation marks if you use the exact words from your source. If you paraphrase someone else's ideas, you still need to cite the source, but you do not need to use quotation marks.

I take ideas from the textbook, but I always change the words.

If the student doesn't give the name of the source, then this is plagiarism. Even when you cite the source, only changing a few words is not acceptable. It is best when you express the ideas in your own words.

If I take ideas from a book, I always say whose ideas they are. The internet is so huge, I can easily cut and paste and get away with it.

It's good that you are acknowledging ideas from books. Remember your lecturer will probably have read far more on the topic of your assignment than you have! However, copying and pasting from the internet is plagiarism too. Students will get caught. Many universities use software that scans assignments and checks them against material on the internet and past assignments that have been handed in.

The whole essay

Is the world a better place today?

a. quotation

b. a sentence supporting the main argument of the essay

c. an example of entertainment

d. one point that goes against the main argument (we call this a counter-argument)

e. an example of what people did to send greetings 100 years ago

f. a summary of the main point of the paragraph

g. examples of causes of death

h. a round-up of counter-arguments then a restatement of the thesis

i. a definition (of the word 'better').

Chapter 10: Small Group Learning

What is the purpose of tutorials?

<12

You have clearly had some good experiences of tutorials. Maybe they suit your learning style. You can see how they are useful.

12–18

You have mixed feelings about tutorials but on the whole can see that they are useful. Maybe you have had some difficulties having your say in tutorials you have been to. In this case, the section on the language of discussions will be really important to you. Maybe small group learning is less important in your culture. Maybe you have had some negative experiences with other students or tutors.

19<

You have quite negative feelings about tutorials. They are an important part of university learning and you will miss out if you do not attend or participate. The section on 'Preparing for tutorials' will be useful for you as this will help you see that tutorials are relevant to you.

Building discussions: reacting to what people say

8. Ask for other people's opinion

What do you think about …?
How do you feel about …?
Do you agree with …?
You haven't said much about this. What do you think?
Are you opposed to …?
I think …. What is your opinion?
What do you think / feel about …?
Would you agree / say that …?
John, what is your opinion on / about …?

6. Add your opinion

I'd just like to say (that) ….
I think/believe/feel that ….
It seems to me (that) ….
I am convinced (that) ….
In my opinion, the main thing is ….
As I see it, the most important point is ….
I feel that the most important consideration is ….
I believe that the highest priority here is ….

7. Not give an opinion

I just don't know.
I don't feel strongly either way.
I'm not sure.
Actually I can see both points of view / both sides.
Maybe (who knows?).

9. Refocus the discussion

Let's move on to the next point.
OK. We've talked about …. What about …?

2. Fully agree with them

\-

Yes, I agree.
Yes, I see what you mean.
That's for sure.
That's a good point.
Absolutely!

5. Disagree with them

\-

I don't agree ....
I don't think so.
Yes, but I think ....
Yes, but don't you think ...?
I agree to some extent, but ....
I'm afraid I must disagree with you.

4. Partly agree with them

\-

It could be that ....
Maybe it is the case that ....
One option would be that ....
I partly agree ....
Probably you're right ....

3. Draw conclusions from what they are saying

\-

Okay, so that means ....
That relates back to what we were saying about ....
The logical extension of that is that ....

1. Check the meaning of what they have said

\-

I'm sorry, I didn't catch that.
Sorry, what was that again?
Do you mean that ...?
Are you saying that ...?
.... Is that what you mean?
In other words, ...
To put it another way, ...

Accounting for this behaviour

a. For students like these, the teacher is the most important person in the room and the focus of their learning in the room. They may not see the point of talking to other students or the point of doing tasks in smaller groups because they want the right answer from the teacher. 3

b. These students may not feel confident and worried about speaking up in front of the whole class. They may be worried about their English language level or their subject knowledge. 5.

c. These students do not seem to be participating actively in the class. They respond when they have to, but are not really involved. 2

d. These students are not actively involved. They may be interested in the tutorial, but are completely passive in the class. Maybe they are unfamiliar with this style of learning. Or maybe they are demotivated. 4.

e. These students are fully involved in the ideas in the class, but communicate only with their friends. 1

Types of question

Students' questions	Type of question
a. Could you please tell us what ... means?	defining
b. What would happen if someone ...?	predicting
c. What if ... had been written in a different century?	hypothesizing
d. Is this similar to the point you made last week about ...?	comparing and contrasting
e. Reading between the lines, is it true that the poet is trying to say ...?	making an inference
f. Can we sum this up by saying ...?	summarizing
g. In your opinion what would be the most likely cause of ...?	evaluating

Chapter 11: Assessment

Ways in which you may be assessed:

___e)_Students are observed doing something, for example teaching a class on a teaching course or making jewellery on a jewellery course, and are graded on their performance.

___a)_Students are assessed throughout the course and have to prepare a folder of short pieces of work that shows what they have been learning throughout their course.

___j)_Students need to write a diary or series of stories to show that they are thinking about the content of the course and learning from it.

___c)_Students have to do an exam in which they write answers of one or two paragraphs. These might be definitions or key ideas on the course.

___k)_This is an exam which students are allowed to do at home. They have a time limit of a week or two weeks in which to complete the exam from the time the exam is set. This type of assessment is common on business courses as it simulates real business situations.

___g)_This is an exam, but you are allowed to bring in your notes and some reference materials.

___l)__In this type of exam you may be given a list of questions a week or two before the exam. During the exam you will be asked to answer only some of them.

___h)_These are long essays that are set throughout the course. You do them at home. Each is set up by the lecturer and has a deadline.

___b)_Students have to write a number of essays in a set time (e.g. three in three hours).

___f)_ Students have to give a short talk to other students on the course. They may have to lead a discussion after the talk.

___d)_This is an exam. Students have to choose the best answer for each question. There may be 60 questions.

___j)__This is common for distance courses. Students have to visit the course website and contribute to a discussion that is usually started by the lecturer.

An example of assessment criteria

Preparation:

- use of literature
- quality of arguments
- integration of theory and case study
- careful reading
- use of primary literature in relation to secondary sources
- imagination in interpretation
- conclusions drawn.

The content of your talk:

- Set out clearly the problem or position to be discussed
- Select what you consider to be the most important aspects of it and explain why
- Consider different ways of approaching it
- Answer questions from the other students or your lecturer about your chosen topic
- Explain and clarify points in the subsequent discussion.

How you talked:

- delivery
- organization of time
- audibility
- structure and signposting
- use of overheads or handouts.

Discussion:

- encouragement and involvement in discussion
- awareness of wider issues raised (including the ability to recognize and stick to the main issue)
- coherence of response to questions
- use of the imagination in interpreting and understanding questions posed to the group.

1 You need to give a presentation, answer questions on your topic and then lead a discussion.

2 The lecturer is most interested in 'academic content and quality of argument / analysis.' Notice how many of the criteria refer to critical thinking skills: quality of arguments; imagination in interpretation; conclusions drawn; selecting what you consider to be the most important aspects of it and explaining why; considering different ways of approaching it; use of the imagination in interpreting and understanding questions posed to the group.

Text patterns in essay feedback

1 Identify the positive comments, detailed comments with criticisms and final positive comment in the following essay feedback:

Positive: You have presented a competent discussion of the article with an analytical approach that conveys aspects of the researcher's work in a systematic way.

Negative: The section that needed more consideration was the final part in which I would have liked to have seen a fuller account of the practical implications of the study. Mostly the essay is well written; however, at times, I found it difficult to follow your argument and had to re-read sections to understand your logic. I felt that more signposting would have helped me with this.

Positive: Overall, though, the assignment was a balanced critique of the issues that arose from the research and it was good to see that you mentioned many of the limitations of this kind of research that we have discussed in class. Well done.

2 If you got the feedback given above, how should you try to improve your next assignment?
This student should:
- Read the question really carefully and make sure he/she has responded to all parts in sufficient depth.
- Be really careful to make sure that their argument is clear by using signposting language (see Chapter 8) or sub-headings. He/she should also spend more time editing for organization.

Spot the criticism

a. 'Your argument was clear in most parts of the essay. A statement that previews the structure of the assignment might have helped me navigate through the essay.'

In some parts the argument was *not clear*. The lecturer wants to see a sentence in the essay's introduction like this:

'In this assignment, I will firstly examine the issue of ..., before ... and finally ....'

If the lecturer needs help 'navigating' the essay, she is finding it hard to read.

b. 'While you mostly followed the recommended referencing conventions, at times this was not the case and I was unsure whether you were referring to sources or claiming these ideas as your own.'

The problem here is the way the student is referring to other writers in the text. This means that when the student writes about someone else's ideas, he or she must say whose ideas they are by including the name of the original writer and a publication date in the text (e.g. (Carter, 1990)) or if the student is using the words of another writer in a direct quote, then they need quotation marks ('...') around the words as well as the writer's name and year. This is a very serious issue. See Chapter 8 on plagiarism.

c. 'This is a well-researched assignment; however, I feel it could have benefited from more time spent proofreading before submission.'

This essay was inaccurate. There may have been typos, missing words, sentence fragments (these are sentences that are not complete e.g. 'Because of the war.'), spelling problems or punctuation errors. See Chapter 8 on proofreading your work.

d. 'Make sure that you answer all parts of the question.'

The student didn't. When writing and after writing, it is important to check the question again and re-read the criteria so that you can make sure you've answered it. Many assignment questions have more than one part e.g. *Describe the chief causes of the rise in global terrorism in the early years of the 21st century and assess the impact of tighter security procedures on everyday life in the West.*

e. 'This assignment is evidence that you have synthesized information from a number of sources. At times, though, I struggled to hear your voice coming through.'

This means that the student needs to give his or her opinion and get this across in their writing rather than just writing what other people have said before. See Chapter 6 on 'Becoming a critical reader'.

f. 'Your literature review is based almost entirely on two sources.'

The lecturer expected the student to read more articles on the topic and synthesize these (bring their main points together).

g. 'While parts of the essay read well and you make some valid points, the essay as a whole fails to read as a coherent whole.'

'A coherent whole' means a complete piece of writing that reads well together. This is a problem with 'coherence' (how the essay is organized). It may be useful for the writer to go back to some familiar essay shapes – e.g. general to specific, or problem to solution, or claim to counter-claim, and fit what they want to say into these shapes.

h. 'This is an excellent description of the process. Your writing is clearly signposted and paragraphs flow seamlessly from one to the next. You follow academic conventions well and clearly have a good grasp of this topic.'

There is no problem with this one.

Revising for exams

When you are revising, choose active, critical and interactive methods. This means you should always make sure you are doing something with the information you are trying to learn and not just repeating it. When possible, try to revise with other people so that you can test each other. The following are useful revision methods: **1, 3, 4, 7, 8 and 9**. Note: 6 is a bad idea because you are unlikely to get exactly the same question in your exam and your learnt example may stop you from thinking through your answer.

Understanding essay questions

WHAT	cell phones – texting communications – at home / in public
HOW	1. Describe the growth in popularity of cell phones. 2. Say how this has changed the way we communicate – i.e. we have discussions in the street / train / car that previously we would have had in private. We can be contacted 24 hours a day and people expect an instant answer. 3. Talk about the effect of this e.g. our private conversations can be heard. Telecom companies (and the police) can track our communications and contacts more easily – privacy law.

What essay questions mean

1.	*Describe how developments in management theory in the 1980s have affected management practice in the 21st century.*	What happened in the field of management theory about 20 years ago? What was the management practice like then? What is it like now? Why is it different? How is it different? Are the changes significant? Why?
2.	*Discuss the controversy over Iris Chang's interpretation of the Nanking Massacre, and account for the strength of the reaction to her work.*	Why is Chang's interpretation controversial? Who agrees with Chang? Who disagrees with Chang? What alternative interpretations are possible?

How would you say this?

You might say: 'Often runners start running much longer distances when they are training for a race. Some of these runners increase their running distances too quickly and do a lot of this running on roads and hard surfaces. When runners run on roads, there is a lot of impact with each stride. This repeated impact causes lots of injuries to the lower leg. One of these injuries is called shin splints …'

Students' experiences of portfolio assessment

a. POSITIVE
b. NEGATIVE
c. POSITIVE eventually
d. NEUTRAL
e. POSITIVE
f. POSITIVE

Chapter 12: Communicating with Lecturers

For and against emailing

Viewpoint	For	Against
Quick to read	Yes each one may be quick	But not if a person gets dozens each day
Quick to answer	Yes if done immediately	But not if they are not given priority
Friendly	Yes if the student chooses polite words	But not if the student writes as if to a fellow student
Clear in meaning	Yes if the student reads it through once	But not if the email is written and sent hastily
Saves time	May save the student time	But the student who takes the trouble to visit may show more commitment

What's a good opening line?

I was just wondering if ...	'Just' – makes the request smaller and therefore easier to say yes to. 'Wondering' – again makes the request sound less serious and less threatening. There is less at stake than 'Can you ...?'
Sorry to be a nuisance, but ...	'Sorry' – this is more common in English than many other languages. Apologizing shows that you respect the person you are talking to and also admits that you are interrupting them.
Excuse me, is it possible ...?	'Excuse me' again makes it clear that you understand the person is busy and you are interrupting them. 'Is it possible?' – it is more abstract and less personal than you / I.
This is just a small request.	This makes the request small and therefore easier to agree to. A good strategy.
Sorry I didn't make an appointment. Do you have a couple of minutes?	As above there is an apology for interrupting the lecturer. Plus 'a couple of minutes' = two or three minutes. This is easy to agree to – even if the request actually takes longer.

What sort of requests do lecturers say 'yes' to?

There's a long waiting list in the library for the book you recommended. Do you mind if I borrow yours?

All except one said they would not lend books to students because the return rate was too low. However, they did say that a request like that would make them look at discussing ways around the problem with the library, such as putting the book as a desk copy only.

I know you are strict about dates for handing in assignments, but, as you can see, I've broken my leg.

All lecturers said that medical reasons were acceptable as excuses for late assignments, especially if they were accompanied by a certificate.

I just missed a bit of your lecture this morning. I wonder if you'd mind running through that last part again with me.

No lecturer took this request seriously.

Would you mind giving me your frank opinion on whether I should advance this subject next year?

Everyone said they would take this request seriously, although one said it would be good to have advance warning to give time to look up the student's marks.

Trouble-shooting lecturer–student dialogues

As you could see, there are similarities in these two dialogues.

Dialogue 1

1 The student leaves silence once the lecturer has greeted him.

2 The student waits too long before letting the lecturer know the topic of the interview.

Dialogue 2

The student comes to see the lecturer because she has a problem with the assignment. The lecturer appears frustrated because she does not know why the student is there and what the student wants. It took three turns for the student to state that she had a problem with the assignment and she took nine seconds to say this. This is a long time for someone who is busy and probably has a queue of people waiting outside their office. It took several more turns for the teacher to find out that the problem was really about the student's writing skills.

Getting your message across

1
   a. Would be a polite start, but until you state your name the person answering may not have a good answer. After all, if there are many students in the class he or she might not recognize your voice and might think you are the person he's just left a message for in administration or computer services.
   b. Yes, it's a good idea to start with your name, but remember to leave some pauses as you state your problem. The lecturer may want to make a suggestion before hearing the whole problem.
   c. It's probably better to let the lecturer decide if the problem is urgent unless of course you mean REALLY serious.

2
   a. Some people are annoyed by a clicking phone. Others are relieved that they don't need to do anything. It's hard to give a definite suggestion here. Just don't keep ringing back and clicking off every five minutes.
   b. Not a good idea unless you are a senior student. Imagine having dozens of students asking you to phone them back. Will you always be there by your landline? You can't expect the university to pay for cell phone calls.
   c. This sounds like a good idea. You could add that you will either phone back or email.

When to talk to your class rep

The following situations are personal issues and should be dealt with in other ways.

Situation 3: You feel that a lecturer is giving you bad marks because they do not like you. *If you don't want to talk to the lecturer directly, contact a counsellor in the Student Union (see Chapter 12). Note: The class rep should not deal with harassment cases.*

Situation 4: You fail an exam and don't understand why. *Talk to your lecturer directly.*

Situation 7: You need extra tutoring with one of your assignments. *Talk to your lecturer or get help from a language advisor.*

Chapter 13: Dealing with Problems

Are you a proactive problem solver?

Add up how many points you have got.

1	a)	1 point	b)	2 points	c)	3 points
2	a)	1 point	b)	3 points	c)	2 points
3	a)	1 point	b)	2 points	c)	1 point
4	a)	2 points	b)	1 point	c)	2 points
5	a)	1 point	b)	3 points	c)	2 points
6	a)	2 points	b)	3 points	c)	2 points
7	a)	3 points	b)	1 point	c)	2 points
8	a)	2 points	b)	1 point	c)	3 points
9	a)	2 points	b)	1 point	c)	3 points

Now read the advice for someone with your scores:

9–13

Your approach to academic problems is an individual one and you tend to stick your head in the sand and ignore problems. If you get a bad mark, you either ignore the problem or you work harder than before but without really addressing the issue. This approach may have worked well for you before, but sometimes it would be a good idea to seek help and take a more proactive approach to academic problems, otherwise things may not get better quickly enough.

14–21

You have a sensible approach to academic problems. You naturally think about things and talk them through with someone before taking further action. This is a good strategy because you are reflecting on the issues, giving yourself time to work things out and using the people around you, but you ARE still dealing with the academic issues that you face.

22+

You tend to overreact to academic problems and take immediate and drastic action. While it is good to do something about your problems, the danger of this approach is that you don't actually address the source of the problem. You should try to reflect about your problems, talk to other students and staff and get some ideas before diving towards a solution that may cause more problems.

Index